THE
RESERVOIR

 Renovaré

In memory of
GARY EDMONDS (1950-2019),
a true reservoir.

Portions adapted from *A Spiritual Formation Workbook: Small-Group Resources for Nurturing Christian Growth*, by James Bryan Smith (HarperSanFrancisco, 1993).

Also referenced and recommended:

Foster, Richard J. *Celebration of Discipline: The Path to Spiritual Growth.* Rev. ed. HarperSanFrancisco, 1998.

Foster, Richard J. *Prayer: Finding the Heart's True Home.* HarperOne, 1992.

Willard, Dallas. *The Divine Conspiracy: Rediscovering Our Hidden Life in God.* HarperCollins, 1997.

Parham, Richella. *A Spiritual Formation Primer.* Renovaré, 2013.

Gaultiere, Bill. *Jesus' Greatest Teaching: Living the Sermon on the Mount.* SoulShepherding.org, 2016.

CONTENTS

Introduction 1

Months 1 & 2: The Big Questions

What Is Spiritual Formation? 4

What Is My Picture of God? 10

What Is My Picture of Myself? 16

What Is My Picture of the Gospel? 22

Is Change Possible? Some Biblical Examples 28

Is Change Possible? More Biblical Examples 34

How Do People Change? Cooperating through Spiritual Disciplines 40

How Do I Follow Jesus? 46

Months 3 & 4: The Prayer-Filled Life

How Did Jesus Pray? 52

How Did Jesus Teach Us to Pray? Part One 58

How Did Jesus Teach Us to Pray? Part Two 64

What Practices Help Nurture a Life Of Prayer? 70

Moving Inward—Seeking the Transformation We Need ... 76

Moving Upward—Seeking the Intimacy We Need 82

Moving Outward—Seeking the Ministry We Need 88

Jesus' Prayer in John 17 94

Months 5 & 6: The Virtuous Life

The Beauty of Holiness 100

Holiness in the Sermon on the Mount 106

What Does a Virtuous Person Look Like? 112

How Can Someone Become Virtuous? Part One 118

How Can Someone Become Virtuous? Part Two 124

How Can Someone Become Virtuous? Part Three 130

Training with Jesus in Holiness 136

Restoring Our Vision of Holiness 142

Months 7 & 8: The Spirit-Empowered Life

Jesus and the Holy Spirit 148

Meet the Holy Spirit.. 154

What Is The Spirit-Empowered Life?............................... 160

Gifts of the Holy Spirit 166

The Holy Spirit at Work in Peter 172

The Holy Spirit at Work in Paul....................................... 178

Practicing the Spirit-Empowered Life.............................. 184

How the Spirit-Empowered Life Connects the Streams 190

Months 9 & 10: The Compassionate Life

Seeing and Acting... 196

Social Justice in the Life and Parables of Jesus................ 202

Christ's Peace, Pace, and Love in Ministry 208

Avoiding the Pitfalls of Self-Righteous Service................. 214

Justice for Every Person.. 220

The Vocabulary of the Compassionate Life 226

Potential Perils of the Compassionate Life....................... 232

Boldness and Perseverance in Doing Good 238

Months 11 & 12: The Word-Centered Life

What Is the Word-Centered Life? 244

Scripture: The Written Word.. 250

Jesus: The Living Word 256

The Gospel: The Spoken Word... 262

Memorize and Teach Scripture 268

Read and Pray Scripture.. 274

Proclaim the Gospel with Words...................................... 280

Proclaim the Gospel with Actions.................................... 286

Months 13 & 14: The God-Saturated Life

How Do We Become More Like Jesus in All Aspects of Life? 292

No Divide Between Sacred and Secular 298

Becoming More Like Jesus in Our Public Actions.............................. 304

Becoming More Like Jesus in Our Relationships............................ 310

Partnering with the Trinity 316

Going Deeper with the Apostles... 322

How Do We Live with Jesus in Our Workplaces? 328

How Do We Live with Jesus at Home? 334

Month 15: Invitations From Jesus

Questions Jesus Asks 340

More Questions Jesus Asks 346

Invitations from Jesus.. 352

More Invitations from Jesus.. 358

Preface

~~~~~~~~~~

Three years ago Gary Edmonds, President of Food for the Hungry, passionately shared with me his concern for the spiritual formation of his staff. He knew first-hand the demanding nature of humanitarian work and how serving the poor can result in burnout. Indeed, this is a serious problem for Christian disaster relief organizations. Staying spiritually healthy—being continually renewed in Jesus—is vital to sustainable social justice work. Gary and I both sensed God's direction for Renovaré and Food for the Hungry to partner together for the spiritual health of their staff.

The Reservoir is the result of that partnership. This fifteen-month workday devotional was written one month at a time by members of the Renovaré staff, and then translated by Food for the Hungry into five languages and distributed for their staff to use individually and in groups where they operate. Hundreds of workers have already been through the devotional with encouraging results. Food for the Hungry and Renovaré are now pleased to offer it to you.

May Christ bless you deeply as you drink from the living water he offers.

Chris Hall
President, Renovaré
Summer 2019

Introduction

Let anyone who is thirsty come to me, and let the one who believes in me drink. As the scripture has said, "Out of the believer's heart shall flow rivers of living water." — Jesus (John 7:37–38)

As followers of Jesus, we want to pour out our lives for others. This is a good and beautiful thing. However, if we are not continually replenished by "living water," we will end up drained, dry, and exhausted.

In the twelfth century, Bernard of Clairvaux diagnosed this very problem. He observed that many well-intentioned people were trying to serve, teach, and give without first receiving from God what they needed to maintain spiritual health. He described these people as "canals," and urged them to become "reservoirs" instead:

If then you are wise, you will show yourself rather as a reservoir than as a canal. A canal spreads abroad water as it receives it, and a reservoir waits until it is filled before overflowing, and thus without loss to itself communicates its superabundant water. In the Church at the present day we have many canals but few reservoirs.

For the next fifteen months, these weekday devotionals will encourage you to drink the living water Jesus promised. We will explore truths and practices designed to help you become a person who "lives in the overflow," continually replenished rather than constantly drained—a reservoir, rather than a canal.

Our focus will be upon six great traditions, or streams, outlined by Richard Foster in his book *Streams of Living Water*. They are found in saints and movements throughout the ages, and most perfectly displayed in the life of Jesus.

These are *The Prayer-Filled Life*, *The Virtuous Life*, *The Spirit-Empowered Life*, *The Compassionate Life*, *The Word-Centered Life*, and *The God-Saturated Life*.

But first, we will explore some big questions about our capacity to receive and overflow with living water. The first two months ask those questions, using the language of spiritual formation.

Before you begin, here are a couple of practical notes.

Weekends for many bring a different schedule. We hope the weekdays-only format of this devotional offers you a sustainable rhythm.

While you can start this devotional anytime, the beginning of a month works best.

You'll notice each month contains only four weeks. When the fifth week of a month arises, consider reviewing the previous weeks of that month—week one on Monday, week two on Tuesday, and so forth—looking for something God may be inviting you to "soak in" a bit longer. Then on Friday, take a few minutes in silence or go for a walk, asking God to bring to mind anything from your times together that might otherwise be forgotten. The Holy Spirit delights to bring truth to our remembrance (John 14:26).

Alright, let's dive in.

Week One

~~~~~~~~

What Is Spiritual Formation?

MONDAY 1/4

WHAT IS SPIRITUAL FORMATION?

Spiritual formation is the process by which the human spirit (will) is given a definite form, or character.... It happens to everyone. — Dallas Willard

The inner being of each one of us (our personality, character, and will) is gradually shaped by everything and everyone we spend time with. Most of us are completely unaware of this formation process. When we do become aware of issues in the way we've been formed (for example, a struggle with anger, pride, or insecurity), we often don't know how the problem developed, or what we can do about it. The good news is that there is something we can do about who we are now, and about who we are becoming. An awareness of our own spiritual formation will allow us to become more intentional about what—and who—we let shape us.

Read: Philippians 4:4–8

Reflect:

1. There are many forces (families, schools, churches, entertainment, politics, advertising, arts, etc.) competing to "form" the human beings within them. Which forces seem to have the most influence on your own formation and that of those around you?

2. What (and who) has most shaped you and the way you see the world?

3. What is one thing you would like to give more influence to in your formation? What is one thing you'd like to see have less power over you?

4. What does the apostle Paul seem to be saying about spiritual formation in today's passage?

TUESDAY

FORMATION IN JESUS

Jesus-centered spiritual formation is the process of being transformed into the image of Christ, through a relationship of intimacy with God, by the power of the Spirit, in order to live a good and beautiful life of faith, hope, love, joy, and peace—a life that will be a blessing to oneself and to others and will glorify God now and for all eternity. — James Bryan Smith

In John 4, we meet a woman who has chosen to do the hard work of drawing water at the village well at high noon—the hottest part of the day. Evidently she feels so much shame (and has experienced so much rejection) about the events of her life that she will do anything to avoid having to be around other people.

By the end of the story, this woman has run to tell the entire village about Jesus. How did she transform from being a person drowning in shame to being a community leader? It's a story worth studying if we're interested in learning more about how people change.

Read: John 15:5

Reflect:

1. What do you think Jesus means by the phrase "abide in me"?

2. What does "abiding in Jesus" look like in your life? What *might* it look like?

3. Jesus claims, "Apart from me you can do nothing." Certainly there are people who are productive in various ways apart from Jesus. So what do you think he means?

4. Is the thought of becoming more like Jesus appealing to you? Why? Do you find yourself resisting the idea at any point? Why?

WEDNESDAY

SPIRITUAL FORMATION AS DISCIPLESHIP

Believing in Jesus and discipleship to Jesus are part of the same action.
— Richard Foster

A disciple is a person who has decided that the most important thing in her life is to learn how to do what Jesus said to do. . . . Disciples simply are people who are constantly revising their affairs to carry through on their decision to follow Jesus. — Dallas Willard

One of the ways we can think about spiritual formation centered in Jesus is by using the language of *discipleship*. During the time Jesus lived in Galilee, it was common for students to identify a rabbi they wished to emulate and follow him everywhere he went. They were listening, observing, and imitating—living with him so that they could learn to be like him. Today we are still invited to be disciples of Jesus, progressively and systematically rearranging the details of our lives so that we can spend time with him and learn to be like him.

Read: Mark 1:16–20; 8:34–37

Reflect:

1. What do you think Jesus means when he connects the decision to be his disciple with both saving your life and losing your life?

2. Imagine Jesus walking up to you today, right in the middle of your job, and saying, "Will you follow me?" Would you have to change anything you are currently doing in order to say yes?

THURSDAY

SPIRITUAL FORMATION AS APPRENTICESHIP

Apprenticeship centers on immersion in the culture of the master, experientially learning to do what he did through hands-on training. — Gary Moon

Another way to explore spiritual formation centered around Jesus is to use the model of *apprenticeship*. Apprentices in any craft or trade must pay very close attention to the one they wish to follow. They need practical training—and lots of it! The apprenticeship model is helpful because it reminds us that we need to learn to live our lives the way Jesus lived his. If Jesus stepped away from the busy demands of his life to pray, as his apprentices we should too. If he reached out to the outcast, that's something we need to practice as well. If he quoted Scripture in the wilderness, then we know that part of our learning will be to memorize passages from the Bible. But, as with our discipleship model, we also need to be with him in order to learn from him. So in addition to learning from his earthly life, we also learn from his active presence with us today.

Read: John 13:12–17

Reflect:

1. Have you ever had a chance to either apprentice someone in a craft or be an apprentice yourself? If so, what elements were most important in the process?

2. If you decided that your full-time job was to be an apprentice to Jesus, what (if anything) would change in your daily schedule?

FRIDAY

SPIRITUAL FORMATION AS FRIENDSHIP

Prayer is friendship in action. — M. Basil Pennington

Spiritual practices at their best are practices of friendship. — Trevor Hudson

Many people struggle with the idea of relating to God as a friend because they feel it reduces God's majesty and transcendence. And yet Jesus himself said, "I do not call you servants any longer . . . but I have called you friends" (John 15:15). The beautiful thing about *friendship* as a model for our formation in Jesus is that it reminds us that all our spiritual practices (prayer, study, worship, service, etc.) are not spiritual "techniques," but rather ways of being intentional about spending time with the God who deeply desires relationship with us. As God's friends, we will possess not only the seriousness of disciples and the teachability of apprentices, but also the delight of discovering we are his beloved.

Read: John 15:9–17

Reflect:

1. Are you comfortable thinking of God as your "friend"? Why or why not?

2. In today's passage, Jesus links friendship with him to friendship with others. Why does he make this connection?

3. Which model of spiritual formation (discipleship, apprenticeship, or friendship) makes the most sense to you? Is there one model you'd like to focus on more than you have before?

Week Two

What Is My Picture of God?

MONDAY

WHY IS MY PICTURE OF GOD SO IMPORTANT?

What comes into our mind when we think about God is the most important thing about us. — A. W. Tozer

We become like the God we worship. If I believe that God not only loves, but is love, then the more I center my life on him, the more loving I will become. If, however, I actually hold a picture of an angry God, I will gradually become an angrier person. If I worship a trustworthy God, I will have an easier time trusting God and other people. But if my image is of an unreliable God, I will likely become increasingly anxious and controlling. It's vital to uncover the difference between our *professed* images of God—the things we say we believe about him—and our *default* pictures of God—the ideas we hold deep down, perhaps unaware, that are profoundly shaping us.

Read: Psalm 136

Reflect:

1. What are some dominant pictures of God within the culture?

2. Recall your childhood picture of God. Do you think it still shapes the way you see him now?

3. Choose three words to describe God. What might these three words teach you about yourself and your view of God?

4. Do you find yourself relating to God differently in seasons of stress or difficulty than in happier times?

TUESDAY

GOD IS GREATER (AND BETTER) THAN WE IMAGINE

Great is the LORD, *and greatly to be praised; his greatness is unsearchable.*
— Psalm 145:3

The psalmist tells us that God's greatness is "unsearchable"—his greatness is so vast that we can't begin to understand all of it. This means that while encounters with God are significant, God is always greater than our particular experience of him. It reminds us that while the language we have to describe God is helpful, God will always be more than anything we can say about him. And it helps us see that while our theology and traditions can serve to point us to God, he will always transcend our doctrines and denominations. God is big! The good news is that we will eternally be discovering more and more of his unsearchable greatness.

Read: 2 Chronicles 6:18–21; Acts 17:28

Reflect:

1. Does the idea of God's greatness being "unsearchable" excite you or frighten you? Why?

2. Have the churches you've attended done a good job of remembering the greatness of God? Have they ever tried to reduce God to a more describable size?

3. In 2 Chronicles 6, King Solomon is praying a prayer of dedication over the temple. He recognizes that the temple can't begin to contain God's greatness, but he still boldly asks God to hear the prayers that are prayed there. On what basis, do you think, did Solomon believe he could ask an unfathomably great God to pay attention to his prayers?

WEDNESDAY

GOD'S CHARACTER IS REVEALED IN JESUS

Whoever has seen me has seen the Father. — Jesus (John 14:9)

[Jesus is] the Divine life operating under human conditions. — C. S. Lewis

One of the ways we can check to see if our picture of God is healthy is to ask, Is there anything I believe about God's character that is in conflict with the character of Christ? In his teaching, his actions, his sacrificial death, and his victorious resurrection, Jesus of Nazareth reveals to us the character of God. If we ever wonder if God is truly a God of both unsearchable greatness and unending love, compassion, and goodness, we can look at Jesus and say a resounding yes.

Read: John 14:8–10; Colossians 1:15; Luke 15:1–2, 11–32

Reflect:

1. Do you agree that there is nothing in God's character that is in conflict with the character of Christ? Why or why not?

2. What does Jesus' portrayal of the human father in Luke 15 say about the character of God the Father?

3. Look again at Luke 15:1–2. What were the religious people around Jesus upset about? What do their complaints reveal about their own pictures of God?

4. Reread Colossians 1:15. Is there anything in your own picture of the "invisible God" that seems at odds with the visible "image" of Jesus Christ?

THURSDAY

GOD IS CLOSER THAN WE CAN IMAGINE

And remember, I am with you always, to the end of the age.
— Jesus (Matthew 28:20)

Earlier in the week, we looked at 2 Chronicles 6:18-21 and asked how Solomon could be so aware of God's surpassing greatness and yet still feel confident that God would hear his prayers. In the verse above, Jesus tells us that Solomon's confidence was not misplaced. God is greater than we can fathom, but he's also closer and more accessible than we can imagine. Better yet, for us born after the earthly life, death, and resurrection of Jesus, we know that the kingdom of God is not only magnificent, it has come near.

Read: Psalm 73:28; Acts 17:27-28; Matthew 4:17

Reflect:

1. In Matthew 4:17, Jesus announces that "the kingdom of heaven has come near." What do you think he means?

2. There is evidence that although God draws close to human beings in the Old Testament, when Jesus arrives, in the New Testament, he seems to be announcing an increased level of access. What has changed?

3. Sometimes we use the term "transcendence" (God is above and beyond all things) to talk about God's greatness and "immanence" (God is present, active, and near) to express God's accessibility. Which aspect of God's character do you find harder to understand?

FRIDAY

GOD IS THREE-IN-ONE

The Trinity suddenly filled my heart with the greatest joy. And I understood that in heaven it will be like that for ever for those who come there. For the Trinity is God, God is the Trinity; the Trinity is our maker and protector, the Trinity is our dear friend forever, our everlasting joy and bliss, through our Lord Jesus Christ. — *Julian of Norwich*

Jesus teaches that God is more wonderful—and more complex—than we could ever imagine. Although the Bible never uses the word Trinity, biblical writers teach that God exists in three persons—Father, Son, and Holy Spirit. Remember that the Trinity is not a puzzle to be solved but a wonder to be worshiped. God is one. And God is also three in one, a relationship of love we are invited to enter into by faith.

Read: John 3:17; John 5:17; John 14:26

Reflect:

1. God the Father is distinct from God the Son and God the Spirit, yet all three are one God. Julian of Norwich writes that the Trinity "filled my heart with the greatest joy." How do you find yourself responding to God as Trinity? How might we, by faith, move ever more deeply into the wonder and beauty of the Trinity?

2. God's triune nature tells us that he has never been lonely. Yet he created us to be in relationship with him. Why?

Week Three

What Is My Picture of Myself?

MONDAY  1/18

WHY IS MY PICTURE OF MYSELF SO IMPORTANT?

I know well the deadening effects of not knowing who or whose we are.... When we see ourselves wrongly, we often end up in the muddy pit of worthlessness with its attendant despair. — Trevor Hudson

Dr. Frank Lake specialized in working with missionaries who had become exhausted or bitter in their work. After countless interviews, he concluded that the problem for many of these people was that they were trying to use their work to achieve acceptance—to prove their worth to God, others, and themselves. Lake argued that we can only do healthy, sustainable work when we are operating from acceptance—when we realize there is nothing we can do to make God love us more and nothing we can do to make God love us less. This week we'll ponder whether we are living for or from acceptance.

Read: Psalm 139:1–18

Reflect:

1. Think about a group you've been part of that struggled to work well together. Did any members of the group feel unaccepted? If so, how did that affect the team dynamics?

2. Dr. Lake suggested that it is dangerous to use our work (or our ministry, or our roles as friends and family members) to try to gain acceptance with God or others. Why is that?

3. As you read Psalm 139, the psalmist seems to feel accepted by God. Where do you think he got that sense of acceptance?

TUESDAY

I AM MADE IN THE IMAGE OF GOD

God formed human beings with his own hands. . . . He traced his own form on the formation, so that what would be seen would be of divine form. Humankind was formed as the image of God and set on the earth.
— Irenaeus

Human beings have a unique place in creation. We are the only creatures made in the image of God, breathed into life from his own Spirit. The way we were created brings us into a special relationship with God. As image-bearers of the living God, how we treat ourselves and others matters beyond measure.

Read: Genesis 1

Reflect:

1. At what point in Genesis 1 does God move from calling his creation "good" to calling it "very good"?

2. In Genesis 1:28, God commands his image-bearers to help govern creation with him. How does this mandate relate to your own vocation and way of life?

3. If you could live today fully aware of your unique value as a person who bears the image of God, how would that awareness change your perspective . . . and your actions?

4. If you could see each person you encounter for the next week as God's beloved image-bearer, how might that change your interactions?

WEDNESDAY

I AM GOD'S BELOVED

All I want to say to you is "You are the Beloved," and all I can hope is that you can hear those words as spoken to you with all the tenderness and force that love can hold. — Henri Nouwen

Knowing myself to be beloved of God is slowly becoming more than intellectual conviction; it is gently developing into the core truth of my everyday existence. — Trevor Hudson

Before Jesus began his ministry, his Father declared publicly, "You are my Son, the Beloved; with you I am well pleased" (Mark 1:11). While we might think these words only apply to God's Son, Jesus himself tells us, "As the Father has loved me, so I have loved you" (John 15:9). We too, like Jesus, are the beloved of God. The world is full of voices that tell us we can never have enough or be enough. It's critically important that we rediscover our value as God's beloved image-bearers.

Read: Matthew 17:1–13; John 13:23

Reflect:

1. Why do you think the Father publicly affirms his love for Jesus a second time in Matthew 17:5?

2. How does the apostle John describe himself in John 13:23?

3. Is it possible for you to picture yourself as "the disciple Jesus loves"? Why or why not?

4. Is it possible for you to picture other people as "the ones Jesus loves"? Why or why not?

THURSDAY

I AM ACCEPTED

My deepest awareness of myself is that I am deeply loved by Jesus Christ and I have done nothing to earn it or deserve it. — Brennan Manning

What if we had to wait to come to Jesus until we were worthy of him? We'd never get there! Yet, too often we find ourselves slipping into the mind-set of waiting until we're "just a little better" before approaching the throne of grace. How strange to attempt to earn the acceptance that is freely given to us!

Read: John 3:16; 1 John 4:16–19

Reflect:

1. Do you ever find yourself thinking that God loves you more when you are doing well than he does when you are falling into sin? Read John 3:16 (as familiar as it may be) carefully. Did God send Jesus to the world in order to make the world loveable, or did he send Jesus to the world because he already loved it?

2. If God loves us no matter what, and we are already accepted, why does God care so much that we become holy people?

3. John writes that God's love casts out fear (1 John 4:18). And yet many of us experience fear when we think we are not worthy to come before God. How do our pictures of God influence that fear? How do our pictures of ourselves influence that fear?

4. According to this passage in 1 John, who is always the initiator in our relationship with God?

FRIDAY

I AM INVITED

[God's] invitation has long been on public record. You can hardly look anywhere across the human scene and not encounter it. It is literally "blowing in the wind." A door of welcome seems open to everyone without exception. — Dallas Willard

Author Philip Yancey once said that the plotline of the whole Bible is "God wants his family back." From Genesis to Revelation, God extends invitation after invitation—"not wanting any to perish" (2 Peter 3:9). The truth is, whether you feel close to God or, like the prodigal son, you've been living off in a "far country," you are always loved, wanted, accepted, redeemed . . . and invited to repent—change directions—and come back home.

Read: Matthew 11:28; Mark 1:17; John 15:4

Reflect:

1. Billy Graham identified the three verses above as the "Three Invitations of Christ." He called the one in Matthew 11:28 "The Invitation to Come Rest." What would you call the other two?

2. This week, have you detected any distortions in your picture of yourself that need correction? How about in the way you see other people?

Week Four

What Is My Picture of the Gospel?

THE GOSPEL IS MORE THAN THE FORGIVENESS OF SIN

Can we seriously believe that God would establish a plan for us that essentially bypasses the awesome needs of present human life and leaves human character untouched? — Dallas Willard

The word gospel means "good news." If you ask many Christ-followers, in many parts of the world, "What is the gospel of Jesus Christ?" they will answer that it is the forgiveness of sins so that we can go to heaven when we die. This answer is not wrong—Jesus' life, death, and resurrection make it possible for our sins to be forgiven. But a gospel that solely deals with the forgiveness of sin is incomplete. The good news that Jesus proclaimed is the availability of a completely different kind of life—a life that changes us from the inside out, starting now.

Read: John 10:7–10

Reflect:

1. What do you think Jesus means in John 10 when he says he is the "gate for the sheep?"

2. In verse 10, Jesus says he came that we "may have life, and have it abundantly." Do you think he is referring only to the afterlife? Or do you believe he is saying something about human existence for people living here and now?

3. What picture of the gospel ("good news") are you most familiar with? Is it a gospel primarily concerned with the forgiveness of sins and the promise of heaven in the future, or does it include a full picture of the availability of another kind of life here and now?

TUESDAY

THE GOSPEL OF THE KINGDOM

Jesus came to Galilee, proclaiming the good news of God, and saying, "The time is fulfilled, and the kingdom of God has come near; repent, and believe in the good news." — Mark 1:14-15

Jesus primarily proclaims his gospel by announcing the fact that, with his arrival, the "kingdom of God has come near." In the Lord's Prayer, Jesus also teaches us to pray for God's kingdom to break more and more fully into the world ("Your kingdom come . . . on earth as it is in heaven"). The kingdom of God is the place where God reigns—where what he wants to be done is done. The apostle Paul describes God's kingdom as a kingdom of "righteousness and peace and joy in the Holy Spirit" (Romans 14:17). The invitation of the gospel is for us to take our own little kingdoms (our lives and spheres of influence) and align them with the kingdom of God, so that we can help bring in his kingdom wherever we live.

Read: Luke 4:42–43; Colossians 1:9-14

Reflect:

1. In Luke 4:43, what does Jesus say is the reason he was sent?

2. In the Colossians passage, the apostle Paul lists "redemption" and the "forgiveness of sins" as things we receive in the "kingdom of the Son." What other things from God (aspects of God's kingdom) does Paul list and pray for in that passage?

3. If the kingdom of God reigned completely in your community, what would be different? What would change if God's kingdom took over completely in your own heart?

life worthy of the lord
bearing fruit
growing in knowledge
strengthened
great endurance
patience

WEDNESDAY

THE GOSPEL CHANGES EVERYTHING

Spiritual depth and renewal come, as and when they come, as part of the larger package. But that package itself is about being delivered from evil; about God's kingdom coming on earth as it is in heaven. — N. T. Wright

One of the things that happens when our picture shifts from a gospel that deals solely with the forgiveness of sins to a gospel that announces the availability of the kingdom of God is that we begin to realize that our personal decision to say yes to Jesus has very public—even cosmic— implications. When we decide to follow Jesus, we agree to become a part of his kingdom mission—to bring his truth, justice, love, and libera- tion to every aspect of his creation. We become part of something much bigger than ourselves, and the adventure of kingdom living begins!

Read: Luke 4:16–21

Reflect:

1. Why do you think Jesus chose to read this passage from Isaiah?

2. What do you think Jesus was saying about the nature and purpose of the kingdom of God?

3. Are there areas of your life where you can more fully cooperate with God and his kingdom?

4. Have you been taught to think of the gospel of Jesus more as an invitation to a personal decision or as an invitation to a cosmic mission? Is there a way it can be both?

THURSDAY

THE GOSPEL MEANS ETERNAL LIFE STARTS NOW

You see, the goal of the Christian life is not simply to get us into heaven, but to get heaven into us! — Richard Foster

On Monday, we explored the idea that the gospel means not only the forgiveness of sins but the availability of another kind of life—life in the kingdom of God. Jesus calls this kind of life "eternal life." Notice how he defines "eternal life" in his prayer in John 17:3: "And this is eternal life, that they may know you, the only true God, and Jesus Christ whom you have sent." Jesus seems to be saying that eternal life does not begin when you die, but rather it begins when you come to know the Father through Jesus himself. Eternal life, for those who say yes to Jesus, starts now.

Read: John 14:6; 1 John 5:11; Colossians 3:1–17

Reflect:

1. Consider Jesus' self-description as "the way, and the truth, and the life" (John 14:6). In this passage, do you think Jesus is offering to take us to a destination (i.e., he can "get us to heaven") or that he is the destination himself (eternal life is found in him)? Could it be both?

2. Practically speaking, does it make any difference how we live our lives if we think eternal life starts now rather than after we die?

3. In Colossians 3, how does the apostle Paul describe life in Christ? What does this life include? What does it rule out?

4. Dallas Willard has argued, "The simple and wholly adequate word for salvation in the New Testament is 'life.'" Do you agree or disagree? Why?

#3 Includes.
Forgive others
Love one another
peace of Christ Rule

Exclude
Earthy Desires

FRIDAY

SAYING YES TO THE GOSPEL

I pray that you, being rooted and established in love, may have power, together with all the Lord's holy people, to grasp how wide and long and high and deep is the love of Christ. — Ephesians 3:17–18 NIV

Earlier this month, we explored the idea that we become like the God we worship. We might also say that we live out the gospel we believe. If we think Jesus came only to make a way for us to get to heaven after we die, we will say yes to the gospel and then potentially go on living much as we did before. If, however, we understand that Jesus came to invite us to a completely different life, serving a different king, living in his kingdom, and directly experiencing his love and life and power—our lives will become radically different. We are invited to say yes to the gospel that Jesus actually proclaimed, and to step into the kingdom of God now.

Read: Ephesians 3:14–21

Reflect:
This month, we wrestled with four big questions: What is spiritual formation? What is my picture of God? What is my picture of myself? What is my picture of the gospel?

1. Are you answering any of those four questions differently now than you would have a month ago?

2. Which of the four questions do you think is the most important in your own spiritual formation?

Week One

Is Change Possible? Some Biblical Examples

MONDAY 2\

IS CHANGE POSSIBLE?

People don't believe real life transformation is possible anymore. The whole concept of spiritual formation begins with the question: What's possible? People will live up to or down to their beliefs. — Dieter Zander

The goal of spiritual formation is spiritual transformation. All of us have cracks in our personalities—parts of ourselves that need healing and deliverance in order for us to be able to live and love well. Jesus offers us hope and freedom ("If the son makes you free," he says in John 8:36, "you will be free indeed.") A journey toward progressive healing and wholeness in Jesus begins with the hope-giving conviction that change is actually possible.

The Bible is full of people who went from darkness to light, stubbornness to surrender, fear to faith. For the next several days we'll look at several biblical examples of transformation—with the goal of catching a vision for our own.

Read: Hebrews 12:1–2

Reflect:

1. Can people change? When you have encountered problematic patterns of behavior or thinking (in other people or in yourself), have you tended to be optimistic or pessimistic about the possibility of transformation?

2. The writer of the letter to the Hebrews says that Jesus both initiates and perfects our faith. What do you think he means by the "perfecting" of our faith? Does it sound like this "perfecting" happens in an instant or over a lifetime?

TUESDAY

FROM SHAME TO SHARING: THE WOMAN AT THE WELL

The Samaritan woman grasped what He said with a fervor that came from an awareness of her real need. She had come as a reject. He sent her back being accepted by God Himself. . . . She came living a life of quiet desperation. She ran back overflowing with hope. — Ravi Zacharias

In John 4 we meet a woman who has chosen to do the hard work of drawing water at the village well at high noon—the hottest part of the day. Evidently she feels so much shame (and has experienced so much rejection) about the events of her life that she will do anything to avoid having to be around other people.

By the end of the story, this woman has run to tell the entire village about Jesus. How did she transform from a person drowning in shame to a community leader?

Read: John 4:4–29, 39

Reflect:

1. What role does shame play in culture? Do you know anyone who feels isolated like the woman did at the beginning of this story?

2. What was the woman's "testimony," according to verse 39? What was most significant to her about her encounter with Jesus? What caused her to change?

3. Reread verses 25–26. This exchange is the first time in John's Gospel that Jesus tells anyone that he is the Messiah. Why do you think Jesus chose this woman for such a special revelation?

WEDNESDAY

FROM COWERING TO CONFIDENCE: GIDEON

God does not exist to solve our problems. We exist to stand up with God and count for something in his world. — Dallas Willard

No one expected Gideon to lead a revolt against the oppressive Midianites—least of all Gideon himself! Not only was he a member of the weakest clan of Manasseh, Gideon was also a coward—hiding out, threshing wheat in a winepress to keep it from the sight of the Midianites. Imagine his surprise when the angel of the Lord spoke an unexpected greeting: "The Lord is with you, you mighty warrior" (Judges 6:12)!

From that first encounter until the unconventional battle against the Midianites, Gideon's story was one of transformation from victim to victor. Why did Gideon change?

Read: Judges 6:11–16; 36-40 7:1–24

Reflect:

1. God spends the first part of Judges 7 whittling Gideon's army of thirty-two thousand down to three hundred. Gideon listens and obeys God's commands without asking for a sign. The night before the battle, God offers him the opportunity to receive one more sign of God's presence with them. What is that sign? Why do you think God offered it?

2. How do the words others use about us shape the way we see ourselves? Can you think of a time in your life when you have been encouraged by someone else's view of your abilities? When you have been discouraged?

3. Hebrews 11:32 includes Gideon among the heroes of the faith. He trusted God's voice and acted on that trust. Can you think of a time when you've done the same?

THURSDAY

FROM MOURNING TO GLADNESS: HANNAH

Do you know why the mighty God of the universe chooses to answer prayer? It is because his children ask. God delights in our asking. He is pleased at our asking. His heart is warmed by our asking. — Richard Foster

Hannah longed for a son—not only because her husband's other wife was cruel about Hannah's barren womb, but because her motherly heart yearned to kiss baby toes and caress the baby's head. In her grief and despair, she became angry and bitter. She wept and would not eat.

An encounter at the tabernacle of the Lord in Shiloh transformed her heart and replaced her mourning with gladness. Whom did she meet, and what happened there?

Read: 1 Samuel 1:1-20

Reflect:

1. Eli accuses Hannah of being drunk. What does Hannah's response say about her heart?

2. After talking with Eli, Hannah's countenance was no longer sad. Why did Hannah have so much confidence that her prayer would be answered?

3. A prayer to become pregnant might seem selfish, but Hannah's heart was to bless God when he blessed her. What's the difference between a selfish request and one that glorifies God? Is there anything you have hesitated to ask of God because it felt selfish?

FRIDAY

FROM DESPAIR TO HOPE: THE CRIMINAL ON THE CROSS

A dying man asked a dying man for eternal life; a man without possessions asked a poor man for a Kingdom; a thief at the door of death asked to die like a thief and steal Paradise. — Fulton Sheen

On Calvary, two criminals and Jesus are nailed to crosses. Matthew records that at first both men taunt Jesus (Matthew 27:44). Then Luke tells us that one of the criminals has a change of heart. "Jesus, remember me when you come into your kingdom."

Why this sudden transformation? How could a condemned and dying man find hope in the midst of despair?

Read: Luke 23:32–43

Reflect:

1. What do you think might have happened to cause one criminal to change his mind about Jesus? In rereading these verses, can you note any particular moment that might have made him repent?

2. What does looking at Jesus' final actions and words on the cross tell you about him?

3. Transformation is a lifelong process, but change can begin in the blink of an eye. Can you define any moments in your life in which you went from despair to hope? From unbelief to belief? Did the change last?

Week Two

Is Change Possible? More Biblical Examples

FROM GREED TO GIVING: JACOB

Nowhere will the man or woman who has fallen short of the glory of God find greater encouragement [than in the story of Jacob]. — A. W. Tozer

God likes to choose and change unlikely people. And Jacob has to be one of the least likely. Here is a man who cheats his own brother and father, a man who altogether lacks common decency. Yet Jacob goes down in history as one of the key people God uses as he develops the story of salvation.

Whoever seeks God will find him. But remember that God is always the one seeking us first. Even here in the Old Testament it's clear that God's favor is never earned. Jacob's famous dream with the angels on the ladder happened right after Jacob swindled his blind father. Right then, at Jacob's worst, God shows up and says the unthinkable: "All the families of the earth shall be blessed in you and in your offspring. Know that I am with you and will keep you wherever you go." And Jacob's response shapes the rest of his life: "Surely the LORD is in this place—and I did not know it!" (Genesis 28:14-16).

Read: Genesis 27:21-24; 33:8-11

Reflect:

1. What happened to Jacob that brought about such a dramatic change? Did it happen suddenly or over time?

2. Has there ever been someone, perhaps yourself, you thought would never change who was changed by God?

TUESDAY

FROM INSECURITY TO BOLDNESS: PETER

Humility is the mother of giants. One sees great things from the valley; only small things from the peak. — G. K. Chesterton

Peter always had a form of boldness, a brash personality that rushed into things for better or worse. When his arrogant claim that he would never deny Jesus was tested by fire, it couldn't withstand even a servant girl's questioning. His boldness came from his own strength, and it failed him at a critical moment. You might say he was filled with himself. Later, filled with the Holy Spirit, he preached with fearless humility.

Read: Luke 22:54–62; Acts 3:6–16

Reflect:

1. Why did Peter deny Jesus? What was he afraid of?

2. What role do our mistakes play in our spiritual formation?

3. Was there a time when something humiliating turned into healthy humility?

WEDNESDAY

FROM THIEF TO BENEFACTOR: ZACCHAEUS

Though you are weak and small... you know and can feel God's pure truth in your spirit. Desire only to have that life brought forth in you and to have your spirit renewed and changed by God's power. — Isaac Penington

Zacchaeus had a reputation as a sinner, likely using his position as chief tax collector to defraud people for his own gain. Yet he found in Jesus something attractive, something he was willing to humble himself like a child to see. Jesus said few words to Zacchaeus, but this brief encounter changed everything for the tax collector. What happened in that moment?

Read: Luke 19:1–9

Reflect:

1. What do you think Zacchaeus felt in Jesus' eyes and words that changed him from a man who defrauded people to one who volunteered half of his wealth to the poor?

2. Jesus never had the same conversation twice. He asked the rich young ruler to sell all and give to the poor. He did not ask the same of Zacchaeus. Why does Jesus use a different approach with each person?

3. If Jesus came to your house, what is one question you'd ask him? What do you think his response would be?

THURSDAY

FROM SELF-DECEPTION TO SELF-KNOWLEDGE: DAVID

Repentance, not proper behavior or even holiness, is the doorway to grace.
And the opposite of sin is grace, not virtue. — Philip Yancey

Change isn't always a straight line from bad to good. There is progress and regress, victory and defeat. The Bible reflects this. It gives us a full picture of the saints with all their sins and shortcomings. Take David, for example. This man after God's own heart made a tremendous mistake.

Uriah was an honorable soldier in David's army. While he was off in battle, David committed adultery with his wife. When she became pregnant, David arranged for Uriah to be sent to the front of the battle line and then for the army to withdraw so that Uriah would be killed. Afterward God sent his prophet Nathan to David to convict him of his sin, and David repented deeply. What can we learn from this in regard to repentance and change?

Read: 2 Samuel 11:1—12:14

Reflect:

1. In 2 Samuel 12, Nathan tells David a story. Why did he do this instead of confronting David directly? Later Jesus would use stories as well to announce the kingdom of God and to lead people to repentance. Why?

2. Repentance means to turn away from evil and turn toward God. What is the difference between just being sorry and true repentance that leads to lasting change?

3. Read 1 John 1:9. Take a moment to ask God if there is any unconfessed sin in your life. If so, write it down, quietly confess it to God, and then put a line through it as a reminder that Jesus has taken care of it on the cross.

FRIDAY

FROM SONS OF THUNDER TO SONS OF LIGHT: JAMES AND JOHN

Remember that what is most important to God is that we submit ourselves and all that we have to him. This requires that we be willing to endure whatever his will brings to us, to be content in whatever state we are in, and to be ready for every change. — Jeremy Taylor

From fishermen, to disciples, to fathers of the faith, James and John were prominent from the start of Jesus' ministry until the building of his church. Early on they were restless youths eager to be first in the kingdom, ready to rain down fire from heaven on those who wouldn't welcome Jesus. Later James became the first martyred disciple (Acts 12:1–3) and John became known as the apostle of love (John 13:23;1 John 4:7–11). What happened?

Read: Mark 3:16–17; Mark 10:35–41

Reflect:

1. What do we learn about Jesus from how he responds to the brothers' request for a prominent place in his kingdom? Imagine Jesus' face as he responds. Do you see him as angry and irritated or as patient and kind?

2. Jesus said, "You do not know what you are asking." At what point in their journey with Jesus do you think the brothers better understood the kingdom of God?

3. James and John are further examples of the slow work of transformation. Their change started with obeying Jesus' call, leaving their nets, and following him. What "nets" have you had to leave behind to follow Jesus? What nets still entangle you?

Week Three

How Do People Change?
Cooperating through Spiritual Disciplines

WHAT ARE SPIRITUAL DISCIPLINES?

God has given us the Disciplines of the spiritual life as a means of receiving his grace. The Disciplines allow us to place ourselves before God so he can transform us. — Richard Foster

In the past two weeks we have looked at biblical examples of ordinary people who were transformed by encountering the living God. Through them, we see that people really can be changed. Now we want to ask: How do people change? In his letter to the Romans, the apostle Paul tells us thirty-five times that righteousness is a "gift from God"—only God can bring the healing and wholeness we need. The question is not "How can we change ourselves?" but rather "How can we cooperate with God's desire to change us?"

Followers of Jesus throughout the centuries have pointed to certain practices—sometimes called *spiritual disciplines*—as means to help us connect and cooperate with God. Richard Foster has cataloged a list of classic spiritual disciplines: meditation, prayer, fasting, study, simplicity, solitude, submission, service, confession, worship, guidance, and celebration. This week we will look at the role these practices (and others like them) play in our friendship with Jesus and in our journey to becoming more like him.

Read: Galatians 6:7–9

Reflect:

1. Reread Richard Foster's list of disciplines above. Which discipline on that list do you naturally enjoy the most? Which one do you feel least attracted to?

2. Today's passage uses a farming metaphor: we sow our lives to either the Spirit or the flesh. What role does a farmer play in helping seed become wheat? What parts of the process are beyond his control?

3. How does the farming metaphor apply to your own spiritual growth?

TUESDAY

A "NEW AUTOMATIC"

Spiritual formation in Christ is the process through which disciples or apprentices of Jesus take on the qualities or characteristics of Christ himself.
— Dallas Willard

Under pressure, what's inside of us comes out. Think of Peter's denial. He thought he was willing to die for Jesus, but in a high-pressure moment he repeatedly denied that he even knew Jesus. Jesus knew all along what was in Peter, but Peter didn't know until he was tested by fire.

All of us have automatic responses when we're under pressure. Usually when we're hurt, we hurt back. Jesus wants to give us a "new automatic"—to make us the kind of people who are naturally inclined to bless those who hate us and to pray for those who spitefully use us.

This new way of being is supernatural. We can't do it on our own. However, we can put ourselves in a place, through spiritual disciplines, to cooperate with God in our transformation.

Read: 2 Peter 1:3-8

Reflect:

1. Today's passage starts by saying it's only through God's promises that we become "participants of the divine nature." What are some of these promises?

2. Is there an area in your life at work or at home where you would like to automatically respond with more love? Resolve to share this with someone you trust and ask for prayer to be transformed in these areas.

WEDNESDAY

Grace isn't opposed to effort. Grace is opposed to earning. — Dallas Willard

The apostle Paul encourages his spiritual son Timothy to "train yourself in godliness." The invitation is to keep company with God, to work out with God by doing the things Jesus did—solitude, silence, fasting, service. These disciplines don't earn anything with God; they simply make room for God to work in our hearts. As we practice them, the Holy Spirit acts as our encouraging friend and coach. He comes alongside and does in us what we could never do on our own.

Read: 1 Timothy 4:7–16

Reflect:

1. What sorts of activities does the apostle Paul seem to suggest are included in "training in godliness"?

2. What effect do disciplines done in secret—prayer or fasting, for example—have on everyday life at work and home? Why do they have that effect?

THURSDAY

BECOMING LIKE JESUS BY LIVING LIKE JESUS

Our model is the Jesus, not only of Calvary, but of the workshop, the roads, the crowds, the clamorous demands and surly oppositions, the lack of all peace and privacy, the interruptions. Jesus is the divine life operating under human conditions. — C. S. Lewis

Several years ago, many folks around the world wore a bracelet that asked What Would Jesus Do? The idea was that in a moment of decision or crisis a person could look at the bracelet on her wrist and be encouraged to act how she imagined Jesus would act in the same situation.

A more helpful question (though too long for a bracelet!) might be this: *What did Jesus do in his private life that enabled him to respond the way he did in his public life?* The accounts of Jesus' days in the Gospels suggest that he cultivated private habits—prayer, solitude, silence, fasting, and Scripture memorization—that empowered him for a public life of healing, teaching, and preaching.

If Jesus himself felt it was important to make spiritual disciplines a priority, we can be sure they are a good idea for us as well.

Read: Luke 5:15-16; Mark 1:32-39

Reflect:

1. Since Jesus was divine, why did he still need to practice disciplines, like withdrawing alone for prayer?

2. In the Mark 1 passage, the disciples seem aggravated that Jesus left to pray when everyone was looking for him. Do the people in your life encourage or discourage you to make space for spiritual disciplines?

3. In Jesus' life we see moments of tremendous output (healing, teaching, preaching) balanced with moments of intentional input (solitude, silence, prayer). How would you rate the balance between "output" (work/ministry) and "input" in your life?

FRIDAY

PLANNED NEGLECT

Your priorities must be God first, God second, and God third, until your life is continually face to face with God. — Oswald Chambers

A world-class violinist was once asked how she came to master her instrument. "Planned neglect," she responded. When she began violin, she explained, other necessary work came before practicing violin. It wasn't until she decided to neglect everything else each day until after violin practice that she started becoming a virtuoso.

In yesterday's reading, Jesus withdrew for prayer when his disciples thought he should be out ministering. You could say he was practicing "planned neglect" in order to make his relationship with his Father first in his life.

The obligations we have to family, work, and society are secondary to—and dependent upon—connecting with God as our first priority. "Seek first the kingdom of God," Jesus tells us, "and all these things will be added to you" (Matthew 6:33 ESV). So how do we see what we are "seeking first"? We pay attention to how we structure our days and order our thoughts. The spiritual disciplines are wonderful gifts for helping us neglect all else until we seek first the kingdom.

Read: Psalm 16

Reflect:

1. Is the idea of "planned neglect" helpful? How can it be balanced with things that must be done, like caring for young children or meeting a work deadline?

2. If you were to examine your schedule for the past week, what does it say about your priorities?

3. The psalmist David says, "I keep my eyes always on the LORD" (Psalm 16:8 NIV). What practices have you found most effective for keeping your focus on Jesus?

Week Four

How Do I Follow Jesus?

MONDAY 2/22

FOLLOWING JESUS AS SAVIOR

God creates out of nothing. Wonderful you say. Yes, to be sure, but he does what is still more wonderful: he makes saints out of sinners.
— *Søren Kierkegaard*

Why do we need a Savior? Simply put, we cannot save ourselves. Even Paul, a faithful servant of Christ, filled with the Holy Spirit, found his human nature interfering with his pursuit of godliness. "For I do not do the good I want to do, but the evil I do not want to do—this I keep on doing" (Romans 7:19 NIV). Paul knew that the law could convict him of his sin, but only the grace of Christ could save him from it.

The idea of God's provision of a Savior for his people—one who would crush the serpent's head and restore right relationships—goes back to Genesis 3:14-15. Today's passage from Isaiah speaks about the coming Messiah.

Read: Isaiah 49:1-13

Reflect:

1. What are some of the attributes of the Messiah, according to this passage? Can you think of ways that Jesus fulfills these prophecies?

2. To whom does God's salvation come in this passage? Why is this important?

3. Thinking about your life, when do you most recognize your need for a Savior? Can you empathize with what Paul said in Romans 7:19? How?

TUESDAY

FOLLOWING JESUS AS TEACHER

Jesus Christ is alive and here to teach his people himself. He has not contracted laryngitis. His voice is not hard to hear, his vocabulary is not difficult to understand. — Richard Foster

Using sermons or parables, speaking to multitudes or individuals, standing in the synagogue or on a boat, Jesus was always teaching about reality. "They were astounded at his teaching, for he taught them as one having authority" (Mark 1:22). Jesus did not offer mere academic theory. Everything he taught came from the heart and was proven through action.

Even those who don't follow Jesus affirm he was a great historical teacher. But for those who follow him, he is more than that. Jesus is alive. Through the Holy Spirit, he is our ever-present teacher, ready and willing to instruct us in the classroom of life.

Read: John 14:16–17; John 16:7–15

Reflect:

1. Walking with Jesus during his earthly ministry would have been an incredible thing. Yet Jesus said it was better that he "go away." What did he mean? What is better about having the Holy Spirit to teach us rather than having Jesus with us in the flesh?

2. In our daily lives, what kinds of things does the Holy Spirit use to teach us? How can we be good students?

3. Take a moment to pray. In your own words, ask God to help you hear his voice teaching you throughout your day.

WEDNESDAY

FOLLOWING JESUS AS LORD

Salvation apart from obedience is unknown in the sacred scriptures.
— *A. W. Tozer*

Think of Thomas, who would not believe that Christ had risen until he could see and touch the wounds in Jesus' hands and side. When Jesus appeared and offered his wounds for inspection, Thomas could only exclaim, "My Lord and my God!" (John 20:24–28). The power, authority, and influence that Thomas had thought were nailed to the cross and died with Jesus were suddenly, vibrantly alive.

In today's reading, Peter rebukes Jesus while at the same time calling him "Lord." What do we learn from Jesus' response?

Read: Matthew 16:21–27   Luke 9: 23-25

Reflect:

1. Is it possible to accept Jesus as Savior but not accept him as Lord? In other words, when you follow Jesus can you just carry on with life as before?

2. Do Jesus' love, gentleness, and humility give him more authority or less? Why?

3. What does it mean, in practical terms, to "lose your life" for Jesus?

THURSDAY

FOLLOWING JESUS AS FRIEND

A rule I have had for years is to treat the Lord Jesus Christ as a personal friend. His is not a creed, a mere doctrine, but it is He Himself we have.
— Dwight L. Moody

Savior, Teacher, Lord—yes. But Friend? Truly there is no greater miracle than the very Son of God, the one who holds all things together, calling us friends.

Perhaps you are familiar with this passage from John 15. Today, slow down with it. If you're in a group, have two or three different people read it. A person's most important words often come when he or she is close to death. We would do well to listen closely to these words from Jesus, spoken as he neared the hour of crucifixion.

Read: John 15:9–17

Reflect:

1. Jesus said, "I have said these things to you so that my joy may be in you" (John 15:11). What did Jesus' joy look like? Why do you think Jesus wants to share that joy with us?

2. What are some differences between a servant and a friend?

3. How do you feel about calling Jesus a friend? Is it easy or difficult to embrace this aspect of relationship with Jesus?

FRIDAY

FOLLOWING JESUS INTO SIX GREAT STREAMS

When we carefully consider how Jesus lived while among us in the flesh, we learn how we are to live—truly live—empowered by him who is with us always even to the end of the age. — Richard Foster

Beginning next Monday, and for the rest of this devotional, we will be looking at spiritual formation through what Richard Foster identifies as six great streams in the life of Jesus and in the lives of his followers. These six streams are the prayer-filled life, the virtuous life, the Spirit-empowered life, the compassionate life, the Word-centered life, and the sacramental life.

Many people naturally gravitate toward one or two of the streams, but either resist or don't know much about some of the others. All of these streams, however, are present in the life of Christ. Through exploring all six we will gain a balanced framework for becoming more like Jesus.

Read: Ephesians 2:1–10

Reflect:

1. What does it mean to be seated with Christ in heavenly places? What effect does that have on everyday life?

2. Paul writes that we are saved by grace through faith rather than by works. But then he writes that we are created for good works. Why does Paul put these two ideas side by side?

3. God had every right to let us stay dead in our sins. He didn't have to save us, but he wanted to! Take a moment to pray aloud to thank God for his grace. Ask him to help you to "grow in the grace and knowledge of our Lord and Savior Jesus Christ" (2 Peter 3:18) over these coming months.

Week One

How Did Jesus Pray?

PRAYER

Real prayer comes not from gritting our teeth but from falling in love.
— Richard Foster

For the next eight weeks we will swim in the first of the six great streams we find modeled in the life of Jesus—the "prayer-filled life." Prayer is interaction with the God who loves and delights in us. It is what our hearts long for, what we are made for. It is listening, it is talking, it is abiding in the presence of God. We need a teacher—the Teacher—to show us how. And so this week we look at how Jesus prayed. First, though, let's start with a passage from Richard Foster's book *Prayer* to catch a glimpse of the heart of God:

> *Today the heart of God is an open wound of love. He aches over our distance and preoccupation. He mourns that we do not draw near to him. He grieves that we have forgotten him. He weeps over our obsession with muchness and manyness. He longs for our presence. And he is inviting you—and me—to come home, to come home to where we belong, to come home to that for which we were created. His arms are stretched out wide to receive us. His heart is enlarged to take us in.*

Read: John 5:19

Reflect:

1. In John 5:19, Jesus talks about doing "only what he sees the Father doing." What does it mean to see what the Father is doing? How do you think prayer helps us to see that?

2. Take a few minutes to talk with God. Ask God to teach you how to pray and lift up anything else on your heart.

TUESDAY

The soul anchor established in solitude will remain solid when you return to your ordinary life with others. — Dallas Willard

Jesus was a very busy person, yet he always made prayer a priority. One might easily conclude from reading the Gospels that the central focus of Jesus' life was his relationship with the Father. He said that he could do nothing apart from the Father and that his entire mission in life was to do his will. We see this focus in Jesus' daily life. He frequently left the crowds to be alone with the Father, retreating to "a deserted place" (Matthew 14:13) to pray. He became a role model for the disciples; when they looked at Jesus, they longed to be like him, to have the same kind of intimacy with God that he had.

Read: Matthew 14:13-23

Reflect:

1. Matthew 14:22-23 tells us that Jesus made his disciples get into the boat "immediately" while he sent the multitudes away so that he could pray alone on the mountain. Why do you think he went immediately? Why was that need so pressing?

2. Today's passage opens with "when Jesus heard this." The event Jesus heard about was the death of John the Baptist. How do you draw nearer to the Father in times of stress and grief?

WEDNESDAY

THE BUSIER HE GOT, THE MORE HE PRAYED

I have so much to do today that I shall spend the first three hours in prayer.
— Martin Luther

Jesus was a person of prayer. He prayed regularly; he prayed often. The busier he got, the more he talked with God. Why? Because he always looked to the Father for instruction and strength. "I do nothing on my own, but I speak these things as the Father instructed me" (John 8:28).

From God Jesus heard what to do and say. And by spending time with God in intimate prayer, he gained the strength to carry out what was asked of him.

By his actions, Jesus became a model, a "divine paradigm" that we can imitate.

Read: Psalm 46

Reflect:
The Psalms are quoted by Jesus more than any other book of the Old Testament, and no doubt Jesus knew and prayed today's psalm. It's wonderful to imagine Jesus, perhaps alone on a mountain, praying this very psalm. Praying the Psalms is one way to imitate him. Today read Psalm 46 aloud, slowly. On an index card write down a word or phrase that stands out to you. Carry this with you and return to it throughout the day.

THURSDAY

ABBA

Prayer is putting oneself in the hands of God. — Mother Teresa

What set Jesus apart from the disciples was the intimate relationship he had with the Father. Jesus addressed God as "Abba, Father." This manner of addressing God indicates closeness, love, and a trusting relationship like that of children to their parents. Jesus was not afraid to talk with God, to share his deepest feelings.

In the Garden of Gethsemane—at his moment of greatest need—Jesus prayed. His prayer was full of faith: "For you all things are possible." His prayer was honest: "Remove this cup from me." And in the end, his prayer expressed a desire to do the will of God: "Yet, not what I want, but what you want."

Read: Mark 14:32–36

Reflect:

1. Do you think there is a connection between Jesus' address of God as *Abba* and his willingness to surrender to God's will?

2. Take a few minutes to read today's passage out loud, slowly. Listen for a word or phrase that stands out to you. If you'd like, share that word or phrase with a friend and consider why it stood out to you.

FRIDAY

ABBA'S HEART

Jesus wants to make it clear that the God of whom he speaks is a God of compassion who joyously welcomes repentant sinners into his house.
— Henri Nouwen

The most vivid picture of God's tender love comes in the parable of the prodigal son. A wayward son who has squandered his inheritance returns to his father in repentance and remorse, expecting judgment and punishment. Instead he receives a loving welcome and a warm embrace. This is God's nature, what he is like. If in our deepest being we believed God to be this way—a loving, forgiving Father—praying to him and talking with him would not be a chore or a duty, but rather would be our inner desire throughout the day. God longs for us, searches for us—even through Jesus lays down his life for us—in hopes that we will respond to his longing, searching, self-sacrificing love. Once we catch a glimpse of what God is like we will want to spend time with him.

Read: Luke 15:11–32

Reflect:

1. The father in this parable gives us a snapshot of the nature of God. How does this picture match or not match your own understanding of what God is like?

2. How does the way you picture God affect the way you pray?

Week Two

~~~~~~~~~

How Did Jesus Teach Us to Pray? Part One

MONDAY 3/8

LORD, TEACH US TO PRAY

The Lord's Prayer is not so much a command as an invitation: an invitation to share in the prayer-life of Jesus himself. — N. T. Wright

The disciples knew Jesus had an intimate relationship with the Father. So they asked, "Lord, teach us to pray" (Luke 11:1). Jesus responded, in Luke 11:2-4 and Matthew 6:9-13, with what is called "The Lord's Prayer." But a better name might be "The Disciples' Prayer." After all, it's our prayer—the model Jesus gave us to pray.

This might be the most famous prayer in all of history, and things this familiar sometimes become cold and mechanical. Perhaps it's that way for you. Or perhaps it pulses with life within you. Or perhaps you've not spent much time with it before. In any case, there is more here to be discovered. God is a sea into which we can always sail further—and this prayer is a vessel fit to take us there. So let's spend the next two weeks entering in, line by line, to this prayer Jesus gave us.

Read: Matthew 6:9-13

Reflect:
Take a moment to reflect on your honest experience, if any, with this prayer. Is it old, new, stale, or fresh? Consider reading it aloud in three or four different versions of Scripture.

TUESDAY

OUR FATHER

Some people are offended that we are taught to address God as Father. The greater offense may be the little word Our. *In this prayer we are taught to pray, not as individuals, but as the church. — Stanley Hauerwas*

Relationship with God is personal but not private, intimate but not individualistic. When you choose to follow Jesus, you join a community, the church: a community so connected to Jesus that Scripture calls it his very body, the body of Christ. So even when praying alone, one can say "Our Father"—a joyful acknowledgment of joining with the "communion of saints" (followers of Jesus throughout the centuries).

After his resurrection, Jesus met Mary outside the tomb and said to her, "Go to my brothers and say to them, 'I am ascending to my Father and your Father, to my God and your God" (John 20:17). Don't miss this miraculous statement. Jesus makes us part of the family of God, grants us the same access to the Father that Jesus himself has. Orphans no more, we boldly—with reverence and joy—join Jesus in calling God "*Abba*, Father."

Read: Romans 8:14–16

Reflect:

1. What is the best example of an earthly father you've ever seen? What made that person a good father?

2. Choose an adjective that describes God as Father. Write down this sentence, filling in the blank: I praise you, God, for being a _____ Father. Practice praising God throughout the day using this phrase.

gracious
loving
forgiving
understanding

WEDNESDAY

IN HEAVEN

If we only had eyes to see and ears to hear and wits to understand, we would know that the Kingdom of God in the sense of holiness, goodness, beauty is as close as breathing and is crying out to be born both within ourselves and within the world. — Frederick Buechner

God lives in heaven. Where is that? Is it in outer space, or farther? The root meaning of the Greek word for "heaven" is "to cover" or "to encompass." It is the expansive universe and beyond, but it is also the atmosphere that surrounds us. Consider for a moment that second sense of the word. Wave your hands through the air and you have waved them through the heavens.

For those of us who think of God as far away, this is wonderful news. Here's one way we might pray this part of the prayer: "Our Father, always present to us, you are high above all and as near to us as the air we breathe."

Read: Acts 17:27–28

Reflect:
When you pray, do you normally think of God as close—as close as the person next to you or the air around you—or do you think of God as far off? Why? Does where we think about God's location affect the way we pray?

Meditate for a few minutes upon this phrase from today's passage: "In him we live and move and have our being." Throughout the day, say this phrase as a reminder of God's nearness.

THURSDAY

HALLOWED BE YOUR NAME

God has a name. This points to a key difference between persons and things. God is not a nameless energy or abstract idea. — Thomas Oden

Think of a person that is precious to you—perhaps a close friend or spouse or child. When someone is close to your heart, that person's name is like music to your ears. You delight to hear that name, and you delight to hear others speaking well of that person.

In Scripture, someone's name is supremely important. It represents identity and essence. When Moses asked God who he should tell the Israelites sent him, God responded with the name "I AM." Dwell for a moment on this name. Before sun and stars, before sand and sea, before anything visible . . . I AM—the Trinity forever existing in holy community. And this infinite one chose to create us, redeem us, and bring us into the family of God. Truly there is no greater name, no sweeter name.

So we pray, "May your name, God, a name like none other, be cherished and loved."

Read: Exodus 3:13–15

Reflect:

1. God first identifies as the infinite one, "I am," the one without beginning or end. Then God identifies with his people as "the God of Abraham . . . Isaac . . . Jacob." Why do you think God identified in these two ways?

2. It is natural to honor and esteem someone who does great things. Think of applause for a wonderful performance, or a statue that commemorates a hero. What are some qualities about God, or things God has done for you personally, that make you want to honor his name?

FRIDAY

YOUR KINGDOM COME, YOUR WILL BE DONE,

ON EARTH AS IN HEAVEN

God's kingdom is not a place, but rather a relationship. It exists wherever people enthrone Jesus as lord of their lives. — *J. I. Packer*

What is a kingdom? It's where the king rules—where what the king wants to be done is done. In the kingdom of heaven, what God wants to be done is always done. On earth, God has given people free will to choose good or evil. And Satan still "prowls around like a roaring lion" (1 Peter 5:8). That means a lot of places on earth don't look like the kingdom of heaven . . . yet. So we pray for God's will to be done within and without, in our hearts and in the earth.

A great place to start asking God for his will to be done is in our own little kingdoms—our homes and workplaces, anywhere we are from day to day. So we pray, "God, may your rule be completed all around me. May what you want done be done in my home, my workplace, my children's school."

Read: Mark 1:14–15; Luke 10:8–9

Reflect:

1. In today's passages, Jesus proclaims, "The kingdom of God has come near." In Luke 10:9, Jesus tells his disciples to "cure the sick" as they proclaim that message. In what way does healing show that God's kingdom has come near?

2. Describe a place or system in the world (or in your life) where things are in chaos or dysfunction. Then describe what it would be like for righteousness, justice, and peace to rule in that place. Take a few moments to pray that God would bring what you described into reality.

Week Three

How Did Jesus Teach Us to Pray? Part Two

4th PARTITION

MONDAY 3|15

GIVE US THIS DAY OUR DAILY BREAD

It would be concerning if a child was found stuffing food into her pocket
because she believed her parents wouldn't give her food tomorrow.
— Dallas Willard

"Do not be afraid, little flock," Jesus says, "for it is your Father's good pleasure to give you the kingdom" (Luke 12:32).

The security of riches is an illusion. If we put our trust in things that wear out or can be lost, our hearts can never fully be at peace. So God invites us into true security and peace, to be like a little child who eats food today without worrying about food tomorrow. This is how it was in the Garden of Eden. And this is what Jesus teaches us: our good Father will provide at our moment of need. So we pray, "Give us today what we need for today."

Read: Luke 12:22–32

Reflect:

1. In your experience, do those in poverty struggle with worry more or less than those who are not in poverty?

2. Can people whose physical needs are already met for today still pray "Give us this day our daily bread"? If so, what does it mean in that context?

3. One way to trust God is by giving, especially in secret. Look for an opportunity this week to give away something—money or food or time—in secret or to someone who can't repay you.

DEPENDANCE

TUESDAY

FORGIVE US OUR DEBTS, AS WE ALSO HAVE FORGIVEN

OUR DEBTORS

Harboring unforgiveness is like drinking poison and expecting the other person to die. — Unknown

When speaking of forgiveness, Jesus often put together two things: receiving forgiveness from God and offering forgiveness to others. The apostle Paul tells us "that while we still were sinners Christ died for us" (Romans 5:8). So God forgives us first. Then from that place of being forgiven God expects us to turn and forgive others.

Forgiveness isn't saying that the wrong someone has done against you is right. Forgiveness is releasing the offender to God and relinquishing the right to retaliation and resentment. Numerous medical studies have linked unforgiveness with depression, stress, and illness. When we harbor unforgiveness, we become a prisoner. In forgiving another, we set ourselves free.

Here is one way to pray this line of the Lord's Prayer: "Forgive us for the ways we impose upon you, God, as we forgive those who impose upon us."

Read: Matthew 18:21–35

Reflect:

1. Jesus linked receiving forgiveness from God with forgiving others. Why do you think he was so adamant that we forgive one another?

2. Let's take a few minutes today in quiet. Grab a pen and a sheet of paper. Ask God if there is anyone against whom you are harboring unforgiveness. Write down the individual's name and what he or she has done. Then release that person to God with a simple prayer, "I choose to forgive and bless _____ in Jesus name." You might find the hardest person to forgive is yourself. If so, write down your name and what you have done and forgive yourself as God has forgiven you.

WEDNESDAY

LEAD US NOT INTO TEMPTATION, BUT DELIVER US FROM EVIL

Do not, I beseech you, lead me in your providence where I shall be tempted; for I am so feeble, that maybe the temptation may be too strong for me, therefore, today make a straight path for my feet. — Charles Spurgeon

The late singer and songwriter Rich Mullins openly shared his struggle with temptation. He used to travel alone and he would often find himself, or even put himself, in places of temptation. His spiritual director said, "It's not that you're bad, it's that you're human. Take a friend with you when you travel."

It's good to overcome temptation, but better still, when possible, to be led on a path around it. This part of the prayer is best prayed with the simplicity of a child: "Keep us, Father, out of trouble, and save us from everything bad."

Read: Matthew 18:1–7

Reflect:

1. In today's passage, Jesus says, "Whoever becomes humble like this child is the greatest in the kingdom of heaven." What kind of humility does a child have that most adults don't have?

2. Temptations have more power when they are kept secret. Do you have a trusted friend in whom you can confide? If so, give that person a call this week and ask if you can share your temptations and pray together. If you have no such person, ask God to provide someone.

THURSDAY

THE KINGDOM, THE POWER, AND THE GLORY ARE YOURS FOREVER

Any kingdom that defines glory in terms of a bloody cross is obviously peculiar. — Stanley Hauerwas

God can will whatever he pleases. Whatever he says goes. So what does the creator of the universe do with this infinite power? He showed his power by laying it aside, becoming one of us, dying the worst imaginable death, and then rising again to defeat death forever. God deserved our praise before he did any of this. But when we reflect upon how he's displayed his power through the cross, how can we help but give him praise?

So we pray, "God, you are the one who is in charge, who can do anything, and who deserves all the glory now and forever."

Read: Philippians 2:5–11

Reflect:

1. Jesus compared the kingdom of God to a tiny mustard seed, and he showed his power in humility. How is this different than the world's kingdoms and power? Why do you think God chooses to demonstrate his kingdom and power in ways so different than the world?

2. Today's passage says, "Let the same mind be in you that was in Christ Jesus." What is one specific way that you can have the mind of Christ today toward your coworkers, your spouse, your friends, or your kids?

FRIDAY

AMEN

In testimony of our desire, and assurance to be heard, we say, Amen.
— Westminster Shorter Catechism

Sometimes we say "Amen" simply as a way to signify that we're done praying, like saying "Goodbye" at the end of a phone call. But "Amen" means much more than that. It's a way of testifying that we are in agreement with God, that we know God hears us.

Sometimes it's helpful to take something familiar and put it into new words. So let's close this section on the Lord's Prayer with a paraphrase written by Dallas Willard:

Dear Father always near us,
may your name be treasured and loved,
may your rule be completed in us—
may your will be done here on earth
in just the way it is done in heaven.
Give us today the things we need today,
and forgive us our sins and impositions on you
as we are forgiving all who in any way offended us.
Please don't put us through trials,
but deliver us from everything bad.
Because you are the one in charge,
and you have all the power,
and the glory too is all yours—forever—
which is just the way we want it!

Read: Matthew 18:19

Reflect:
Pray Dallas Willard's version of the Lord's Prayer out loud. Did these familiar ideas become new when you prayed the new words? Did you notice anything else about praying Dallas's version? How might you write the Lord's Prayer in your own words?

Week Four

What Practices Help Nurture a Life of Prayer?

MONDAY 3/22

SILENCE

Be still and know that I am God ... Be still and know that I am ... Be still and know ... Be still ... Be. — From Psalm 46:10

Do you find using words safer than allowing for silence in your life? In your prayer life? Wordless prayer can be surprisingly challenging. When we feel we want to pour out our lives to God—all our praise and worry and pain and joy—we naturally seek words that express the tumbling thoughts that fill our minds. We need to know that God is listening.

We need both spoken and wordless prayer. Wordless prayer is listening prayer. We take a moment to quiet our souls and offer ourselves to the Holy Spirit in a particular way—as people who listen. When we practice silence in prayer, we disengage from the outside and inside noise and prepare our hearts to hear that "gentle whisper" of God (1 Kings 19:12 NIV) without interference.

Read: 1 Kings 19:1–18

Reflect:

1. Why do you think that the Lord caused the wind, earthquake, and fire to precede his voice? How did Elijah react to these phenomena?

2. Set a five-minute timer. Then sit in quiet with the Lord. If your mind wanders, have grace for yourself, and try using a phrase (for example, "The Lord is my Shepherd") or picture (for example, of Jesus in a green field leading you as his lamb) to return your mind to God.

3. If you haven't already, consider designating a place in your home to pray. It can be as simple as a comfortable chair or a floor pillow in a corner. Spend a few minutes there each day this week in silence before the Lord.

TUESDAY

SOLITUDE

Loneliness is inner emptiness. Solitude is inner fulfillment. — Richard Foster

God has forever existed in community—Father, Son, and Holy Spirit. And we who bear God's image are made for community with others. There are times, though, when our souls need to withdraw from others to fellowship alone with the living God.

Jesus calls this the "secret place" (Matthew 6:6 NKJV). In solitude, we release our need for acceptance by others and we receive what we need from the Lord. It's where, as David says in today's psalm, God "restores my soul." Solitude isn't an escape from people and real life. It equips us to be with people and do our daily work in a healthier way.

Read: Psalm 23

Reflect:

1. Solitude comes easier for some than others. Are you an introvert or an extrovert? Do you find the times when God draws you away from others to be refreshing or difficult?

2. Our families and community can present challenges to practicing solitude in prayer. Take a moment now to put a specific time and place on your calendar to get away with God. It could be as simple as an hour in the park. Don't set out to study, or read, or get anything done. This is a time to simply be present to God.

WEDNESDAY

SCRIPTURE MEDITATION

The amount of time we spend with Jesus—meditating on His Word and His majesty, seeking His face—establishes our fruitfulness in the kingdom.
— Charles Stanley

The Word of God is more accessible today than ever before, but that very accessibility can lead us to take it for granted. The technology that brings Scripture to our fingertips in endless translations can also make the Bible just one of many options that grab our attention. To enjoy the riches of God's Word fully, we must take time to meditate upon it.

This practice comes with many blessings. First, it slows us down to consider fully what God is speaking into us. Secondly, it changes us from the inside out. Lastly, it strengthens us to be fruitful for the kingdom. In today's reading, the psalmist leads us through some ways to meditate upon God's Word.

Read: Psalm 77

Reflect:

1. The psalmist finds comfort in continually remembering and meditating upon God's mighty works. Why does he need this consolation?

2. What kinds of wonders have you seen God do in your life, work, or community?

THURSDAY

PRACTICING THE PRESENCE OF GOD

There is not in the world a kind of life more sweet and delightful than that of a continual conversation with God; those only can comprehend it who practice and experience it. — Brother Lawrence

You may recall that Jacob once awoke from a dream and declared, "Surely the Lord is in this place—and I did not know it!" (Genesis 28:16). This is forever true. God is in this place, in whatever place you find yourself: at work, at home, at school, at church. God is as close as the nose on your face. Closer even. Through the indwelling Holy Spirit, God makes his home inside you. Our job is to recognize God's presence and join King David in saying, "I keep the Lord always before me" (Psalm 16:8).

Read: Psalm 16

Reflect:

1. David goes on to say, in Psalm 16:8, that because the Lord "is at my right hand, I shall not be moved." What does it mean to have God at your right hand? Why did that cause David to be unshaken?

2. Today, try living out this wisdom from Brother Lawrence: "God does not ask much of us, merely a thought of Him from time to time, a little act of adoration, sometimes to ask for His grace, sometimes to offer Him your sufferings, at other times to thank Him for the graces, past and present, He has bestowed on you, in the midst of your troubles to take solace in Him as often as you can. Lift up your heart to Him during your meals and in company; the least little remembrance will always be the most pleasing to Him. One need not cry out very loudly; He is nearer to us than we think."

FRIDAY

WHAT CAN HINDER OUR PRACTICE OF PRAYER?

Distraction is the curse of our age. The desperate need today is not for a greater number of efficient people, or busy people, but for present people.
— *Nathan Foster*

Most of us live in the midst of jobs and families and responsibilities. These are all good things. God provides these contexts as a place to form our character. Because there's so much good work to do, it's easy to put prayer at the bottom of the list. Sometimes good can be the enemy of best.

In this information age, we have an added responsibility. Our computers and phones give us tremendous power—power to research and to communicate instantly. Along with that power comes the tremendous potential for distraction.

Guilt is never a life-giving motivator. So let's set before our minds what is true: God invites us into a conversational relationship with him that leads to sustainable joy, peace, and life. When we wake up early to pray, or turn off our phone for a while to be more present to God, we join Mary and say yes to the best thing.

Read: Luke 10:38–42

Reflect:

1. What specifically is the "better part" that Mary chose?

2. Do you think Martha could have done her many tasks without a distracted heart? Why or why not?

3. Take a few moments to consider what distractions might prevent you from keeping company with God. Write down one or two practical steps you might try this weekend to be less distracted and more present to God and others.

Week 1

~~~~~~

Moving Inward—Seeking the Transformation We Need

MONDAY 4|5

3/29 EASTER READINGS JOHN 13: 1-17
MARK 8: 27-33
8: 34-38
14: 32-42
15: 33-47
JOHN 20: 19-28
MATH 28: 1-10

PRAYER: THE KEY TO GOD'S HEART

He prayeth well, who loveth well. — Samuel Coleridge

Richard Foster sat at a library desk neck-deep in books from across the centuries. The task of writing a book on prayer felt increasingly overwhelming. Who was he to write such a book? How could one begin to describe in a single book the depth of a conversational life with God? But then he caught a glimpse of God's heart. He describes what he saw at that moment in the opening pages of his book *Prayer: Finding the Heart's True Home.*

This month we'll work through different kinds of prayer outlined in that book. Remember that prayer isn't just one more activity to add to our list. It's a gift, a way of responding to and interacting with the lover of our souls. It's the key to the home in which we were created to dwell. Foster writes:

> *For too long we have been in a far country: a country of noise and hurry and crowds, a country of climb and push and shove, a country of frustration and fear and intimidation. And he welcomes us home: home to serenity and peace and joy, home to friendship and fellowship and openness, home to intimacy and acceptance and affirmation.*

Read: Matthew 6:7–8

Reflect:

1. Jesus tells us that God knows everything we need before we ask him. That means prayer is more than simply exchanging information. Why, then, do we pray? CONNECTION, THANKSfullNESS, INTERSESSION

2. Spend a few moments in prayer—whether silently or out loud. Specifically, ask God to deepen your life of prayer and bring you to a closer friendship with him.

TUESDAY

SIMPLE PRAYER

Lay before Him what is in us, not what ought to be in us. — C. S. Lewis

Nothing stops prayer in its tracks like feeling inadequate. How are we finite creatures to approach the eternal Creator? And if we do come, are we really to bring our little troubles? Surely the God of the universe has more important things to deal with than our trivialities. So our thinking goes. But it is a limitation of earthly kings to have no time for small matters. God has no such limitation. His power affords him total presence to every person and every situation at all times. He's big enough to care for small situations. His love is strong enough to embrace us where we are, not where we wish we were.

In "Simple Prayer," we come like a child to God with whatever is on our minds, big or small. It's the first kind of prayer we pray, and one we never outgrow. Foster says:

> *Simple Prayer involves ordinary people bringing ordinary concerns to a loving and compassionate Father. There is no pretense in Simple Prayer. We do not pretend to be more holy, more pure, or more saintly than we actually are. We do not try to conceal our conflicting and contradictory motives from God—or ourselves. And in this posture, we pour out our heart to the God who is greater than our heart and who knows all things (1 John 3:20).*

Read: Matthew 19:13–15

Reflect:

1. Why do you think the disciples wanted to stop the children from coming to Jesus?

2. What is it about children that Jesus wants us to emulate? How can we apply that to the way we come to God, how we talk to God, and what we talk to God about?

WEDNESDAY

PRAYER OF EXAMEN

You might have the impression that your everyday life is . . . dreary. It isn't.
Daily life is rich and meaningful. Every encounter, every challenge, every
disappointment, and every delight is a place where God can be found.
— Jim Manney

In the "Prayer of Examen," we ask the Holy Spirit to help us take an honest look at our recent past, perhaps the last twenty-four hours or the last week, to find God and God's blessings. We also review moments that didn't go well, for which we ask God's forgiveness and grace to correct.

Asking for God's guidance here is key. God helps us see little gifts that we might otherwise overlook. And in seeing our sin, the Spirit keeps us from the ditch on one side of defending ourselves and the ditch on the other side of self-punishment and shame. Rooted in the love of Christ, the Prayer of Examen grows healthy self-awareness that helps us love others more.

Read: Psalm 139:23–24

Reflect:
The Prayer of Examen is often used before bed or first thing in the morning. Today let's practice it by reviewing the last forty-eight hours. Have paper and pen ready and move slowly through the steps.

First, ask the Holy Spirit to guide your time.

Second, ask God to bring to mind specific things from the last two days that you're thankful for and write them down.

Third, ask for God's help to recall shortcomings in the last two days and write those down.

Forth, ask and thank God for his forgiveness and healing.

Lastly, pray about the day to come. Ask God for grace to be present to him in every conversation and circumstance.

THURSDAY

〰〰〰〰〰

PRAYER OF RELINQUISHMENT

It is wonderful what miracles God works in wills that are utterly surrendered to Him. — Hannah Whitall Smith

At the core of what makes us human is our will, the ability to choose. The goal of spiritual formation is not to destroy the will but to transform it so that over time we come to naturally will what God wills. The "Prayer of Relinquishment" says "Thy will be done." This prayer isn't resignation, a sigh of "Whatever happens, happens." This prayer is agreement with God, our will becoming like God's will that we might live our life as Jesus would live it. Foster says:

> *The Prayer of Relinquishment is a bona fide letting go, but it is [also] a release with hope. We have no fatalist resignation. We are buoyed up by a confident trust in the character of God. Even when all we see are the tangled threads on the backside of life's tapestry, we know that God is good and is out to do us good always. That gives us hope to believe that we are the winners, regardless of what we are being called upon to relinquish. God is inviting us deeper in and higher up. There is training in righteousness, transforming power, new joys, deeper intimacy.*

Read: Luke 22:39–44 ✓

Reflect:

1. Surrendering one's will to God would seem to make us less free, yet the Scriptures testify that surrender leads us to true freedom and life. How does surrender to God increase our freedom?

2. At the start of Jesus' ministry, God the Father said, "This is my beloved Son" (Matthew 3:17 ESV). How did knowing how much he was loved help Jesus surrender to God's will, though doing so was costly? How can knowing how much God loves you help you to surrender?

FRIDAY

COVENANT PRAYER

The truth is that we only learn to pray all the time everywhere after we have resolutely set about praying some of the time somewhere. — John Dalrymple

Modern culture avoids covenant and commitment. On the one hand, it can feel stifling—We want to do whatever we want whenever we want! On the other hand, it can feel intimidating—Will we follow through with our commitment? The truth is that commitment and discipline bring freedom. A musician can know the joy of improvising because of hours of structured practice.

In the spiritual life, we want to be people who pray without ceasing, ever in sweet communion with our Maker who loves us. That is possible. But it starts with a specific time and a specific place. Mornings, in particular, set the tone for the day. "Early will I seek thee," says the psalmist (Psalm 63:1 KJV). Many Christian traditions throughout history have fixed times to pray at morning, afternoon, and night. Like a compass, these set times of prayer bring us back to the path of life.

Read: Psalm 57:7–11 ✓

Reflect:

1. Do you find it difficult to commit to regular times of prayer? Why or why not?

2. Today through this weekend, consider trying this simple exercise: If you have a phone or watch, set an alarm for midday. Noon perhaps. Decide now what you will pray when the alarm sounds. You might pray the Lord's Prayer, Psalm 23, or a simple prayer such as "Thank you, God, that you are always with me."

Week 2

~~~

Moving Upward—Seeking the Intimacy We Need

MONDAY  4|19

THE PRAYER OF ADORATION

Adoration is the spontaneous yearning of the heart to worship, honor, magnify, and bless God. We ask nothing but to cherish him. We seek nothing but his exaltation. We focus on nothing but his goodness. — Richard Foster

This week we move from prayers that focus on our inward condition to ones we use to set our sights upon the beauty of God. The first of these upward prayers is the "Prayer of Adoration."

Adoration is the natural, spontaneous response of a heart that sees the beauty of God. So if adoration is spontaneous, how can we practice it? Like many things in the spiritual life, adoration happens intentionally but indirectly. Space must be made for it. And thankfulness is the space in which adoration grows. Scripture shows over and over that remembering God's deeds leads to praise, to adoration. Setting our minds upon what God has done—his specific work in our lives—opens our eyes to who God is. God's goodness becomes tangible instead of abstract. "I will call to mind the deeds of the LORD; I will remember your wonders of old" (Psalm 77:11).

Read: Psalm 27:1-6 ✓

Reflect:

Let's take a few moments to stir up adoration by giving thanks. Ask God to bring to mind good things. When something comes to mind, simply say it aloud and then affirm it by responding: "Thank you, Lord." Your thanksgiving could be as simple as "For this morning's beautiful sunrise . . . Thank you, Lord." Or as profound as "For the cross of Christ taking away my shame and guilt . . . Thank you, Lord."

TUESDAY

PRAYER OF REST

Rest. Rest. Rest in God's love. The only work you are required now to do is to give your most intense attention to His still, small voice within.
— *Madame Jeanne Guyon*

Rest is often thought of as the opposite of labor, something perhaps earned after hard work. But biblical rest is the opposite of hurry, heaviness, and anxiety. It is freedom from the need to control circumstances and people. It is not laziness or passivity, but an active trust in God. Rather than being something we earn, rest is a gift God gives for our freedom and health.

The "Prayer of Rest" involves agenda-free times of stillness before God, simply enjoying his company. It's a form of prayer that tends to thrive when we keep the Sabbath (whether that means setting aside a weekly day of rest or simply intentional resting for shorter periods of time throughout the week.) The Prayer of Rest comes to us as a gift. Jesus said, "The sabbath was made for humankind, and not humankind for the sabbath" (Mark 2:27).

Read: Matthew 11:28–30 ✓

Reflect:

1. Jesus invites us, "Come to me, all you that are weary and are carrying heavy burdens, and I will give you rest." What makes people weary?

2. Describe a person who has received the rest of Jesus . . . What does his or her daily life look like? How does one practically go to Jesus to receive his rest?

3. Rest is a state of the heart we carry with us throughout the week. Peace. Well-being. Shalom. One way to cultivate an unhurried heart is through intentional inactivity—times of sabbath. Take a moment now to mark on your calendar a day to rest with God for a few hours, perhaps spending time in nature.

WEDNESDAY

LITURGICAL PRAYER

When you don't have to think all the time about what words you are going to say next, you are free to fully enter into the act of praying.
— Lauren Winner

Liturgical prayer, written rather than spontaneous, offers many gifts. It gives us words when we have none. It puts in our mouth what saints have prayed through the ages and makes our prayer corporate rather than individualistic. It alleviates the burden of being original or clever. And it can help cultivate a holy reverence for God. It isn't in competition with spontaneous prayer, but rather another means God gives us to draw near to him. Richard Foster writes:

> *Over the centuries an unfortunate and, in my opinion, completely unnecessary division has arisen among Christians. On the one side are those who stress liturgy and sacrament and written prayer. On the other side are those who stress intimacy and informality and spontaneous prayer. And each group looks at the other in pious condescension. It is here that we need the holy conjunction "and." We need not be forced to choose one over another. Both are inspired by the same Spirit. . . . Ours is a spirituality that can embrace both.*

Read: Deuteronomy 6:1–9 ✓

Reflect:

1. In today's passage, God commands the reciting of his commandments. Why? What was the promised result for those who kept God's commandments?

2. Do you find it difficult or easy to use written prayers? Why?

3. The Shema—"Hear, O Israel: The Lord is our God, the Lord alone" (Deuteronomy 6:4)—was likely recited by Jesus, like all Jews, at least twice a day. Try setting an alarm for later today to remind yourself to pray.

THURSDAY

UNCEASING PRAYER

There is no mode of life in the world more pleasing and more full of delight than continual conversation with God. — Brother Lawrence

Praying without ceasing may at first appear burdensome, even impossible. Modern life is demanding, with days full of responsibilities regarding work and family. How could one possibly talk with God constantly? The testimony of ordinary saints through the ages is that continual prayer does indeed take practice and effort. But, in a divine paradox, the more our attention is set on the things above, the more present and useful we become on earth.

What are some first steps we can take in this journey toward unceasing prayer? One is to use things already in our lives to remind us to turn our attention toward God. Perhaps a bell that rings in a nearby church, a favorite color, or a daily commute to work. Another is to use a "breath prayer"—that is, a prayer that can be prayed in a single breath. The goal, again, isn't to add more things to our busy lives. The goal is to abide in Jesus the vine (John 15:5) so that we can be fully alive and fruitful.

Read: 1 Thessalonians 5:15–18 ✓

Reflect:

1. Does the idea of "praying without ceasing" feel burdensome or inviting? Why?

2. Take two minutes to write down a short prayer. The prayer can be your own or one from Scripture. Two examples: "Abba, I belong to you," and "Teach me your way, O Lord" (Psalm 86:11). Throughout today, return to the prayer. A pebble put in a pocket or a string tied around a finger or wrist might be useful as a reminder.

FRIDAY

THE PRAYER OF THE HEART

Tenderness is what follows when you ... experience that you are deeply and sincerely liked by someone. — *Brennan Manning*

God is holy, high, and infinite. We do well to bow before God's strength and power. Jesus invites us to do that and more, to enter into something we could hardly imagine: intimate friendship with God. The breath prayer of "Abba, I belong to you" is a prayer of the heart. (It's worth noting how many types of prayer overlap and intertwine!) Whether with words or "sighs too deep for words" (Romans 8:26), in these prayers we draw near to our tender Father and Friend. Foster writes:

> *The Prayer of the Heart is the prayer of intimacy. It is the prayer of love and tenderness of a child to Father God. Like the mother hen, who gathers her chicks under her wings, we, through the Prayer of the Heart, allow God to gather us to himself—to hold us, to coddle us, to love us (Luke 13:34).*

Read: Romans 8:26-27 ✓

Reflect:

1. Today's passage says that when we don't know how to pray, the Spirit prays for us. What does this mean? Has there been a time when you've been aware of the Spirit praying for you in this way?

2. This week many types of prayer were covered. The point isn't to become an expert on prayer but to explore ways to be with the God who longs to be with us. Today, let's try an exercise. Imagine God is there beside you, smiling upon you—then God speaks a blessing over you. What words might God say in this blessing? Write them down. (You may find it helpful to read Numbers 6:24-26.)

Week 3

Moving Outward—Seeking the Ministry We Need

MONDAY

THE RESERVOIR BEGINS TO OVERFLOW

The world writhes under the pain of its arrogance and self-sufficiency. We can make a difference if we will. — Richard Foster

The first week of this month we explored inward prayer—prayer that creates space for the Spirit to begin to transform us. Last week we looked at upward prayer and the way it fosters intimacy with our heavenly Father. In both inward and upward prayer we are allowing ourselves to receive the living water we so desperately need.

This week we'll see the way that living water overflows into outward prayer. Transformation and intimacy can't help but spill out into ministry, and in outward prayer we begin to share God's concern for his world.

Outward prayer often comes much more naturally than any other kind. And that is fine, for whatever is in our hearts must be prayed out or left to fester. But in this study we've looked at inward and upward prayer first to remind ourselves that we are not meant to minister out of "spiritual bankruptcy," but rather out of the sort of abundance that comes from transformation and intimacy. So let's dive into a week of transformative, intimate, ministry-focused prayer!

Read: Ephesians 3:14–21

Reflect:

1. What does the apostle Paul pray for on behalf of the Ephesians? Jot down a list of the requests he makes.
2. Read the passage aloud with these requests in mind, then offer it up as a prayer over your day.

TUESDAY

PETITIONARY PRAYER

Whether we like it or not, asking is the rule of the Kingdom.
— C. H. Spurgeon

Something Jesus emphasized repeatedly is that we should ask God for whatever we need. When we ask on behalf of others, we call that "intercessory prayer." When we ask for ourselves, we label that "petitionary prayer."

We might expect that in a section on the outward prayer of ministry we would bypass asking for ourselves altogether. But to do so would be to live inauthentic lives. We are needy people, and we are meant to bring those needs to our Father.

When Jesus' disciples asked him how they should pray, he taught them the "Lord's Prayer" (Matthew 6:9–13). As we saw in our devotionals last month, that prayer consists of a series of six petitions that include grand-scale requests ("Your kingdom come. Your will be done.") as well as practical needs like food and safety ("Give us this day our daily bread"). With his teaching on prayer, Jesus seems to be telling us that there is nothing too big or too small to bring to the Father.

Read: Matthew 7:7–11 ✓   7:12 Do to others what you would have them do to you

Reflect:

1. In today's passage, Jesus strongly encourages asking and seeking. Have you ever felt reluctant to pray for your own needs? If so, what do you think creates that reluctance?

2. Consider one specific thing you need—something concrete so it will be clear when the answer comes. Perhaps you need shoes or a computer. It doesn't have to be "spiritual." Ask the Father and write it down with today's date somewhere you will see it in the coming days.

WEDNESDAY

INTERCESSORY PRAYER

If we truly love people, we will desire for them far more than is within our power to give them, and this will lead us to prayer. — Richard Foster

A story in Exodus 17 gives us a vivid picture of intercessory prayer. With his people under attack, Moses instructs his best military leader, Joshua, to gather troops and enter into battle. But Moses himself does not go to the war zone. Instead, he climbs to the top of a hill with his brother Aaron and their friend Hur.

There he holds up his hands in prayer for the battle—and soon realizes that the Israelites' success depends on keeping his arms raised. When Moses' arms grow weary, Aaron and Hur support him on each side so that he can pray in this way until victory comes at sunset.

When loved ones are in need, when global tragedies strike, we may wish we could do more than simply pray. No doubt we are often called to add practical action to our prayers. But the Exodus story reminds us that intercessory prayer itself is the most powerful action we can take—and that we can expect it to require stamina, perseverance, and, sometimes, friends to pray alongside us.

Read: Exodus 17:8–13

Reflect:

1. When you encounter a crisis, is it more natural for you to take a "Joshua" role (leading teams, heading to the front lines) or a "Moses" role (staying behind the scenes and praying)?

2. Prayer and action aren't opposed to each other; they go hand in hand. In this season, do you sense God calling you to add more action to your life of prayer or more prayer to your life of action?

THURSDAY

PERSISTENCE IN OUTWARD PRAYER

Then Jesus told them a parable about their need to pray always and not to lose heart. — Luke 18:1

The invitation to outward prayer is a wonderful gift. And yet it also raises the troubling issue of seemingly unanswered prayers. From our earthbound perspective it can be impossible to see what is happening in the heavenlies. We may become afraid to pray at all for fear of disappointment.

Jesus' teaching on prayer has a striking emphasis on persistence. In Luke 11, he tells the story of a man who knocks on his friend's door until the friend provides food. In Luke 18, he describes a widow who won't stop calling upon a judge until he grants her justice.

Is Jesus urging us to "nag" God until we get what we want? No, he's teaching us to stay in conversation with our Father no matter what. Even when it might seem that God is silent or absent, Jesus assures us that is not the case. So Jesus asks us to keep the lines of communication open in prayer. Even our prayers of lament are ultimately prayers of relationship and faith, and they are much better than silence.

Read: Psalm 69:1-4; 13-18

Reflect:

1. Psalm 69 is a psalm of lament. How do you feel about the complaints expressed in the psalm? Do you think there is a place for that sort of raw honesty in your prayer life?

2. Is there a situation in your life where it seems that God has long been silent? Can you discuss it with him again—trusting, on the basis of his "steadfast love" (Psalm 69:13, 16), that God is still interested and involved?

FRIDAY

PRAYING IN JESUS' NAME

This is pure grace, that God tells us how we can speak with him and have fellowship with him. We can do it by praying in the name of Jesus Christ.
— *Dietrich Bonhoeffer*

Our own intercessory prayer is possible because Jesus himself is now in heaven interceding for us with the Father (Romans 8:34). Jesus "opens the door and grants us access into the heavenlies," writes Richard Foster. "Even more: he straightens out and cleanses our feeble, misguided intercessions and makes them acceptable before a holy God. Even more still: his prayers sustain our desires to pray, urging us on and giving us hope of being heard."

So when we pray, we pray in Jesus' name. Because Jesus intercedes for us, we can be confident our prayers of intercession for others will be heard.

Praying in the name of Jesus also means praying in the *way* of Jesus. It means learning to want what he wants for other people and the world. The more we allow Jesus to transform us in inward prayer, and the more we discover his heart in upward prayer, the more we will come to pray like him in our outward intercession.

Read: John 14:13–14

Reflect:

1. If asking in Jesus' name means asking in Jesus' way (wanting what he wants for the world), how might that alter the way you pray?

2. Try this exercise. Ask God to bring to mind a person to pray for. This may take a few moments. Simply be still and wait. Once you have the person in mind, ask Jesus what he desires for this person. Again, wait and listen. When a thought comes to mind of how to bless that person in a specific way, then pray for that person.

Week 4

Jesus' Prayer in John 17

MONDAY

FOR THE BENEFIT OF OTHERS

We should seek not so much to pray but to become prayer.
— *Saint Francis of Assisi*

Since our goal is to learn to pray in the Jesus way, most of this week we will look at John 17, Jesus' longest recorded prayer. Some call this chapter the "holiest of holies" because it reveals the innermost heart of our Lord.

Before we dive into John 17, however, let's gain a greater understanding of how prayer and action are woven together in Jesus' life. We'll do that by looking at a story about his friend Lazarus.

When Lazarus got sick, his sisters sent messengers to Jesus asking him to come. After getting word, Jesus said, "This illness does not lead to death" (John 11:4) and waited two days to start his journey. Even in this waiting, we see the intimacy of Jesus' prayer life, his ability to listen to and obey the Father regarding matters of timing. By the time Jesus arrived, Lazarus had died. Jesus wept, showing that, even with the coming resurrection, he still enters into our present suffering. After having the stone seal removed from the tomb, Jesus lifted his eyes toward heaven, paused, and prayed.

Read: John 11:38–44

Reflect:

1. Look back at the beginning of this story in John 11:1–6. Why did Jesus wait two days before returning to Lazarus? How does his waiting show his trust in the Father?

2. Notice how Jesus stops and prays, and then commands action: "Lazarus, come out!" Jesus' disciples would later follow the same seamless movement from prayer into action: "In the name of Jesus Christ of Nazareth, stand up and walk" (Acts 3:6). How do prayer and Spirit-filled action go together?

TUESDAY

JESUS PRAYS FOR HIMSELF

There is no voice which has ever been heard, either in heaven or on earth, more exalted, more holy, more fruitful, more sublime, than the prayer offered by the Son of God Himself. — Philipp Melanchthon

The hour has come. Jesus has finished his earthly ministry and is giving a farewell discourse to his disciples. It concludes with John 17, his longest recorded prayer.

Throughout the Gospels we see Jesus retreating for hours of prayer. This time he allows his disciples to listen in. Jesus allows this prayer to stretch out, visible through the ages, for our benefit. While you read our passage for the day, keep this question in mind: facing certain torture and shameful death, for what and for whom does Jesus pray first?

Read: John 17:1–5

Reflect:

1. Many of us bow to pray, which is a fitting act of reverence and can help us focus. Jesus, however, often looked up while he prayed. Why do you think he did this? How does the posture of our body affect the way we pray?

2. Jesus prayed, "Glorify your Son" (John 17:1). To "glorify" means to cause the worth of something to become visible and acknowledged. Why did Jesus ask for this?

3. How did Jesus define "eternal life"? Do we have to wait for death to enter into it? Why or why not?

WEDNESDAY

JESUS PRAYS FOR HIS DISCIPLES

Joy, not grit, is the hallmark of holy obedience. — Richard Foster

With Judas having fled, Jesus here prays for his eleven disciples in the upper room. This prayer is rich and deep. A slow and thoughtful reading yields many treasures. One is that Jesus longs for the unity of his disciples. Another is that he desires for them to have his joy made complete in them.

Whenever Jesus repeats something, we know it's important. In John 15:11, Jesus told his disciples he wanted them to have the same joy that he had. Now, in John 17:13, he prays for that same thing. This word for "joy" means gladness, happiness, calm delight. Here Jesus is on the brink of a horrific death, betrayed by one of his closest companions, talking about gladness. It's astounding. The writer of Hebrews says it was "for the joy set before him [that] he endured the cross" (Hebrews 12:2 NIV). What kind of joy was this that could sustain the Son of Man in the face of such suffering?

Read: John 17:6–19

Reflect:

1. Why is joy—gladness, cheerfulness, calm delight—so important to Jesus? What do you think is the "joy set before him" that sustained him on the cross?

2. Let's linger on joy for a moment more. Imagine the face of Jesus. It is a face free from anxiety or hurry. His eyes are full of compassion and his smile says, "I'm glad you are here." Close your eyes and take one or two minutes in quiet to linger with this picture. End with this simple prayer: "Father, I desire the joy of Jesus. Please do whatever it takes to make that joy a reality in me."

THURSDAY

JESUS PRAYS FOR ALL BELIEVERS

The purpose of God's gifts is to unite us in a unity which is like the unity of the Father and the Son. — Thomas Aquinas

Jesus finishes his prayer in John 17 by praying for all those who will believe in him through his disciples—that's us! Again we find Jesus using repetition, now praying that all Christians would be one, just as he prayed the eleven would be one.

Jesus says we will come to this unity by interesting and perhaps uncomfortable means: glory. What kind of glory? The glory of being a son or daughter of God (John 1:12), and the glory of doing the works that Jesus did (John 14:12). Unity comes as each of us focuses on who we are in Christ and the work God has given us to do, rather than focusing on the faults of others.

Read: John 17:20–26

Reflect:

1. Jesus says in this passage that the world will know that God sent Jesus and that God loves them when Christians are one—when we are unified. Why is that? How does unity lead to love?

2. Can you think of a person you have met, or have read about, in whom the glory of Christ is evident? A person who radiates the love of God? What effect does that person have on the world around them?

FRIDAY

INTERCESSION OF THE HIGH PRIEST

Jesus Christ carries on intercession for us in heaven; the Holy Ghost carries on intercession in us on earth; and we the saints have to carry on intercession for all men. — Oswald Chambers

"We do not have a high priest who is unable to sympathize with our weaknesses. . . . Let us therefore approach the throne of grace with boldness" (Hebrews 4:15-16). Now that we have considered Jesus' "high priestly prayer" in John 17, we find ourselves once again considering how his intercession for us continues today.

Perhaps the idea of a priest brings to mind someone set apart, unreachable. The author of Hebrews goes to great lengths to make Jesus' priesthood accessible to us. The atoning sacrifice of Jesus was done once and lasts forever. His intercessions for us are unending.

Read: Hebrews 7:23-27

Reflect:

1. Do you find it difficult or easy to approach God boldly? Why?

2. It can be easier to agree with someone powerful than to make a stand on our own. Jesus, our high priest, is always interceding for us. So we can come into agreement with what he is saying about us to the Father. As we conclude these two months on prayer, we invite you to approach the throne of grace with boldness, agreeing with Jesus about what he has accomplished and what he prays for us. Examples: "Father, I agree with Jesus that I am cleansed from all my sin." "Father, I agree with Jesus that I have been given every spiritual blessing."

Week 1

~~~~~~

The Beauty of Holiness

MONDAY  5|3

JESUS AND THE VIRTUOUS LIFE

You shall be holy, for I am holy. — 1 Peter 1:16

For the next two months we will turn our attention to holiness and virtue. We'll look at what holiness is and why it's worth pursuing. We'll look at sin and why it's worth avoiding. And we'll learn that while holiness is a gift to us from the Holy Spirit, there are concrete ways to offer our "bodies as a living sacrifice" (Romans 12:1) so that the holy fruit of love, joy, peace, patience, kindness, generosity, faithfulness, gentleness, and self-control (Galatians 5:22–23) overflows in our lives. That will lead us into a study of Jesus' Sermon on the Mount, which we find recorded in Matthew.

Today, though, let's start with the story of Jesus' temptation in the wilderness. The end of Matthew 3 is included in the reading to remind us that before the temptations of the devil came the affirmation of Father God: "This is my Son, the Beloved, with whom I am well pleased." God affirms identity; Satan questions it. Jesus' responses to the devil's three temptations tell us much about the nature of sin and the importance of purity.

Read: Matthew 3:16—4:11

Reflect:

1. Jesus fasted for forty days. Do you think that made him spiritually weaker or stronger by the time the devil came to tempt him? Why?

2. In the first two temptations, Satan asks Jesus to prove his divinity. Jesus had the power to do so, so why didn't he yield to these requests?

TUESDAY

WHAT IS TRUE HOLINESS?

Holiness means the ability to do what needs to be done when it needs to be done. — Richard Foster

In the life of Jesus, we see how God desires holiness, purity, and virtue in our lives. A holy life is one that is functional and healthy and whole. But holiness, or purity of heart, is not merely obedience to certain rules. Jesus chastened the Pharisees for outwardly obeying God's law while neglecting the "word of God" (Matthew 15:6)—that is, the spirit of the law.

The Israelites defined holiness as a way to separate the clean from the unclean. Later, the Pharisees in particular refined the definitions of holiness in terms of outward rituals. Washing properly, not working on the Sabbath, eating only certain foods, avoiding the company of sinners—all these were the way to holiness. But Jesus openly challenged this division between inward purity and outward ritual. "It is not what goes into the mouth that defiles a person, but it is what comes out of the mouth that defiles" (Matthew 15:11). Jesus turns our attention away from ritual purity and points to the purity of heart from which flows unshakable obedience to God.

Read: Matthew 15:10–20

Reflect:

1. Why did Jesus criticize the Pharisees for focusing on outward action rather than on the inner source of action?

2. In some contexts, "holiness" can mean self-righteousness or arrogance. Does 'holiness' connote a positive or negative quality for you? How does the culture perceive holiness?

WEDNESDAY

SIN IS SLOP   *HEALTH*
                WHOLENESS

Do not let sin control the way you live. — Romans 6:12 (NLT)

Holiness is something God wishes for us simply because it is the best way to live. The commandments of God are not meant to turn our lives into a dull drudgery but to make them whole and full. God's plan completes and integrates our lives; sin disrupts and fragments our lives. While sin seems appealing on the surface—the fulfillment of all our desires—beneath the surface lurks poison that will ultimately destroy us.

Writer and philosopher Dallas Willard taught that sin is "slop." Sin stains and ruins our souls. We are drawn to it and tempted by its whispers of pleasure only to find that it offers a short season of delight and a long—sometimes lifelong—season of pain. Because God knows this, he prescribes a way of living that helps us resist the seductive and destructive clutches of sin. Living a holy life is not limited to "super saints"; rather, it is healthy and functional for everyone.

Read: James 1:12–21

Reflect:

1. If sin is destructive, why is it so appealing?

2. Richard Foster describes the holiness stream as cultivating a life "that functions as it should." Have you ever associated holiness with a life that functions well? Does that association make sense to you?

THURSDAY

HOLINESS IS GIVEN BY THE HOLY SPIRIT

When I sin, it is from me and is done on my own, but when I act righteously, it is wholly and completely of God. — *Charles Spurgeon*

No amount of human reasoning, no amount of strenuous trying on our own will ever produce the fruit of holiness. It may produce the appearance of holiness, for a time, but not the fruit. Fruit on a tree grows from the life within the tree. The fruit of the Spirit—an unforced inclination toward that which is good and right—comes from the life of the Spirit within us.

This truth is a great relief! It lifts the burden of making spiritual growth happen in our own strength. It guards us against the pride of thinking our progress is due primarily to our efforts. Understand that cooperation with God is necessary for growth. But our cooperation is like a seed (if it had a choice) partnering with the farmer by staying in the ground. "Neither the one who plants nor the one who waters is anything, but only God who gives the growth" (1 Corinthians 3:7).

Read: John 16:13; 2 Thessalonians 2:13

Reflect:

1. Paul, echoing Jesus, mentions that the Spirit sanctifies us (makes us more like Jesus) through the truth. How does having a truth revealed to our hearts—for instance, that God always desires the best for us—affect the way we live?

2. Throughout Scripture we're told to ask. "If any of you is lacking in wisdom, ask God," James says (James 1:5). "Ask, and it will be given you," Jesus told his disciples (Matthew 7:7). Take a few minutes now to pray, aloud or silently, to ask God for the Holy Spirit to reveal truth to your heart. Keep your eyes open today for how God specifically answers this prayer.

FRIDAY

～～～

PROGRESS IS POSSIBLE

We all, who with unveiled faces contemplate the Lord's glory, are being transformed into his image with ever-increasing glory, which comes from the Lord, who is the Spirit. — 2 Corinthians 3:18 (NIV)

There are days when we feel spiritually stuck, days when old habits return or mean words fly out of our mouths. It can be tempting to think change is impossible. It's good to remind ourselves of the truth—that while the completion of our transformation into the likeness of Christ comes in the next life, it starts now. Genuine freedom and change and growth are not only possible but promised for those in Christ (Philippians 1:6).

In *Streams of Living Water*, Richard Foster says:

> *The salvation that is in Jesus Christ is not limited to the forgiveness of sins; it is also able to break sin's power. We are "created in Christ Jesus for good works, which God prepared beforehand to be our way of life" (Ephesians 2:10). Sin no longer needs to reign in our mortal bodies. We can walk in newness of life.*

As today's reading suggests, we can yield our arms and legs and eyes and ears and brain to God as "instruments of righteousness." We can be "conformed to the image of his Son," Jesus.

Read: Romans 6:12–14; 8:29

Reflect:

1. What does it mean to "present your members to sin"? And what does it mean, in day-to-day life, to "present your members to God as instruments of righteousness"?

2. In what ways have you seen God genuinely change you, or someone you know? Take a few minutes to reflect. Offer a prayer thanking God for the work he has done and asking him for grace for deeper transformation.

Week 2

Holiness in the Sermon on the Mount

MONDAY  5/16

LIFE IN THE KINGDOM OF HEAVEN

Repent means to change the way you've been thinking and acting. Notice how you've been thinking and then add to those thoughts the fact that it is now possible for you to begin living in God's kingdom right now, right where you are. — Dallas Willard

Jesus is the greatest teacher the world has ever known. And his discourse in Matthew 5–7 is perhaps his greatest teaching. In it he paints a picture of true holiness—a holiness that flows out of the heart. For the next few weeks we will explore this teaching, often called the Sermon on the Mount.*

Our reading today comes just before the sermon. "Repent," Jesus says, "for the kingdom of heaven has come near." The call to repent is a call to think differently. And heaven is not just a place we go after we die. It is the realm God inhabits, which includes the very air we breathe. Jesus proclaims that this kingdom, the kingdom of God, "has come near," just as the book you are reading right now has come near. This invitation from Jesus sets the stage for the sermon to come.

Read: Matthew 4:17–25

Reflect:

1. True holiness is beautiful. Ordinary fishermen see something in Jesus that they are willing to leave career and family to follow. Describe what you think they saw in him that was so compelling.

2. In Matthew 4:23–25 we find Jesus "proclaiming the good news of the kingdom and curing every disease." How are these two things related?

---

* Dallas Willard's book *The Divine Conspiracy* (Harper, 1998) and Bill Gaultiere's booklet *Jesus' Greatest Teaching* (SoulShepherding.org, 2016) informed months 5 and 6.

TUESDAY

WHO IS WELL OFF?

In this great sermon Jesus is not teaching systematically or exhaustively. He is not giving us a system of doctrine or of moral rules. Rather, he is aiming to convey a certain spirit to us, a spirit that will transform our minds.
— Richard Foster

In his teaching, Jesus answered questions that every great moral teacher must answer. One of these questions is "Who is well off?" The assumption in Jesus' day, as it often is now, is that the ones blessed by God are the rich, the powerful, the outwardly righteous. Jesus turns this upside down. He says that in the kingdom of heaven even the poor in spirit, the meek, and those hungry for righteousness are happy and blessed.

Often this passage (called "The Beatitudes") is taught as a new kind of law—a list of things for us to live up to. In this way, it can become burdensome. If, instead, we read this list as a proclamation of good news to a group of outcasts, it becomes good news to us as well. No matter who we are, we are well off because the kingdom of heaven is available to us in Jesus.

Read: Matthew 5:1–10

Reflect:

1. It's likely that Jesus is speaking to uneducated, "unimportant" people. How does that affect the way you read the passage?

2. Take a few minutes to pray, thanking God that his kingdom is now available in Jesus to everyone, including the least. Ask that the Holy Spirit would reveal the truth to you as we study the Sermon on the Mount.

WEDNESDAY

COMING REWARDS

No suffering that the Christian endures for Christ is ever in vain.
— *Billy Graham*

The kingdom of heaven is available now in Jesus, and in the age to come it will be fully revealed. In that day, all things will be made right. What we see dimly in a mirror now will be revealed face to face (1 Corinthians 13:12), and what we do now will be repaid (Romans 2:6–8).

That's how Jesus can say to those who will suffer on his account, "Rejoice and be glad, for your reward is great in heaven" (Matthew 5:12). He knows this isn't the end of the story. He knows the Father sees and will reward every good thing that's done in secret. Later we see this coming alive in Jesus' disciples: "They rejoiced that they were considered worthy to suffer dishonor for the sake of the name" (Acts 5:41).

Read: Matthew 5:11–12

Reflect:

1. In the Acts 5 passage mentioned above, the disciples had just been flogged for professing their faith. Yet they didn't seem to be pretending to rejoice—rejoicing flowed out of them. How can that be?

2. Have you ever been persecuted for doing something right? If so, how did it feel?

THURSDAY

A LIFE THAT CAUSES OTHERS TO WANT GOD

But God chose what is foolish in the world to shame the wise; God chose what is weak in the world to shame the strong. — 1 Corinthians 1:27

The people Jesus is teaching aren't rich or famous or highly educated. Yet Jesus says, "You are the salt of the earth. . . . You are the light of the world" (Matthew 5:13–14). Like a great king who calls forth bravery out of meager soldiers, Jesus calls forth these unlearned disciples to a life that causes people to thirst for and glorify God.

Acts 4:13 records this being lived out: "When they saw the boldness of Peter and John and realized that they were uneducated and ordinary men, they were amazed and recognized them as companions of Jesus."

Read: Matthew 5:13–16

Reflect:

1. What kind of good works would cause people to glorify God instead of exalting us?

2. Imagine Jesus saying, "You are the salt of the earth. . . . You are the light of the world." Does this feel empowering or burdensome? Why?

FRIDAY

PAUSING AND REFLECTING

It is the glory of God to conceal things, but the glory of kings is to search things out. — Proverbs 25:2

In just one week we have read through Scriptures that a person could study for a lifetime. Now is a good time to pause and remind ourselves of a couple of things.

First, we want to remember that while we often read God's Word in small sections, God's heart is revealed through Scripture as a whole. When putting a puzzle together one may focus for a time on a small piece, but it's good to always have the big picture in view. Keeping in mind all of Scripture, and especially all of what Jesus said, protects us from errors that arise by overemphasizing one part.

Second, we should be assured that while the meaning of Scripture may be initially hidden from us, we can trust the Spirit to reveal it as we humbly seek the Lord. The goal isn't to have the right answer, but to grow in friendship with God as the Holy Spirit reveals truth to us.

Read: Matthew 5:1–16

Reflect:

1. Today, take a moment in silence to ask God to reveal himself through Scripture. Have a pen and paper handy. Then read today's Scripture aloud, slowly. Write down any phrases that you sense the Holy Spirit may be inviting you to explore more deeply. Thank God for these invitations as you pray.

Week 3

What Does a Virtuous Person Look Like?

MONDAY 5/17

RELYING ON GOD FOR INWARD GOODNESS

Therefore the Law has become our tutor to lead us to Christ, so that we may be justified by faith. — Galatians 3:24 (NASB)

Another important question every great teacher must address is "Who is a good person?" Jesus answers that in the next section of the Sermon on the Mount, which we will look at this week.

The crowds may have wondered how to interpret the Law of Moses now that the kingdom of heaven has come near. Is the law now irrelevant? Jesus says it isn't, that he came not to abolish the law but to fulfill it. Then he goes on to set an even higher standard than Moses. The scribes and Pharisees, after all, were the most respected religious teachers of Jesus' day. If anyone was righteous, it must be them. And yet Jesus says that to enter the kingdom of heaven one must have a righteousness that exceeds theirs. How is this possible?

Read: Matthew 5:17–20

Reflect:

1. In Galatians 3:24, Paul says that the law was our "tutor" until Christ came. What did the law teach us? And how did Jesus fulfill the law and the prophets?

2. Is Jesus telling us that if we try hard enough we can be more righteous than the scribes and Pharisees, or is he saying something else?

TUESDAY

MOTIVES OF THE HEART

One who is slow to anger is better than the mighty, and one whose temper is controlled than one who captures a city. — *Proverbs 16:32*

"Unless your righteousness exceeds that of the scribes and Pharisees . . ." Jesus says, and then immediately he provides examples of what that means.

"You have heard . . ." Where did they hear it? In the Law of Moses, which concerned outward action.

"But I say . . ." Jesus now moves beyond outward action to motives of the heart. The Pharisees addressed symptoms. Jesus addresses the root cause.

The root of murder is anger. The root of adultery is lust. Even if anger and lust don't result in "spectacular" sins, they still destroy the soul. Sooner or later their effects will bleed out in depression, in addiction, or in a hurtful outburst toward a loved one.

It was common in that day for men to divorce women for any reason whatsoever, leaving their wives in a vulnerable state. Giving a certificate of divorce was the "legal" way for a man to do this. But in all of these matters Jesus wants more than legality—he wants love. He wants to make our hearts a wellspring from which right action naturally flows.

Read: Matthew 5:21–32

Reflect:

1. In verses 23–24, Jesus says that making a relationship right is even more important than a religious service. Why is that?

2. One way to cooperate with God in ridding your heart of anger and lust is confession. If you struggle in one of these areas, write down the name of someone to whom you can confess your struggle and contact that person this week. Healing comes through confessing our sins to one another (James 5:16).

WEDNESDAY

~~~~~~~~~~~~~~

SAYING WHAT YOU MEAN

Do not lie to one another, seeing that you have stripped off the old self with
its practices and have clothed yourselves with the new self, which is being
renewed in knowledge according to the image of its creator.
— Colossians 3:9–10

Why is it so difficult for us to simply say yes or no? Perhaps we're afraid
we'll disappoint other people or damage our own reputation. Perhaps
we need something from another person, so we use flattery or empty
promises to try to get our way.

It was common in Jesus' day to make an oath to assure someone of
the speaker's honesty. Instead of swearing by God, which would bring
judgment, people would swear by heaven, earth, Jerusalem, or their
own heads. Jesus, always going to the heart of the matter, says simply
not to make oaths at all. Instead, be a person who speaks plainly, trusting the God who made heaven and earth and the hairs on your head.

Read: Matthew 5:33–37

Reflect:

1. Why are oaths unnecessary for those who follow Jesus?

2. In what kinds of situations in your own life—when you talk to
   others or when others talk to you—is it tempting to not speak
   plainly? Pray this simple prayer, "God, help me always to say what I
   mean and to speak the truth in love, even when it is hard."

THURSDAY

~~~~~~~~~~

RESPONDING TO INJURY WITH MERCY

See that none of you repays evil for evil, but always seek to do good to one another and to all. — 1 Thessalonians 5:15

In most contexts today, "An eye for an eye" sounds like harsh revenge. In Jesus' day, however, it was considered reasonable; and these kinds of punitive measures kept tribal conflicts from escalating. Jesus, layering upon the previous examples, tells us another way: the way of the kingdom of God.

Later Jesus would live out what he taught in the most extreme way imaginable. He allowed the creatures he made to nail him to a cross, and proclaimed, "Father, forgive them, for they do not know what they are doing" (Luke 23:34).

Read: Matthew 5:38–42

Reflect:

1. What is accomplished by "turning the other cheek" or "going the second mile"? Why is Jesus calling us to live this way?

2. Consider how you might "go the second mile" without allowing others to take advantage of you. What are some examples?

3. Should you always prevent others from taking advantage of you? Why or why not?

Month 5: The Virtuous Life

FRIDAY

〜〜〜

BLESSING YOUR ENEMIES

Have we not come to such an impasse in the modern world that we must love our enemies—or else? The chain reaction of evil—hate begetting hate, wars producing more wars—must be broken, or else we shall be plunged into the dark abyss of annihilation. — Martin Luther King Jr.

Every people in every time and place has enemies. For first-century Jews, it was Rome—a foreign power holding God's people under subjection. Yet Jesus, to crown his definition of what a virtuous person looks like, tells believers across the ages that we must love our enemies.

An enemy is someone who is against us and who is thwarting our will. Large-scale enemies are usually easy to recognize: an oppressive ruler, for example. But sometimes our day-to-day enemies are the most difficult to spot, and to love: a spouse who is unkind, a neighbor who doesn't like us, even our own hearts, which can condemn us.

To love is to want the best for someone. Jesus wants to make us the kind of people who want the best even for those who want bad for us. This change in desires alone breaks the cycle of hate. And only the Spirit of Jesus in us can help us do it.

Read: Matthew 5:43–48

Reflect:

1. This teaching, along with others, can lead to the impression that Christians are called to be "unassertive" or even "wimps." Is that what Jesus is teaching here?

2. Spend a few minutes in silent prayer today. Grab a pen and paper. Ask God, "Is there someone who is my enemy—who wishes me ill and for whom I wish ill?" Write down anyone who comes to mind. Then write a short prayer of blessing upon that person.

Week 4

~~~

How Can Someone Become Virtuous? Part One

MONDAY 5/24

DO GOOD WORKS FOR GOD ALONE

Nothing disciplines the desires of the flesh like service, and nothing transforms the desires of the flesh like hidden service. — Richard Foster

In the spiritual life, training is better than trying. Here in Matthew 6, Jesus provides a training program for the virtuous life.

For example, many of us are naturally driven by pride. We want others to see us in a favorable light. We can try to make pride less of a driving force in our lives, but any success is usually short-lived. Instead, Jesus tells us to train to overcome pride by using an exercise program of service in secret.

God desires to lift off the burden of having to manage what others think of us. Doing good works for others without calling attention to ourselves is a way to give God that burden. Service in secret helps turn our attention away from our own needs and toward pleasing our heavenly Father.

Read: Matthew 6:1–4

Reflect:

1. How do you feel if you do something good for someone and they don't thank you? And how do you feel if someone else takes credit for something good you did? What do these feelings reveal?

2. Based on everything you know about God, what sort of reward do you think Jesus is referring to in this passage?

3. Consider asking God for one opportunity to serve someone secretly in the next twenty-four hours—and then stay alert!

TUESDAY

PRAY SECRETLY AND SIMPLY

Prayer is talking to God about what you and God are doing together.
— Dallas Willard

Another key ingredient in Jesus' holiness-training program is prayer. Just as he warns us not to impress others by our giving or serving, he urges us not to make a show of our praying. God wants genuine conversation and connection, not a display of how religious we are.

Jesus also warns us against "heaping up empty phrases" in prayer—against trying to impress other people, or even God, with our eloquence or passion. The prayer he teaches us to pray, the Lord's Prayer, is only fifty-seven words in the original Greek.

"Just talk to me," Jesus seems to be saying. No pretense. No show. Just real conversation. Entering into an authentic dialogue with a holy God is bound to move us toward holiness.

Read: Matthew 6:5–15

Reflect:

1. Jesus warns us against empty words, but in the Lord's Prayer he does offer us a script. What makes a prayer empty? What makes it genuine?

2. Is praying aloud in a group always wrong? If not, what kind of praying aloud is Jesus warning against? What kind of praying aloud in a group is healthy?

3. This section in the Sermon on the Mount is about bringing glory to God rather than to ourselves. Why do you think Jesus emphasizes forgiving others here in verses 14–15?

WEDNESDAY

FAST SECRETLY AND JOYFULLY

Fasting helps express, deepens, confirms the resolution that we are ready to sacrifice anything, even ourselves, to attain what we seek for the kingdom of God. — Andrew Murray

There seems to have been a consensus in Jesus' day that fasting was an important spiritual discipline. But once again Jesus puts a new twist on common religious practice. He says that people who make it obvious that they are fasting are hypocrites. Jesus points out the irony of undergoing a discipline of self-denial while glorifying yourself in the process.

Instead, Jesus suggests, God-followers should keep the fact that they are fasting hidden. In this way they can fast both from food and from the approval of others. He knows firsthand that in training ourselves to rely upon God alone, we are given "food to eat that [others] do not know about" (John 4:32).

Read: Matthew 6:16–18

Reflect:

1. In your view, what is the value of fasting?

2. It might be possible to take from this passage the idea that Jesus wants us to conceal hunger or pain—to pretend things are OK. Is that the point of this teaching? If not, what is the point?

3. Consider setting a day on the calendar when you will fast one meal. If a food fast is not possible for health reasons, consider a day without television or your smartphone. Remember, fasting earns nothing from God. It simply helps our bodies and hearts agree with the truth that "One does not live by bread alone, but by every word that comes from the mouth of God" (Matthew 4:4).

THURSDAY

STORE UP TREASURES IN HEAVEN

Aim at Heaven and you will get Earth "thrown in": aim at Earth and you will get neither. — C. S. Lewis

A famous financial talk-show host recalled a childhood event that shaped her life. When her father's business caught on fire, she watched him run into the flames to retrieve his metal cash register. Her father's willingness to burn his hands and risk his life for cash convinced her that money—and the financial security it represents—are the most important things in human existence.

Most of us would deny that money is the most important thing. But many of us allow the need for financial security to drive our choices and consume our thoughts.

Jesus is clear on this matter. You can't live your life for money and God. It's one or the other. It's not that wealth is bad in and of itself. In fact, much good can be done with money. It's just that money, if not handled correctly, is a tyrannical master. Every person must decide who gets to call the shots in his or her life—money or God.

Read: Matthew 6:19–24

Reflect:

1. In verses 19–21, Jesus contrasts earthly and heavenly treasures. If money and material goods are earthly treasures, how would you describe heavenly ones?

2. In verses 22–23, Jesus compares a healthy and unhealthy eye. In biblical times, the expression "unhealthy eye" meant stinginess or greed, while a person with a "healthy eye" was considered generous. What do you think Jesus is saying about how the way we look at the world affects our whole being?

FRIDAY

REST IN GOD'S PROVISION FOR TODAY

Do not be afraid, little flock, for it is your Father's good pleasure to give you the kingdom. — Luke 12:32

Only God can transform us into virtuous people, but Jesus tells us how to cooperate with God. We can serve others in secret, displacing pride from the throne of our life. We can pray—really pray—not for show but for relationship. We can fast from things that normally sustain us, including the approval of others. And we can choose to center our lives around God rather than around financial provision, trusting him for our security and well-being.

Moving toward holiness, it seems, has something to do with moving away from self-reliance. If we're honest, we realize that our sense of self-reliance is an illusion anyway. But it is a comforting illusion, and giving it up can be unsettling.

Perhaps that's why Jesus moves next into a teaching about trust and instructs us not to worry. While worry is futile, he says, God is trustworthy. Jesus invites us to be people who come to him day after day for what we need to live and flourish.

Read: Matthew 6:25–34

Reflect:

1. What does this passage say about the physical needs of human beings? What does Jesus seem to be saying about God's attitude toward our need to eat and be clothed?

2. Jesus says not to worry about tomorrow. Does that seem like a reasonable suggestion? Why or why not?

3. Prayerfully call to mind one thing you are tempted to worry about. You may find it helpful to share this with someone you trust. Pray aloud, on your own or perhaps with that person, to release it: "Father, I release _____ into your care."

Week 1

~~~~~~

How Can Someone Become Virtuous? Part Two

MONDAY

JOIN THE COMMUNITY OF LOVE

The person who loves their dream of community will destroy community,
but the person who loves those around them will create community.
— Dietrich Bonhoeffer

This month we are going to continue exploring the gift of holiness and the way it leads us into a life of virtue. For the first two weeks we will be working with the second half of the Sermon on the Mount, recorded in Matthew 7. But first, let's consider why it's important we do this work with other people.

It has always been God's plan to create a community that displays his glory. The Bible starts with two people in a garden (Genesis 2). It concludes with a city full of all people groups (Revelation 21). But we don't have to wait for that perfected future to live with others in the kingdom of God. It starts now. What does it look like when a community lives out the Sermon on the Mount? Today's passage provides a vivid example.

Read: Acts 2:42–47

Reflect:

1. In today's passage, everything the group is doing—selling what they own, sharing with each other, breaking bread, praising God—seems to be coming from an overflow of their hearts, not some law or ideal they are striving to live up to. What motivated this radical lifestyle? (Reading a little earlier in Acts 2 may be helpful.)

2. Life with others can be exciting at first—a new job, a new neighborhood, a new project, getting married, having children. As time goes on, though, getting along with others can prove very difficult. What sustains healthy community beyond the initial "honeymoon" phase?

TUESDAY

DON'T CONDEMN PEOPLE

Encourage always, give advice once in a great while, rebuke only when absolutely necessary, and condemn never. — Richard Foster

Condemnation happens when we love being right more than we love another person. It happens when we, like the Pharisees, value the letter of the law more than the spirit of the law. It happens when we look at someone's appearance and judge that person's heart—something only God sees. Jesus speaks to this simply and directly: don't do it.

Instead, Jesus says, remove the log out of your own eye—which, perhaps in this context, is self-righteous contempt and anger—and then you'll have the vision and compassion to help someone else.

Read: Matthew 7:1–5

Reflect:

1. Just as it's wrong to condemn others, it's wrong to condemn ourselves. How can we look at our own issues—the log in our own eye—with love instead of condemnation?

2. Is it hard or easy for you to be with people you disagree with? Why?

3. Pray that God would help you see others today with his eyes. Then, as the day goes on, return to this prayer if you feel tempted to judge someone.

WEDNESDAY

ONLY OFFER WHAT IS HELPFUL

The problem with pearls for pigs is not that the pigs are not worthy. It is not worthiness that is in question here at all, but helpfulness. — Dallas Willard

"Don't throw your pearls before swine." This phrase, in many cultures, has come to mean "Don't waste your time offering wisdom to people who aren't worthy and wouldn't appreciate it." Context here, as always, is important. Jesus is in the midst of talking about how we are to help people rather than to self-righteously condemn them. Here is how Dallas Willard, in his book The Divine Conspiracy, continues the quote above:

> *Pigs cannot digest pearls, cannot nourish themselves upon them. Likewise for a dog with a Bible or a crucifix. The dog cannot eat it. . . . What a picture this is of our efforts to correct and control others by pouring our good things, often truly precious things, upon them— things that they nevertheless simply cannot ingest and use to nourish themselves. . . . The point is not the waste of the "pearl" but that the person given the pearl is not helped.*

Read: Matthew 7:6

Reflect:

1. Do you agree with Willard's interpretation of this verse—that it's about helpfulness, not worthiness? Why or why not?

2. Remember an experience in which you tried to help someone, but they didn't want—or weren't ready for—your help. What happened?

THURSDAY

SIMPLY ASK

Asking is indeed the great law of the spiritual world through which things are accomplished in cooperation with God and yet in harmony with the freedom and worth of every individual. — Dallas Willard

Some read the Sermon of the Mount as simply a collection of Jesus' sayings that may or may not relate to each other. If, instead, we read it as a progression presented by a master teacher, even these familiar passages take on fresh meaning—or rather, the meaning that Jesus originally intended.

We typically relate the phrase "Ask, and it will be given you" to asking God for what we need in prayer. But Jesus is also talking in this context about how we relate to people. Asking, in regard to God and others, is the way of the kingdom. A good request, free from the desire to manipulate or the fear of rejection, respects the dignity and free will of another person. It is a gentle yet powerful force.

Read: Matthew 7:7–11

Reflect:

1. Have you ever thought of this passage as applying to people as well as to God? How do you feel this principle of asking relates to yesterday's topic of offering what people need?

2. Do you find it difficult to ask others for what you need? Why or why not?

3. Take a few minutes to pray. Ask God for something specific—something measurable so that you will know when the request is answered. Then keep alert over the coming days to see how God answers.

FRIDAY

PRACTICE THE GOLDEN RULE

The Golden Rule of the New Testament is a summing up of what everyone . . . had always known to be right. — C. S. Lewis

Mosaic law was stated primarily in negative terms: don't kill, don't steal, don't covet. Jesus here sums up the entire law in one positive statement: "Do to others as you would have them do to you."

Restating the negative law with a positive statement isn't just being clever. It's another way Jesus shows how one's righteousness must "exceed that of the scribes and Pharisees" (Matthew 5:20). We must move beyond simply abstaining from evil into actively loving each other. It's true we want others not to harm us. But we also hope they would do good things that benefit us. That is Jesus' call to us—to actively pursue the good of others. We can only live that way if we allow the grace of God to transform our naturally self-seeking habits.

Read: Matthew 7:12; Leviticus 19:18

Reflect:

1. What are some specific examples of the way you want people to act toward you?

2. Take a few minutes today to pray. Have a pen and paper handy to write anything you sense God saying. You might pray something like, "God, is there someone in my life with whom you'd like me to more intentionally practice the Golden Rule?"

Week 2

~~~~~~~

How Can Someone Become Virtuous? Part Three

MONDAY 6/7

ENTER THE NARROW GATE THAT LEADS TO LIFE

Two roads diverged in a wood and I—I took the one less traveled by, and that has made all the difference. — Robert Frost

Roman roads in Jesus' day were well paved and well patrolled, often built by Roman legionaries. These roads were the safest and surest way to reach one's destination and were traveled by many. They were surely the route of choice. The narrower roads of Judea were a much tougher affair to navigate and travel.

Thieves and murderers roamed the Judean byways and lay in wait for the unwary or unprotected pilgrim.

Despite the inherent dangers of the journey, Jesus exhorts his audience to avoid the safer, well-protected, well-traveled way. Instead, he offers them a gate that is narrow and a road that is hard. If we take this less-traveled road (by choosing to follow Jesus and ordering our lives accordingly), we will likely be misunderstood and at times mocked. People traveling the easier road will likely view us as foolish, impractical, naïve, misguided, wrongheaded; the list of possible negatives seems endless.

Read: Matthew 7:13–14

Reflect:

1. Jesus speaks about two ways of life. Think back to a time in your life when you intentionally chose the narrow way. How did that shape your life going forward?

2. Do you think it is harder today to live walking along the narrow way than it was a generation or two ago? Why or why not?

3. What are the joys of walking in the narrow way? The challenges?

TUESDAY

LOOK FOR THE FRUIT OF GENUINE LOVE

A tree is known by its fruit; a man by his deeds. A good deed is never lost; he who sows courtesy reaps friendship, and he who plants kindness gathers love. — Basil the Great

A virtuous life is one that bears good fruit. Fruit does not just appear; it grows out of a long process, from seed to vine to flower to fruit. It is the end result of the planter's patient tending and the rhythms of nature. Without this tending, the fruit never comes, or it comes and rots.

Have you ever bitten into a perfectly good-looking apple and discovered that it was rotten inside? Sometimes it's impossible to detect bad fruit until you get up close. In today's Scripture, Jesus warns us against trusting only the outward appearance of goodness in others—especially those who would teach or prophesy to us. The foremost factor in discerning good fruit from bad is to look for love. Is this teacher or leader speaking in love? Do his or her actions show Christ's love?

Read: Matthew 7:15–20

Reflect:

1. Jesus warns us against wolves in sheep's clothing. What sort of clothing might the wolves be dressed in today? How do you discern deception?

2. Sometimes an unhealthy fear of deception can make us reject anything unfamiliar, even things that God wants to show us. Have you ever experienced this fear? How might this fear be overcome?

3. How can being grounded in Scripture and a praying community protect you from false teaching?

WEDNESDAY

GOOD DEEDS ARE NOTHING WITHOUT LOVE

Do ordinary things with extraordinary love. — Mother Teresa of Calcutta

Imagine a marriage in which the spouses are "going through the motions." The husband may bring small gifts to the wife and the wife may help her husband, but they both know something is missing. They have lost their foundation of love.

Our relationship with Jesus is likened to marriage (Ephesians 5:22–33). Jesus wants more than good deeds. He wants our hearts. Note Paul's emphasis in his benediction to the Ephesians: "Grace be with all who have an undying love for our Lord Jesus Christ" (Ephesians 6:24).

Read: Matthew 7:21–23; 1 Corinthians 13

Reflect:

1. How is "doing the will of the Father" related to 1 Corinthians 13? What connections can be made between those Jesus "never knew" (Matthew 7:23) and a "clanging cymbal" (1 Corinthians 13:1)?

2. These passages shows us that love is more than just doing the right things. So what does it mean to love Jesus?

3. Loving God is a response: "We love because he first loved us" (1 John 4:19). Take a few moments to pray and ask God for a deeper revelation of his love for you, that your love may grow in response.

THURSDAY

BUILD YOUR HOUSE ON ROCK

*Get wisdom; get insight: do not forget, nor turn away from the words of
my mouth. Do not forsake her, and she will keep you; love her, and she will
guard you. — Proverbs 4:5–6*

Jesus offers a solid foundation on which to build one's life. His teaching is more than information or common sense; it is true wisdom that enables us to live rightly and freely. But it's up to us to put his words into practice. Otherwise we are like the fool so often described in Proverbs. The fool doesn't lack mental ability—he might be intelligent. The fool lacks moral judgment. He takes the easy way, the way that works for now but doesn't withstand the storms of life.

Jesus invites us to build the home of our hearts in him—a home that will be a steady shelter for us and others in times of trouble.

Read: Matthew 7:24–27

Reflect:

1. Why do you think the foolish builder chose to build his house on sand? Why do people sometimes build their lives on poor foundations?

2. What are some storms that can cause spiritual casualties in your own life (e.g., doubts, failures, conflicts, illness, apathy)?

3. Take a moment to reflect on the last few weeks of devotionals. Jesus refers to "everyone then who hears these words of mine and acts on them." Are there any specific portions of the Sermon on the Mount that you feel the Lord is asking you to act on?

FRIDAY

FOLLOW THE ASTOUNDING TEACHER

Live in such a way that men may recognize that you have been with Jesus.
— Charles Spurgeon

Charles Spurgeon wrote this about the ending of the Sermon on the Mount: "He touched their conscience; his teaching came home to them; they could not help feeling that it was true. Besides, he did not keep on quoting Rabbi This and Rabbi That, but he spoke from his own knowledge: 'He taught them as one having authority, and not as the scribes.'"

So the multitudes, astounded by Jesus' teaching, followed him after he came down from the mountain and everywhere he went. Until the way became too narrow, the teaching too hard. Then many left. When Jesus asked his disciples if they were going to leave him too, Peter spoke from the heart: "Lord, to whom can we go? You have the words of eternal life" (John 6:68). And so this is the virtuous life: to follow the astounding teacher, to remain with him, to listen and do the will of his Father in heaven—which is to love God and your neighbor.

Read: Matthew 7:28—8:1

Reflect:

1. When was the last time you felt "astounded" by anything? When was the last time you felt "astounded" by Jesus?

2. If you are able, obtain an audio recording of the Sermon on the Mount and listen to it, or ask a friend to read it aloud. Close your eyes and try to place yourself in first-century Palestine, sitting on a hill on the shore of the Sea of Galilee. What astounds you as you listen to the words with fresh ears?

Week 3

Training with Jesus in Holiness

MONDAY  6/14

A PRACTICAL PLAN

Jesus indeed said that without him we can do nothing. (John 15:5) But we can also be sure that if we do nothing it will be without him. So he commands us to "abide in the Vine." (15:1–7) We must find a way to do that.
— Dallas Willard

So how do we actually pursue holiness? How do we follow what Jesus said? That's what we'll look at this week.

All effective efforts toward personal transformation—whether they involve growing spiritually, developing new skills, or dropping bad habits—follow a general pattern: vision, intention, and means. To illustrate, let's use the example of learning another language.

First, to learn a new language one must have a vision of how life will be better when that language is learned. Perhaps knowing a new language opens up ministry or work opportunities. Second, one must intend and decide to actually do something to bring the vision into reality. A vision without intention is merely a daydream. Finally, one must find practical means to bring the intended vision into reality. In this example, the means would be language classes, audio CDs, immersion in another culture, and so forth. As it is with language learning, so it is with growing spiritually.

Read: 2 Peter 1:3–11

Reflect:

1. Peter says that God has given us everything we need for "life and godliness." Then he goes on to say, "You must make every effort . . ." How do grace and effort go together?

2. Do you feel an intentional plan is needed for spiritual growth in the same way that a plan is needed to learn a language? Why or why not? Have you always felt that way?

TUESDAY

VISION

The vision of our life in the kingdom of God, is the place we must start. This is the vision Jesus brought. It was the gospel he preached. — Dallas Willard

Let's apply the pattern of vision, intention, and means to spiritual transformation. Today we'll look at the first part: vision.

Jesus came announcing that the kingdom of God is available. He used parables to give us a vision of the kingdom: the kingdom of God is like this or like that. And he invited others to follow him by telling them what life would be like: "Follow me, and I will make you fish for people" (Matthew 4:19).

Life in the kingdom of God, life with God, is abundant life. It's a life of goodness, beauty, and truth. That doesn't mean it's a life without hardships. In fact, Jesus says, "In the world you face persecution." But he goes on to say, "Take courage; I have conquered the world!" (John 16:22). Having a solid vision of this abundant life with Jesus moves us toward intending to actually do what he said.

Read: Matthew 13:44–46

Reflect:

1. In today's passage, a man—"in his joy"—sells all that he has to buy the treasure in a field. The opportunity was too good to miss. What does this tell us about the kingdom of God?

2. What about Jesus is compelling to you? What was the vision of life in the kingdom of God that made you want to start following him? What vision makes you want to still follow him today?

WEDNESDAY

INTENTION

People who do not intend to be inwardly transformed, so that obedience to Christ "comes naturally," will not be transformed. God will not pick us up and throw us into transformed kingdom living, into "holiness."
— Dallas Willard

Hopefully we've caught a compelling vision of what life is like abiding with Jesus in the kingdom of God—a life of more love, joy, peace, patience, and kindness; a life content with much or with little.

But a vision doesn't naturally drift into reality. One must intend to act on the vision. Our resolve must be firm but humble, knowing we'll need God's help to follow through. This is an important step. "I have decided to follow Jesus. . . . No turning back," goes an old song. The intention, the decision, is what readies us to use whatever means are necessary to bring the vision into being.

Read: Luke 14:25–33

Reflect:

1. How does today's passage about counting the cost go along with yesterday's passage about acting from joy? Can one be both serious and joyful in a decision? Describe what that looks like.

2. Thinking back to our recent study, is there a specific part of the Sermon on the Mount that you want to intentionally work on with Jesus for the next few months? Perhaps it's speaking more truthfully ("Let your word be 'Yes, Yes' or 'No, No'"), or worrying less, or having more compassion for others ("Do to others as you would have them do to you"). Write out a simple prayer telling God your intention and asking for his help, and then put it someplace where you will see it often.

Vision
Intension
Means

THURSDAY

MEANS

The clear vision and the solid intention to obey Christ will naturally lead to seeking out and applying the means to that end. That is the natural order in human life. — Dallas Willard

Continuing the quote above, Willard says: "By finding such means we are not left to ourselves, but have rich resources available to us in the example and teachings of Jesus, in the Scriptures generally, and in his people through the ages. They include such practices as solitude, memorization and meditation upon Scripture, fellowship and account-ability to others, and so forth."

And so we find ourselves back at the spiritual disciplines. It's worth repeating that the disciplines earn us nothing with God. They simply put us in a place to receive God's grace, which transforms us. And that's an important place to be, because God does not force his grace upon us. He waits for us to use the means he has provided. When we do, he blesses us far beyond the effort we put in.

Read: Philippians 4:4–9

Reflect:

1. In today's passage, Paul tells us not to worry. What means—practical steps—does he recommend to help us learn not to worry?

2. Paul says, "Keep on doing the things that you have . . . seen in me." Name one or two followers of Jesus you admire. What means do they use to follow Jesus?

3. Yesterday's exercise was to write out a prayer of intention—something you desire to work on with Jesus. Today take a few minutes to write down ways to work out that intention. For example, write a plan to memorize Scripture (e.g., each day recite a passage ten times out loud), or schedule a day next month to fast or a day next quarter to spend in solitude.

FRIDAY

EMPOWERED TO LIVE HOLY LIVES

The time allotted to our life is redeemed by opening ourself to God and His kingdom through non-legalistic practices that break internal bondages and gives us new habits and character. — Dallas Willard

Passages like Matthew 5-7, Romans 12, 1 Corinthians 13, Galatians 5:22—6:10, Philippians 2:1-11—and today's passage from Ephesians—show us what an apprentice of Jesus looks like.

Followers of Jesus may read these passages with longing and desire, but perhaps also with hopelessness or guilt—"I'll never be like that." The pattern discussed this week (vision, intention, means) empowers us to cooperate with God. And with empowerment comes hope. Thanks be to God!

With that, let's read today's passage not as a burdensome list of laws but rather as an inspiring talk delivered by a coach who loves his team. With bold words, the coach strengthens the players' hearts and calls them to the joy of playing at their full capacity. In response, the team shouts "Yes!" Given fresh vision, they set an intention to put in the practice so that when game time comes, and that critical play is at hand, they find themselves ready and able.

Read: Ephesians 4:20—5:2

Reflect:

1. Paul talks about being "renewed in the spirit of your minds" (Ephesians 4:23). He says something similar in Romans 12:2. Why is renewing your mind so important? What are some practical ways to do this?

2. Paul says to the believers at Ephesus, "Be imitators of God, as beloved children" (Ephesians 5:1). How does being loved make a child want to imitate his or her parent? What are some things about God you want to imitate?

Week 4

Restoring Our Vision of Holiness

MONDAY

JESUS AS THE FACE OF GOD'S HOLINESS

[Jesus] is the image of the invisible God, the firstborn of all creation.
— Colossians 1:15

For nearly two months we've been exploring the invitation to receive holiness from God and allow it to reshape our lives until they are functional, healthy, and virtuous. Yet we may still experience some resistance when it comes to the word holiness. South African pastor and author Trevor Hudson has been known to ask, "If there was a door in this room marked 'holiness,' would you be excited to walk through it?"

We tend to think of holiness as something boring, bland, and judgmental. In Jesus, God's holiness is given a human face—and it is not at all boring, bland, or judgmental! Our study on holiness concludes this week by looking at the holiness of Jesus.

Read: Luke 4:31–35; John 6:66–69

Reflect:

1. In today's passages, both the demon and Peter recognize Jesus as "the Holy One of God." What was it about Jesus that caused them to recognize and declare his holiness?

2. Have you, in the past, been attracted to the idea of "becoming holy"? Why or why not?

TUESDAY

A HOLY INVITATION TO BECOME OURSELVES

The more we let God take us over, the more truly ourselves we become.
— C. S. Lewis

If Jesus gives God's holiness a human face, what can his earthly life tell us about holy living? The first thing we might notice is that Jesus was always completely himself—free of pretense or duplicity. Perhaps part of what it means for us to be holy is to become more authentically ourselves.

When John the Baptist pointed people to Jesus, he cried, "He must increase, but I must decrease" (John 3:30). We might read that Scripture and be tempted to think that the more of Jesus we have in our lives, the more our own personalities will fade away into a generic Christlikeness. But we must remember that John became even more completely his confrontational, unshaven, locust-eating self in Jesus' presence. It was not that John became less himself, but rather that his whole self now pointed to Jesus.

Holiness is, among other things, a wholeness given to us by God. We should expect to become more wholly ourselves as God works within us.

Read: 2 Corinthians 3:12–18

Reflect:

1. The apostle Paul talks about "unveiled faces" in this passage. Have you ever known someone who seems to have an "unveiled face"?

2. All of us have parts of our personalities that have been broken or distorted by sin (either the sin we have committed or the sin that has been committed against us.) As God heals individuals' brokenness, what do you think will happen to their personalities? Will they become "themselves"?

3. Pray that God will move you toward becoming holy in your own unique way.

WEDNESDAY

A HOLY INVITATION TO LOVE OTHERS

There is no holiness but social holiness. — John Wesley

The second thing we might notice about holiness in Jesus' life is the way he related to other people. He mingled easily and lovingly with the social outcasts whom the Jewish religious leaders avoided. He cultivated close and lasting friendships with both men and women. And when he became stern, it was with people who hurt others—like the money changers who were exploiting people in the temple (Matthew 21:12-13).

Steady, unconditional love was the mode of Jesus' life.

As we grow in holiness, then, we can expect to become people increasingly motivated by love. And if we really want to know how we are progressing in the life of holiness, we can ask our friends and family how we are doing at loving them.

Read: John 13:1-5, 12-15, 34-35

Reflect:

1. Why do you think Jesus took the time to wash the disciples' feet the night before his crucifixion?

2. Take a few moments for silent reflection. If someone were to ask your family how you are doing at loving them, what might they say? Is there a person whom you struggle to love well in your thoughts or actions? Ask God for increasing holiness—and therefore increasing love—in that area of your life.

THURSDAY

A HOLY INVITATION TO PUT GOD AT THE CENTER

Jesus said to them, "Very truly, I tell you, the Son can do nothing on his own, but only what he sees the Father doing; for whatever the Father does, the Son does likewise." — John 5:19

The third thing we might notice about Jesus' holiness is the way he calibrated his life to the heartbeat of his Father. "My food is to do the will of him who sent me and to complete his work," he told his disciples (John 4:34). From making prayer a constant priority, to the total surrender of his own will at Gethsemane, Jesus' focus never wavered.

Holiness for us, then, involves centering our lives upon the Father, just the way Jesus did. Fortunately, Jesus has given us the Holy Spirit to help us say yes to such a radical invitation.

Read: Luke 22:39–44

Reflect:

1. In today's reading, Jesus goes to the Mount of Olives the night before his crucifixion to pray through his anguish and surrender his will. Luke notes that it was Jesus' "custom" to go to the Mount of Olives to pray. Why might that be important?

2. Spend a moment or two of silence asking the Lord to show you if there is an area of your life you have not yet surrendered to him. If there is, write it down and commit to discussing it with him further.

Month 6: The Virtuous Life

FRIDAY

HOLINESS: A LIFE OF VIRTUE, THAT FUNCTIONS AS IT SHOULD

You thought you were going to be made into a decent little cottage: but He is building a palace. He intends to come and live in it Himself. — C. S. Lewis

For the last two months we have focused on holiness and virtue. This week we have explored how holiness makes us more whole and authentic, makes us better at loving others, and involves centering our focus upon God.

In earlier weeks we discovered that Jesus' Sermon on the Mount shows us what virtue looks like in action. We have come to see that virtue—the fruit of a holy life—is more than a rote moral code. We will let Richard Foster help us with some final definitions:

> *Simply put, virtue is good habits that we can rely upon to make our lives work. (Conversely, vice is bad habits we can rely upon to make our lives not work.) When the old writers spoke of "a virtuous life," they were referring to a life that works, a life that functions well.*

Centered on our heavenly Father, empowered by his Holy Spirit, we are invited to become more and more like Jesus, each in our own unique way. We do it by saying yes to the holiness God has for us, and then by cultivating the habits that allow us to live into all he offers.

Read: Romans 12:1-2

Reflect:

1. One definition of *holy* is "set apart," which Paul echoes in his statement, "Do not be conformed to this world." Why is being holy—not be conformed to the world—so important?

2. What has stood out the most to you from our reflection on holiness and the virtuous life?

3. Take some time to review your prayer of intention and the means by which you intend to become more like Jesus. Thank God for the work he is doing in your life to make you holy.

Week 1

~~~~~~~~

Jesus and the Holy Spirit

MONDAY 6/28

FROM BIRTH TO BREATH

The early Celtic Christians called the Holy Spirit "the wild goose." And the reason why is they knew that you cannot tame him. — *John Eldridge*

The Holy Spirit is perhaps the least understood member of the Trinity. The Father and Son we can picture at least in earthly terms, but even our metaphors for the Spirit—the wind, a bird—are elusive. Who is the Holy Spirit? What is the Holy Spirit's role in our lives? What does a Spirit-filled and Spirit-led life look like?

For the next eight weeks we will explore these questions. There is nowhere better to start than with Jesus. His life began by the Spirit, and after his resurrection he breathed on his disciples and said to them, "Receive the Holy Spirit."

Read: Matthew 1:18; John 20:19–22

Reflect:

1. Jesus is the only human who was—and ever will be—conceived by the Holy Spirit. Why is this important?

2. If someone asked you "Who is the Holy Spirit?" what would you say?

3. As we begin this new section, take a few moments to pray and ask God to help you to better know the Holy Spirit.

TUESDAY

THE BAPTISM

I baptize you with water for repentance, but one who is more powerful than I is coming after me; I am not worthy to carry his sandals. He will baptize you with the Holy Spirit and fire. — John the Baptist (Matthew 3:11)

There is little record of Jesus' life before age thirty. As far as we know, he did no miracles. Although Jesus lived in relative obscurity, he "grew in wisdom and stature, and in favor with God and man" (Luke 2:52 NIV).

When John baptized Jesus, a wonder and mystery occurred: like a dove, the Holy Spirit descended and rested upon Jesus. This one who had "emptied himself" (Philippians 2:7) is here filled with the Spirit that would guide and power his ministry.

Read: Luke 3:21–22

Reflect:

1. If Jesus was conceived by the Spirit, why do you think it was necessary for the Holy Spirit to descend and rest upon him?

2. A voice from heaven said, "You are my Son, the Beloved; with you I am well pleased." This is prior to Jesus doing any public ministry. Why is it important to know your identity in God before doing ministry?

WEDNESDAY

THE WILDERNESS

Of all the days of Christ's life in the flesh, these [days in the wilderness] seem to come nearest to ... the heavenly life, and this prepared him for Satan's assaults. — Matthew Henry

Assured of his identity ("You are my Son"), and with the Holy Spirit resting upon him, Jesus is led by the Spirit into the wilderness. Immediately the devil attacks his identity: "If you are the Son of God . . ." But Jesus withstands the temptation and emerges not only "full of the Holy Spirit" (Luke 4:1) but "filled with the power of the Spirit" (Luke 4:14).

Read: Luke 4:1–14

Reflect:

1. Why would the Spirit lead Jesus into the wilderness?

2. Do you think the fasting and testing in the wilderness contributed to Jesus being "filled with the power of the Spirit" (Luke 4:14)? How so?

3. Have you ever felt like God led you into a wilderness season of life? What was the result?

THURSDAY

REJOICING IN THE HOLY SPIRIT

Jesus ... was leaping for joy in the Spirit, for now it was clear to him and the others that the power ministry of the promised Holy Spirit was transferable to ordinary disciples. — Richard Foster

Spirit-filled joy—cheerfulness, happiness, delight—was a defining quality of Jesus. It caused religious leaders to say he was a glutton and drunkard; it made sinners flock to him (Matthew 11:19). That kind of joy is what Jesus wants for all who follow him.

Near the end of his life, Jesus told his disciples, his friends, to keep his commandments and abide in his love (John 15:9–10). As they looked to their radiant master, he told them where this obedience and abiding would lead: into joy. "I have said these things to you so that my joy may be in you, and that your joy may be complete" (John 15:11).

Read: Luke 10:1, 17–21

Reflect:

1. The Greek word for *rejoice* in today's passage literally means to jump for joy. Is it hard or easy for you to imagine Jesus jumping for joy? Why?

2. In this passage Jesus says that God revealed things not to the wise but to "infants"? What does that mean? And what about that reality made Jesus so happy?

FRIDAY

~~~~~~

IT IS TO YOUR ADVANTAGE THAT I GO AWAY

Those in whom the Spirit comes to live are God's new Temple. They are, individually and corporately, places where heaven and earth meet.
— *N. T. Wright*

Imagine being one of the twelve disciples. To walk with Jesus, watch him heal, hear him teach, look into his eyes unstained by sin—could there be anything better? Yes, says Jesus. And his name is the Holy Spirit.

Bewilderment must have filled the disciples when Jesus said, "It is to your advantage that I go away." Yet it was true. Jesus wanted more for his friends than they could imagine. His earthly body had limitations: it could only be in one place at one time. He wanted to be personally and fully present to all his followers all the time. And not just walking beside, but dwelling within. They still thought about the temple being in Jerusalem. Jesus had wonderful news for them, and for us: the temple is you.

Read: ~~Matthew~~ John 16:7; 20:17

Reflect:

1. Why do you think it was necessary for Jesus to ascend to send the Holy Spirit?

2. Sometimes we may wish we could have a conversation with Jesus in the flesh. Is that kind of conversational relationship available with God now through the Holy Spirit? Or is it different?

3. Take a few minutes to pray and thank God for dwelling inside you. Perhaps you might pray to be more filled with the Holy Spirit and able to hear the quiet voice of the Spirit more clearly.

Week 2

~~~~~~~

Meet the Holy Spirit

MONDAY 7|12

THE SPIRIT OF TRUTH   SPIRIT OF TRUTH

I may know all the doctrines in the Bible, but unless I know Christ there is not one of them that can save me. — Charles Spurgeon

Before Jesus went away and sent the Holy Spirit, he taught the disciples about the Holy Spirit. The Gospel of John records this teaching in what Bible scholars call the five Paraclete sayings, which we'll look at this week. The word translated "Advocate" that Jesus uses to describe the Holy Spirit in these verses is from the Greek word paraclete. It originally referred to an advocate in the legal sense—one who pleads a client's case before a court. The root of the word means "to call alongside," which denotes the helping character of the Holy Spirit.

The Holy Spirit, as we see in today's reading, is "the Spirit of truth." He affirms what is good and pure and true and holy. However, the world—all those systems and people who base their beliefs on what can be measured and observed—cannot see the Spirit, so it doubts his existence. But believers recognize the Spirit because he lives within them.

Read: John 14:15–17

Reflect:

1. Take a moment to recall a time when a person has helped you or advocated for you. How did that make you feel? What does sending the Holy Spirit as an advocate and helper say about God's heart for you?

2. The word *truth* appears more times in the Gospel of John than in any other book of the Bible. What is truth? And why is truth so important?

3. The religious teachers in Jesus' day knew facts about God, but their bondage was so great that Jesus said the devil was their father (John 8:44). Truth, Jesus said, sets us free (John 8:32). How is cooperating with truth different than merely knowing the right answers?

TUESDAY

THE HOLY SPIRIT AS TEACHER

God's mind is revealed in Holy Scripture but we can see nothing without the spectacles of the Holy Spirit. — *Thomas Manton*

The Holy Spirit functions as a teacher. We learn to pray with the help of the Holy Spirit. He helps us discern our spiritual gifts and then guides us in their proper use. Love, joy, peace, patience, kindness, and more come into our lives through the Holy Spirit's teaching. Like our earthly teachers, the Spirit reminds us and corrects us.

"The Holy Spirit," Jesus said, "will teach you everything." That means the Holy Spirit wants to guide us not only in spiritual matters but in every area of life. Jesus is the smartest person to ever walk our planet; and, through the Holy Spirit, he is present to teach us. Saints through the ages have discovered that practicing the presence of Jesus—being aware of and in conversation with him throughout each day—has made them more effective and joyful in all areas of their life and work.

Read: John 14:25–27

Reflect:

1. We learn from human teachers in a classroom or on the job by being attentive to what they say and do. What are some settings in which we learn from the Holy Spirit? How can we be attentive to the Spirit in those settings?

2. Jesus says the Holy Spirit will remind us of things. How does this relate to our responsibility to read the Scriptures and study?

3. Here's a simple prayer you might consider praying: "Holy Spirit, I recognize your presence in my life. Help me stay present to Jesus today. Teach me through what I read, conversations I have, work I perform, and situations I observe. Amen."

WEDNESDAY

THE HOLY SPIRIT TESTIFIES TO CHRIST

We are witnesses to these things, and so is the Holy Spirit whom God has given to those who obey him. — Acts 5:32

The Holy Spirit functions as a witness who "testifies" about Jesus Christ. When we hear the gospel—the "good news" that Jesus Christ was born, lived, died, and rose from the dead—the Holy Spirit witnesses to our spirit that the good news is true and prompts us to accept it. It's truly a miracle: the Holy Spirit makes us who were dead in our sins able to hear and receive the truth that brings us to life.

Today's passage highlights the "called alongside" nature of the Holy Spirit. Jesus said that the Holy Spirit "will testify on my behalf. You also are to testify." Testifying is work we do together, but the Holy Spirit's work goes far beyond ours. We share who Jesus is and what he's done in our life. The Holy Spirit convicts, enlightens, and saves. That takes the pressure off of our sharing the good news—the results are in God's hands.

Read: John 15:26–27   TESTIFY / WITNESS

Reflect:

1. God would surely do a more effective job of telling people about Jesus if he did it himself directly, without us. Why do you think God has chosen to involve us in testifying about Jesus?

2. Ask God for an opportunity to share the good news of Jesus with someone. Keep your eyes open for an answer to that prayer, and then share with ease, knowing that it's the Holy Spirit's job to work in that person's heart.

THURSDAY

~~~~~~

THE HOLY SPIRIT CONVICTS THE WORLD

It is the Holy Spirit's job to convict, God's job to judge, and my job to love.
— Billy Graham

In addition to being an advocate who defends believers, the Holy Spirit is a prosecutor who will "prove the world wrong" about its relationship to God—particularly about "sin and righteousness and judgment." We must always remember that it is the Spirit's task to convict, not ours.

Eugene Peterson's paraphrase of John 16:8-11 from The *Message* may help clarify this passage:

> *When he comes, he'll expose the error of the godless world's view of sin, righteousness, and judgment: He'll show them that their refusal to believe in me is their basic sin; that righteousness comes from above, where I am with the Father, out of their sight and control; that judgment takes place as the ruler of this godless world is brought to trial and convicted.*

Read: John 16:4-11

Reflect:

1. The world is full of all kinds of sin. Why is refusing to believe in Jesus the basic sin of the world?

2. Where does the world believe righteousness comes from? Where does Jesus say it comes from? FROM THE FATHER

3. There are times when it's necessary and appropriate to call someone to account for something he or she has done wrong. How can we do this in such a way that allows the Holy Spirit room to work in the person's heart?

FRIDAY

THE SPIRIT WILL GUIDE YOU INTO ALL THE TRUTH

If the Spirit of him who raised Jesus from the dead dwells in you, he who raised Christ Jesus from the dead will give life to your mortal bodies also through his Spirit that dwells in you. — Romans 8:11

This week's passages provide a clear picture of the role and work of the Holy Spirit in our lives. Christ's departure meant that all believers, by the work of the Holy Spirit, could now have individual union with Christ. By this work, each believer becomes a member of Christ's spiritual body. What's more, the Spirit is now given to empower us in our ministry. The Spirit provides us with the ability to experience the abiding presence of God, receive all truth, hear the testimony concerning Christ, convict the world of its sin, and have authority over the fallen world.

What a treasure we have in the Holy Spirit! God withholds no good thing from us. All that the Father has belongs to Jesus. And the Holy Spirit takes what belongs to Jesus and declares it to us. Praise be to God the Father, God the Son, and God the Holy Spirit.

Read: John 16:12–15

Reflect:

1. Jesus sent the Holy Spirit to tell the disciples things they weren't yet capable of hearing. What kinds of things do you think these were? How do you think they became ready to hear? How does that relate to what the Spirit wants to tell you?

2. The Holy Spirit is a person, not an idea, and a person can only be truly known by firsthand interaction. Take a few minutes to pray for whatever is on your heart regarding the Holy Spirit. Do you desire to know the Spirit in a deeper way? Ask. It's a prayer Jesus promised to answer (Luke 11:13).

Week 3

~~~~~~~

What is the Spirit-Empowered life?

MONDAY 7|19

A VITAL AND EXCITING LIFE

The truth of the matter is this: God wants to be active in our lives; to endow us with supernatural abilities; to see us live with love, joy, peace, and so on.
— *Richard Foster*

Often Christians earn a reputation as killjoys, people afraid of happiness and excitement. But reading the book of Acts demolishes that stereotype. There we see Jesus' disciples filled with the Holy Spirit, doing the very things Jesus did—healing the sick, casting out demons, and boldly and joyfully proclaiming the good news of the kingdom of God.

Far from being sad and dull, the Spirit-empowered life is joyful, vital, and exciting. We turn our attention to that life this week.

Read: Acts 3:1–10

Reflect:

1. Sometimes we may try to be faithful disciples on our own, without the power of the Holy Spirit. Describe what that looks like. What is the result of striving to follow Jesus in our own strength?

2. Do you believe that the Holy Spirit can empower you to live the same kind of life and do the same kinds of things that the apostles did in the first century? Why or why not?

TUESDAY

~~~~~~

A LIFE THAT BEARS THE FRUIT OF THE SPIRIT

The fruit of the Spirit is a gift of God, and only He can produce it. They who bear it know as little about it as the tree knows of its fruit. They know only the power of Him on whom their life depends. — Dietrich Bonhoeffer

Consider a tree. It doesn't bear fruit of its own will. Rather, it simply functions as it was made to function. If its fruit is missing or poorly formed, the fruit-grower knows that something is wrong.

You may remember from the Sermon on the Mount a section about false prophets. How do we discern them? Jesus says simply, "You will know them by their fruits" (Matthew 7:16). Likewise, followers of Jesus are known by their fruit. Psalm 1 says that those who delight in the law of the Lord "are like trees planted by streams of water, which yield their fruit in its season."

Read: Galatians 5:22–25

Reflect:

1. What words would you use to describe the process of a tree going from seed to sapling to bearing fruit? How do these apply to our spiritual life?

2. Take note of which word Paul places first in his list of the fruit of the Spirit. Why do you think he does this? What implications might we draw from this?

3. Read through the fruit of the Spirit again. Is there one aspect in particular that stands out to you, perhaps one you wish to grow in? Write out a prayer to ask for the power of the Spirit in that area.

WEDNESDAY

A LIFE OPEN TO THE RENEWING WORK OF THE SPIRIT

To renew your mind is to involve yourself in the process of allowing God to bring to the surface the lies you have mistakenly accepted and replace them with truth. To the degree that you do this, your behavior will be transformed.
— Charles Stanley

Have you ever seen a snake shed its skin? As the snake grows, the old skin stretches until it can no longer contain the snake. The snake then glides across a rough surface to leave its old skin behind. The shed skin is often full of parasites and surface wounds that get left behind as the snake emerges renewed.

A Spirit-empowered life constantly stretches us. Our "old skins"—bad habits of thinking and relating to one another—are getting sloughed off. Sometimes the process is uncomfortable, even painful. But take heart. What God wants to make us into is well worth the process.

Read: Titus 3:1–7

Reflect:

1. Scripture speaks often of the power of the Holy Spirit. In today's passage, Paul gives examples of a Spirit-renewed life that may not sound powerful: *be subject to authorities, avoid quarreling, be gentle, show courtesy.* How is the power of the Holy Spirit evident in these qualities?

2. Have you ever experienced a time where you were aware of the Spirit's work in your life and it surprised you—for example, a time when you may have normally been angry but responded in love, or a time when you said something you hadn't planned to say and it blessed someone else? Thank God that the Holy Spirit is at work in your life. Rob/Jessica

THURSDAY

~~~~~~~~~

A LIFE OF WORSHIP

*Worship must be Christ centered, Holy Spirit led, a response to the Father ...
and always lead to transformation.* — *Tim Hughes*

For the Samaritan woman whose story is told in today's passage, worship was location dependent. Her main question was one of place: Where should we worship? But Jesus, as he so often does, interacts with a better question: How should we worship?

Places and forms of worship can be helpful. But ultimately worship—ascribing worth and honor to God in whatever we do, say, or sing—is about the heart. The Holy Spirit, as our teacher, wants to reveal to us God's goodness, beauty, truth—and most of all his love. We need only ask. And when God's love and beauty and truth are seen, it is only natural to respond in thankfulness and worship.

Read: John 4:19–24

Reflect:

1. What does it mean to worship God "in spirit and truth"?

2. Jesus said, "The hour is coming, and is now here." What happened in the coming of Jesus that allows us to worship in spirit and truth?

3. Do you desire to grow in the area of worship? Ask the Holy Spirit to show you today God's goodness, beauty, truth, and love in specific ways. When that prayer is answered, when your heart leaps at beholding something good, offer a simple prayer of worship—like "Thank you, Lord," or "You are amazing, God."

FRIDAY

A LIFE THAT USES SPIRITUAL GIFTS IN LOVE

Signs, wonders, miracles and healings, revelations and visions—these are all part of our walk with the Spirit. They become a witness to nonbelievers and an affirmation of hope to believers. — Richard Foster

One of the mysteries of coming to faith in Jesus is that we are given spiritual gifts by the Holy Spirit. In today's passage, Paul outlines a few of them.

It is possible to use our spiritual gifts in unhealthy ways, disconnected from relationship with Jesus (Matthew 7:21–23). Gifts can also be overemphasized or even fabricated. But God's desire is that we use spiritual gifts motivated by love and in relationship with Jesus. This is good for everyone! We receive the joy of serving, others receive the encouragement of being served, and God receives the glory in it all.

Read: 1 Corinthians 12:1–11

Reflect:

1. Which of these spiritual gifts are you familiar with? Which are unfamiliar?

2. Depending on culture and denomination, spiritual gifts can be a divisive topic. What have been your own experiences with the spiritual gifts?

3. What are your spiritual gifts? If you are unsure, consider praying and talking with a pastor, friend, or colleague to identify how the Holy Spirit has gifted you.

Week 4

~~~~~~~

Gifts of the Holy Spirit

MONDAY 8/2

THE GIFT OF WISDOM

To one there is given through the Spirit a message of wisdom, to another a message of knowledge by means of the same Spirit.
— 1 Corinthians 12:8 (NIV)

In our last devotional, we looked at the apostle Paul's partial list of spiritual gifts in 1 Corinthians 12:1–11. There Paul makes it clear that each follower of Jesus receives at least one gift, which is meant to be used for the sake of the community. All these gifts can be identified in the life of Christ, yet Paul makes it clear that each of us has different gifts. Only together do we make up the body of Christ. That's why we need each other and can celebrate one another's gifts.

In today's passage, we see a vivid example of the gift of wisdom in Jesus' life. While we all have access to God's wisdom in our lives (James 1:5), some believers are also given a special measure of wisdom by the Spirit (1 Corinthians 12:8). When we lack wisdom, God may provide it to us directly through his Spirit, or he may draw us deeper into relationship with himself and his people by making wisdom available to us through other members of the body of Christ.

Read: Matthew 22:15–22

Reflect:

1. Do you think the "wisdom" described in James 1:5 is different than the "wisdom" described in 1 Corinthians 12:8? Why or why not?

2. Do you know anyone who has an unusual depth of wisdom? Describe that person. Does he or she have an openness to the Holy Spirit?

3. In today's passage, Jesus has extraordinary insight in a difficult situation. He knows the motives of those around him and responds with grace and truth. Can you think of a time you needed wisdom and received it? Did it seem to come from your own mind, or from another source?

TUESDAY

THE GIFT OF MIRACLES

The more we let God take us over, the more truly ourselves we become.
— C. S. Lewis

Today's passage tells the story of the wedding at Cana, Jesus' first miracle in the Gospel of John. Notice the delightful details. Jesus works a wonder at least in part, it would seem, to oblige his mother. And he not only turns water into wine, but he also turns it into the best-tasting wine of the extended party. God's goodness is extravagant and abundant.

John tells us that Jesus' miracle "revealed his glory" (John 2:11). The revelation seems to have included not only the fact that Jesus is God, but also the reality that God is good.

Read: John 2:1–11

Reflect:

1. What was the purpose—or purposes—of Jesus' miracle at Cana? Do those purposes tell us anything about the reason a miracle might take place today?

2. Have you ever seen a miracle firsthand? How would you describe it? How did you know it was a miracle?

3. Can you think of someone who needs a miracle? Perhaps this person is yourself. Please take a few moments to pray for God's goodness and power to be made manifest today.

WEDNESDAY

~~~~~~~~~~~~

THE GIFT OF DISCERNMENT

... to another the discernment of spirits ... — 1 Corinthians 12:10

In the Gospels, Jesus encounters a lot of people with agendas. Some of them he protects (see John 8:3–11). Some of them he challenges (see John 2:13–16). All of them he loves (see Mark 10:21).

Jesus, filled with the Holy Spirit, has the discernment both to read the hearts of those around him and to know what they need. His insight into people is never used to harm or manipulate, but only to bring wholeness, justice, and healing.

Read: Mark 2:1–12

Reflect:

1. In today's passage, Jesus "perceived in his spirit" what the scribes were thinking. How did he use this discernment? What was the result?

2. How is using discernment different than criticizing or judging someone?

3. Is there a situation for which you currently need discernment? Take some time to pray that the Holy Spirit would either grant you discernment directly or bring someone to you that has the needed gift.

THURSDAY

~~~~~~~~~

THE GIFT OF HEALING

… to another gifts of healing by the one Spirit… — 1 Corinthians 12:9

Anyone who has spent time in the hospital knows the difference a caring doctor or nurse can make. Too often medical personnel, suffering from time constraints and compassion fatigue, rush in and out of hospital rooms to treat their patients without really seeing them or interacting with them. They may prescribe the right medicine, but the dignity of the patient is overlooked in the process.

Jesus was a different kind of "Great Physician." Not only could he heal his "patients" simply with a word, but his encounters with them were also remarkably personal. No matter how many crowds clamored for his attention, his interactions with the sick were personal, attentive, and insightful. It seems Jesus loved people too much to merely heal their bodies—he wanted to heal mind, soul, and spirit as well.

Read: John 5:1–9

Reflect:

1. What question did Jesus ask the sick man at the pool? What was the significance of the question?

2. Jesus could have waved his hands over large groups of people and healed them, but most of the stories reported in the Gospels are one-on-one encounters. Why do you think that is?

3. Spend some time today praying for the healing of body, mind, and soul in situations where you know it is needed.

FRIDAY

THE GIFT OF JOY

The fruit of the Spirit is … joy … — Galatians 5:22

The apostle Paul makes it clear that the gifts of the Holy Spirit he lists in 1 Corinthians 12:1–11—all of which can be seen in the life of Jesus—will be spread out among the body of Christ. The fruit of the Spirit, however, can be cultivated in the life of every believer (Galatians 5:22–23).

The fruit of joy, according to the apostolic witness, is one of the hallmarks of the followers of Jesus. It seems to pop up most vibrantly in the midst of hardship (see Acts 16:25; 1 Thessalonians 1:6), which is how we know it is not the natural product of human effort, but a gift of the Holy Spirit.

Read: John 15:1–11

Reflect:

1. Think of the most joyful person you know. Has that person had an easy life?

2. We've looked at John 15 before. What does "abiding in Jesus" look like for you today?

3. Spend some time praying, thanking God for things that make you joyful in the present, and asking that your joy may be complete (John 15:11).

Week 1

The Holy Spirit at Work in Peter

MONDAY

THE COMING OF THE HOLY SPIRIT

When the Advocate comes, whom I will send to you from the Father, the Spirit of truth who comes from the Father, he will testify on my behalf. You also are to testify because you have been with me from the beginning.
— John 15:26–27

When the Holy Spirit came upon the apostles on the day of Pentecost, what immediately happened? They began to speak in other tongues, or languages, as the Spirit enabled them, surrounded by "a sound like the rush of a violent wind" (Acts 2:1-4).

There has been much debate about the nature of these languages, but one thing is clear. *The Spirit was speaking.* "Devout Jews from every nation under heaven" *heard* what the apostles—Peter included—were saying *in their native languages* (Acts 2:5-6). Peter then explained to the crowd that the Spirit was being poured out (Acts 2:14-16). *Filled* with the Holy Spirit, Peter was *testifying* to the truth, fulfilling Jesus' teaching in John 15:26-27.

A distinct pattern is perceptible when the Spirit descends on the early church. Did you notice it? The Spirit empowers. The Spirit bears testimony to the truth found in Jesus. The Spirit enables people to hear and respond to the message. This pattern appears in Peter's own life throughout the book of Acts.

Read: Acts 2:1-13

Reflect:

1. What has the Spirit taught you as he has testified to the truth found in Jesus?

2. How have these truths concretely changed your thinking and living?

TUESDAY

PREACHING THAT CUTS TO THE HEART

God was executed by people painfully like us, in a society very similar to our own. — Dorothy Sayers

The truth Peter powerfully preached was clear and specific. "God has made this Jesus, whom you crucified, both Lord and Messiah" (Acts 2:36 NIV).

Some listening to Peter might have collaborated with Rome as Pilate ordered Jesus' crucifixion. Innocent blood had been shed, the blood of God's own Son. Now, through the convicting work of the Spirit, the horrific reality of what had been done began to sink in.

What were these people to do? They made no excuses. No one said "I couldn't help it" or "It's not my fault." Rather, they were "cut to the heart" (Acts 2:37) as Peter called them to repentance and its gracious fruit, forgiveness.

Those who crucified Jesus were not unlike us. We too need heart surgery—a lancing of our diseased heart's infection with the Spirit's scalpel.

Read: Acts 2:14–39

Reflect:

1. Place yourself among the crowd at Pentecost. How do you imagine you might have responded to Peter's preaching?

2. Can you remember a time when your heart was cut by the Spirit—not to harm you, but to save your life?

3. Take a moment to ask the Holy Spirit, "Where am I most likely to make excuses rather than to receive forgiveness?" Try to be as specific as possible. Write down your answer. Keep this in prayer throughout the week.

WEDNESDAY

A PRAYER FOR BOLDNESS

The priests and the captain of the temple guard and the Sadducees came up to Peter and John while they were speaking to the people. They were greatly disturbed because the apostles were teaching the people, proclaiming in Jesus the resurrection of the dead. — Acts 4:1–2 (NIV)

Peter and John were in a tough situation. They were under Jesus' orders to preach his resurrection, but the temple authorities wanted them to stop. Remember that these Jewish leaders were the very persons who had demanded that Pilate execute Jesus. Peter and John were facing the same terrifying possibility.

Remember, also, Peter's history of cowardice. After promising he would bear faithful witness to Jesus, he had failed miserably. In his time of testing, Peter had denied Jesus three times.

Now, in this new time of testing and threats, Peter and John prayed for boldness (Acts 4:29).

We are bold when, through the power of the Spirit, we willingly do something for Christ's sake that could cost us dearly. Bold witness to the resurrection—in Peter's day and ours—might well come with a cost: public humiliation and disgrace, physical harm, imprisonment, even the loss of our own lives. In the book of Acts we see Peter living a consistently bold life. The chances he took were determined by the power of the Spirit, not by his natural strengths and weaknesses.

Read: Acts 4:23–31

Reflect:

1. Peter's denial of Jesus was only a few months prior to today's passage. What caused this change in Peter?

2. How do you act when you are afraid?

3. What are some weaknesses or fears the Spirit may be nudging you to move beyond?

THURSDAY

A VISION FROM THE HOLY SPIRIT

God has chosen to endow men and women with specific and necessary abilities that build the body of Christ. — James Bryan Smith

In today's passage, the Holy Spirit is at work, touching both Peter and Cornelius by means of a vision. What is especially interesting is that neither of these men doubts the reality of the vision they have received. Their expectation for how the Spirit works includes surprising means like dreams and visions.

What is the purpose of the visions? The Spirit is at work advancing the kingdom of God. Peter and Cornelius must meet each other. The Spirit is initiating a significant conversation. For years Peter has been prejudiced against the Gentile people. He could not imagine God welcoming Roman soldiers such as Cornelius into God's kingdom and family.

Peter's perspective on who has a rightful place in the kingdom of God has to be broadened by bringing him together with Cornelius. To do that, the Spirit uses a vision—a direct means of telling each what he wants them to do.

The result? The gospel is proclaimed, and the kingdom is advanced.

Read: Acts 10:1–23

Reflect:

1. On occasion, God chooses to use a dream or vision to communicate with people. Why do you think he chooses that means? Do you see a pattern for when and why he does this?

2. Have you ever experienced the direction of God through a dream or a vision? If not, do you believe that God still acts in this way?

FRIDAY

GENTILES RECEIVE THE HOLY SPIRIT

Then God has given even to the Gentiles the repentance that leads to life.
— Acts 11:18

In yesterday's passage, Peter saw a sheet descending from heaven, seemingly held by its four corners. It was filled with unclean animals. The Lord commanded Peter to kill and eat. At first, Peter refused. The Lord's response was quick and direct. "Do not call anything impure that God has made clean" (Acts 10:15 NIV).

In today's passage, we see that Peter learned his lesson well. Cornelius, an "unclean" Roman soldier, invites Peter into his home and Peter willingly comes into an "unclean" space. Why? The Lord wants Cornelius to listen to Peter's teaching. Cornelius invites Peter to speak.

What are the first words out of Peter's mouth? "I truly understand that God shows no partiality" (Acts 10:34).

Peter's mind and heart have been transformed through the power of the Spirit. What had been unimaginable to the Jewish Peter is now possible as his understanding of God's purposes has dramatically expanded. The church will be a community composed of Jews *and* Gentiles! No one will be excluded because of race or ethnicity.

Read: Acts 10:24–38

Reflect:

1. The Holy Spirit loves to break down barriers between people. What are some significant barriers between people in the world today that are hindering the spread of the gospel?

2. Are there people or people groups that you have considered beyond the Holy Spirit's loving touch? Who are the "Gentiles" in your culture or your own life?

Week 2

~~~~~~

The Holy Spirit at Work in Paul

MONDAY 8/9

A DRAMATIC TURN   Robin

Saul, Saul, why do you persecute me? — Acts 9:4

Can you imagine his shock? For months Saul (later and better known as Paul; see Acts 13:9) had zealously destroyed the church, thinking he was serving God. He arrested, imprisoned, and perhaps even executed Christians. There was blood on Saul's hands.

Saul believed his actions were serving the purposes of God. He knew his Bible well. Moses taught that "anyone hung on a tree is under God's curse" (Deuteronomy 21:23). Jesus died on a tree, a Roman cross. Surely, Saul thought, this man isn't the blessed one of God.

And now suddenly, unexpectedly, Saul's world is turned upside down. Jesus speaks to him from heaven and asks only one question: "Saul, Saul, why do you persecute me?" What was Saul to do?

What should we do when we realize we have sinned in a terrible way? Thankfully, Saul serves as a wonderful example. He trusted that Jesus would know what to do with his sin. Under the Holy Spirit's guidance and empowerment, Saul turns to Christ rather than away from Christ. He was to learn—and then preach—that Jesus had acted on his behalf at the very place that had made so little sense to Saul: the cross.

Read: Acts 8:1–3; 9:1–9

Reflect:

1. What inner motivations do you think drove Saul to persecute the church? How do you think he perceived God during that time?

2. Can you identify times when you thought you were serving God, but later realized you were not?

TUESDAY

A LIFE CHANGED BY THE HOLY SPIRIT

It is no longer I who live, but it is Christ who lives in me. And the life I now live in the flesh I live by faith in the Son of God, who loved me and gave himself for me. — Galatians 2:20

In our reading for today, two more visions are described, which apparently occur in succession. Paul, who had been blinded by the Damascus road vision, receives another vision. He sees a man named Ananias who will come to Paul, place his hands on Paul, and pray that Paul receives his sight.

Next, the Lord addresses Ananias in a vision and commands him to go to Paul as Christ's emissary (Acts 9:12). Initially, Ananias is reluctant to do so. He knows Paul's reputation—"how much evil he has done" (verse 13). Jesus is insistent, though. "Go! This man is my chosen instrument . . ." (verse 15 NIV).

Paul's sight is restored by Jesus in more than one way. His physical sight returns. *And his spiritual sight is vastly expanded.* Jesus has a special task in mind for Paul. Paul will be the apostle to the Gentiles, just as Peter was the apostle to the Jews. Jesus, through the Holy Spirit, is laying the groundwork for the church's expansion into the Roman Empire. Further visions and miracles will occur as the kingdom of God invades the kingdom of the empire.

Read: Acts 9:10–22

Reflect:

1. Paul receives his vision of Ananias while still physically blind. What is the significance of that?

2. Think of someone in your life who needs a special touch from the Lord to expand his or her spiritual sight. Pray Ephesians 1:17 (NIV) for this person: "I keep asking that the God of our Lord Jesus Christ, the glorious Father, may give you the Spirit of wisdom and revelation, so that you may know him better."

WEDNESDAY

POWER ENCOUNTER AT CYPRUS

[Paul] knew how to discern the movements of the Spirit, and he knew how to work in cooperation with those movements. That knowledge produced a Spirit-empowered life. — Richard Foster

As the church leaders at Antioch worship and fast, the Holy Spirit instructs them to "set apart" Paul and Barnabas "for the work to which I have called them" (Acts 13:2). Then, sent by the Holy Spirit, these two missionaries sail to Cyprus.

At first things go well, and they preach the word of God in the Jewish synagogues at Salamis. Even the Roman proconsul Sergius Paulus is open to Paul's message. Suddenly opposition erupts as a sorcerer named Elymas opposes Paul and tries to turn the proconsul from the faith.

Paul, *filled with the Holy Spirit,* knows who he's dealing with and pronounces God's judgment. Elymas is blinded by the hand of the Lord. This power encounter between the kingdom of God and the kingdom of Satan was no contest. Why? Because the Holy Spirit was fighting on Paul's behalf.

Paul later prays that we experience the power of the Spirit as we serve Christ in the world. "I pray that, according to the riches of his glory, he may grant that you may be strengthened in your inner being with power through his Spirit" (Ephesians 3:16).

Read: Acts 13:1–12

Reflect:

1. Why do you think Paul dealt so directly and harshly with Elymas?

2. When you read a passage like this, how do you feel? Encouraged? Afraid? Empowered? Offer this reaction up to God in prayer.

THURSDAY

~~~~~~~~~~~

EXORCISM AT PHILIPPI

[The girl was proclaiming] quite good—even accurate—advertising for Paul and his team. But Paul had no need for that kind of publicity.
— Richard Foster

The world of the Roman Empire was wildly superstitious, at least partly because ancient peoples like the Romans knew that supernatural evil existed and could be used to harm and exploit.

In this case, a young slave girl, perhaps still in her teens, is possessed by an evil spirit. We don't know what caused this possession to occur. We do know, however, that this wicked spirit enabled her to know some things about the future, an ability exploited by her cruel owners.

Paul tolerates the girl's shouts for many days. Finally, "in the name of Jesus Christ" he commands the spirit to come out. Immediately the spirit leaves, robbing the girl's owners of an unjust income. Paul is then seized by her owners and brought before the authorities.

A distinct pattern in Paul's ministry is emerging: Paul and his companions announce the way of salvation and the presence of the kingdom; devilish opposition arises; a power encounter occurs, in which the power of Christ through the Holy Spirit drives out the demonic presence; the kingdom of God expands; and often Paul personally suffers.

Read: Acts 16:16–24

Reflect:

1. In yesterday's story, Paul acted immediately with the sorcerer. Here Paul allows several days to pass, then casts the demon out, and neither the girl nor her owner is made blind. Why did he approach this situation differently?

2. The extension of God's kingdom always involves resistance. Have you experienced this resistance? In what ways?

FRIDAY

EXTRAORDINARY WORKS AT EPHESUS

It is instructive to see that extensive teaching and miraculous manifestations went hand in hand. — Richard Foster

Miraculous manifestations of the Holy Spirit occur throughout the book of Acts. If we tried to remove them from our Bibles with scissors, we would have a book filled with holes, whose storyline makes little sense.

The truth of Paul's teaching is always verified by manifestations of the Spirit's power. People speak in unknown languages. Miracles are the norm rather than the rarity. Even the dead are raised.

The Spirit refuses to be domesticated by either our desires or our fears. The Spirit is fire. The Spirit is a mighty wind. And as we see in today's text, the Spirit is not reluctant to speak, although we may not always understand what the Spirit is saying.

Read: Acts 19:1–7

Reflect:

1. How might you welcome the Holy Spirit more deeply into your life? Are there barriers that need to come down?

2. Richard Foster writes, "While the particular manifestations will be tailored to our individual needs and personalities, we are all to enter into life in the Spirit." What might life in the Spirit look like in your life?

Week 3

Practicing the Spirit-Empowered Life

MONDAY 8/16

THE WIND BLOWS WHERE IT CHOOSES MARK

The kingdom of God depends not on talk but on power.
— 1 Corinthians 4:20

"The wind blows where it chooses," Jesus said to Nicodemus (John 3:8). Though we cannot see the wind, we observe its effects as trees bend and leaves fall.

Do we decide when the wind blows and when it doesn't? We cannot control the wind's power, but occasionally it controls us. When the winds of a hurricane roar, we head inside! Just as we cannot control the wind, so we must not domesticate the Spirit.

Saints through the ages—those in whom the Holy Spirit has been strongly at work—have a remarkable combination of both wind-like freedom and loving self-control. The same Holy Spirit who is free like the wind is also grounded like a tree, bearing the fruit of love, joy, peace, patience, kindness, and more.

Read: John 3:1–8

Reflect:

1. What qualities of the wind are in the life of a person who is filled with the Spirit?

2. Can you identify times in your life when you were tempted to control the Holy Spirit rather than allow the Spirit to control you?

3. Take a few moments to pray and thank God for the times when the Spirit has guided you. Ask God to make you even more sensitive to the Spirit's leading.

TUESDAY

NO GIMMICKS

The only trouble is that in the spiritual life there are no tricks and no short-cuts. Those who imagine that they can discover spiritual gimmicks and put them to work for themselves usually ignore God's will and his grace.
— Thomas Merton

As Peter stresses in today's reading, God is concerned about the kinds of people we are becoming through the power of the Spirit. The power of the Spirit is given to us to transform wickedness into goodness, cruelty into kindness, self-indulgence into self-control, hatred into love.

People characterized by faith, goodness, knowledge, self-control, endurance, godliness, kindness, and mutual affection will be safe, wise, and discerning as they seek the power of the Spirit.

Wise Christians know the Spirit refuses to be manipulated through gimmicks, formulas, or techniques. The Spirit does not come at our beck and call. Rather, as we saw in yesterday's reading, the divine wind of the Spirit blows where it desires to blow. So, while we reject all spiritual gimmicks, let's hoist our sail to the wind and receive the Spirit's empowerment.

Read: 2 Peter 1:3–9

Reflect:

1. What's the difference between manipulation of the Holy Spirit and receptivity to the Holy Spirit?

2. What are some gimmicks or techniques that you have seen used, or been tempted to use yourself, in your relationship with God? What is the result of using these?

WEDNESDAY

FIND ROLE MODELS 8/18 Susan - Ref.

We learn to keep in step with the Spirit as we pattern our lives on the insights, faith, and practices of those wiser and more experienced than us, those whose gifting and character reflect the generosity and power of the Holy Spirit. — Chris Hall

In Acts 11:24, Barnabas is described as "a good man, full of the Holy Spirit and of faith." Church history is full of people like Barnabas: disciples who have manifested the character and power of the Holy Spirit, apprentices of Jesus whose lives and practices we can imitate.

From the perspective of ancient Christians such as John Chrysostom, bishop of the church at Constantinople in the late fourth century, we do well to identify examples of the Spirit-filled life who can guide, discipline, and encourage us as we seek to live well before God.

Of course, Jesus is our chief teacher and example. Christ showed his disciples—and to us—how to serve and how to live. "I have set you an example, that you also should do as I have done" (John 13:15).

Our role models for the Spirit-filled life might be well-known Christians, such as Francis of Assisi. Or they might be people known only to us: members of our families or close friends.

Read: Acts 11:19–26

Reflect:

1. Are there Christians you have known or read about who have served you as role models or guides in the life of the Spirit? Who are they, and how did they help you? Try to be as specific as possible.

2. Are there Christians who have been less helpful as you have sought to go deeper with God? How so?

THURSDAY

BY THE SPIRIT, PUT TO DEATH THE SINS OF THE FLESH

Put to death, therefore, whatever belongs to your earthly nature: sexual immorality, impurity, lust, evil desires and greed, which is idolatry.
— *Colossians 3:5 (NIV)*

Are there particular sins that you would like to see disappear from your life? Perhaps you would like to live a life free from anger . . . or greed . . . or lust. We all struggle with character traits or habitual behaviors that disrupt our family life or work experiences. Is change possible?

Paul invites us to put to death sins such as greed and lust. He promises the Holy Spirit will help us to do so. So we ask ourselves very directly, *What in us needs to die?*

Paul is confident that these sinful habit patterns can disappear from our lives through the power of the Spirit. What are some concrete steps toward freedom from sin that we can take?

If it's greed, we give things away. If it's anger, we ask the Holy Spirit why we are angry. If it's lust, we pray for courage to share our struggle with a close friend. As we take steps toward freedom, the Holy Spirit is there to guide and empower.

Read: Romans 8:12–13

Reflect:

1. Paul says that we put sins to death "by the Spirit." How is this different than simply trying in our own strength not to sin?

2. Take a few moments for quiet reflection. You might pray, "Holy Spirit, is there a sin that you want to help me put to death?" Pause to write down anything that comes to mind. And then pray, "Holy Spirit, what specific steps can I take to move toward freedom? Is there a friend who can help me?"

FRIDAY

Christian spirituality is a life of radical dependence on the Spirit. The biblical vision is a life lived in radical dependence on God and in deep mutual interdependence with others. — Gordon Smith

Imagine the Holy Spirit walking alongside you, holding your hand, guiding you along the pathways of life. The Holy Spirit understands how fast you can walk. He doesn't want you to stumble. The Spirit is in no rush. He would rather walk slowly than quickly.

A relationship with God takes time, doesn't it? Formation into the image of Jesus cannot be hurried. James Houston said, "Spiritual formation is the slowest of all human movements."

Think of trustfully leaning into the Spirit through each moment of the day. The Holy Spirit longs for us to depend on him. He is not interested in spiritual self-help programs in which we rely solely on ourselves. No, lean into the Holy Spirit, depend on the Holy Spirit, and welcome those people whom the Holy Spirit graciously brings into our lives. Keeping in step with the Holy Spirit is a community affair.

Read: Galatians 5:25

Reflect:

1. What does it look like on a day-to-day basis to be "keep in step with the Spirit" (Galatians 5:25 NIV)?

2. Have you sensed times when you were trying to grow too fast in your relationship with God?

3. Are you tempted to think your spiritual formation depends only on you? Or, equally problematically, do you think it depends solely on God, with no effort from your side?

Week 4

~~~~~~

How the Spirit-Empowered Life Connects the Streams

MONDAY 8/23

THE HOLY SPIRIT AND PRAYER   Robin

Let us help one another, humbly, prayerfully, lovingly. Let us go hand in hand to the light and fire which the Holy Spirit has so lavishly poured upon us. — Catherine de Hueck Doherty

Can we learn to pray without ceasing? Is it possible to move throughout our day, responsibly carrying out our responsibilities at home and at work, while continuing to pray? Many Christians—ancient and modern—say yes. We simply need to learn how.

One modern Christian, Frank Laubach, developed a method for learning to pray continually. He called it "The Game with Minutes." Laubach writes, "We make Jesus our inseparable friend. We try to call Him to mind at least one second each minute. We do not need to stop our work, but we invite Him to share everything we do or say or think. . . . It is no harder to learn this new habit than to learn [how to type]."

Today, as you continually draw your mind to Jesus, try simple prayers like these: "Lord, watch over _____." "Lord, heal _____." "Lord, protect _____." "Lord, encourage _____."

Read: Ephesians 6:18–20

Reflect:

1. Do you think Laubach's "Game with Minutes" is realistic? Why or why not?

2. Who or what might the Lord want you to pray for continually throughout the day?

TUESDAY

THE HOLY SPIRIT AND HUMAN TRANSFORMATION

*His divine power has given us everything needed for life and godliness,
through the knowledge of him who called us by his own glory and goodness.*
— 2 Peter 1:3

The Holy Spirit delights in transforming God's image-bearers—people like us—into people who look and act like Jesus. The Spirit does so in a variety of ways.

Perhaps most importantly, as Dallas Willard teaches, through the Gospels—Matthew, Mark, Luke, and John—the Holy Spirit touches our minds "to present the person of Jesus and the reality of the kingdom." We respond by faith to the truth graciously offered to us by the Holy Spirit. We are born again.

Our new birth continues to be nourished by the Spirit; we learn to do the kind of works Jesus did through the gifts of the Spirit, and as we are transformed by the Spirit, the fruit of the Spirit appears in our lives (Galatians 5:22–23). We are new people. Or, to use C. S. Lewis's illustration, we are turned from ordinary horses to new winged creatures, soaring over fences which by our own effort could never be jumped.

Read: 1 Peter 1:1–3

Reflect:

1. The term "born again" has become so familiar to many Christians that it has almost lost its meaning. Pause to consider this picture of being born a second time. Why do you think Jesus, and then Peter, speak of becoming a Christian in this way?

2. How have you been transformed by the Holy Spirit? Can you name three ways?

WEDNESDAY

Remember, Lord, all the infants, the children, the youth, the young, the middle-aged, and the elderly who are hungry, sick, thirsty, naked, captive, or friendless in this world. Be with those who are tempted with suicide, those who are sick in soul, those who are in despair. — Lancelot Andrews

People reborn by the Holy Spirit experience renewed, recreated eyesight. People who were once invisible or alien now enter our field of vision. We see where once we were blind. "I once was lost, but now am found; was blind, but now I see," sings John Newton's famous hymn, "Amazing Grace."

Before his conversion, Newton was a slave trader. After trusting Christ, he realized the immense evil he had committed. He "saw" Africans in an entirely new way—and acted accordingly. Love replaced hatred. Compassion replaced exploitation.

Who are the orphans, widows, hungry, friendless, and sick in our very neighborhoods? Who are the invisible people in our town, city, or country—the untouchables too many see as beyond the love of God? "Lord, give us eyes to see and arms to embrace."

Read: 1 John 4:11–16

Reflect:

1. John says, "No one has ever seen God." But then, in the same breath, he says, "If we love one another, God lives in us." How does loving one another help us to "see" the God who is invisible?

2. Who are the invisible people in your town, city, or work whom you pass by every day but do not see?

THURSDAY

THE HOLY SPIRIT AND THE WORD OF GOD

If you continue [dwell, abide] in my word, you are truly my disciples; and you will know the truth, and the truth will make you free. — John 8:31–32

Jesus calls his disciples to dwell, or abide, in his word. How can we dwell in Jesus' words, making them our home? We do so by learning to refocus our attention. Dallas Willard suggests that we "fill our souls with the written Gospels . . . devote our attention to these teachings, in private study and inquiry as well as public instruction."

Focused attention on Jesus' words and actions takes time and requires retraining our mental habits and focus. Willard continues: "We will refuse to devote our mental space and energy to the fruitless, even stupefying and degrading stuff that constantly clamors for our attention. We will attend to it only enough to avoid it."

Try setting a time each day to reading the Gospel of John. Read it again and again. Let Jesus' words sink into your mind and heart. Make this a slow, paced reading. Try memorizing lines or passages that especially catch your attention or warm your heart.

Read: 2 Peter 1:19–21

Reflect:

1. What clamors for your attention every day? During your leisure time, where do you tend to focus your attention?

2. If Jesus was to coach you about your mental habit patterns, what might he say?

FRIDAY

~~~~~~

THE HOLY SPIRIT AND THE INCARNATIONAL LIFE

The whole mass of Christians is the physical organism through which Christ acts. . . . We are His fingers and muscles, the cells of His Body. — C. S. Lewis

The Holy Spirit dwells in human bodies and works in the world through human bodies. As these two months of pondering the Holy Spirit conclude, let's consider the incarnation and what it means for us.

In the incarnation, the Son of God became a human being—joining his divine nature to our human nature in an incomprehensible union. He was always God. But at Bethlehem, things changed. There he was, lying in a feeding trough, wiggling his fingers and toes, his eyes wide open, drinking in the world he created long ago.

Just as Jesus honored God with his earthly body, so Paul calls us to honor God with our bodies. If Jesus was walking on earth today, where would his feet take him? What would Jesus do with his hands? Whom would he touch? What would he build? Walking the streets of Calcutta or New York City, what would he say? What would he read? What would he be thinking?

As Jesus' disciples—his apprentices—these are important questions for us to ask. For as C. S. Lewis rightly emphasizes, we are Jesus' fingers and muscles, his hands and feet, his eyes and ears.

Read: 1 Corinthians 6:19–20

Reflect:

1. Christ bought us with a price, and things with a price have value. How does a person usually treat a valuable possession? How does knowing you are Christ's valuable possession help you to yield your body to him?

2. Take some time to thank God for your body. Ask the Holy Spirit to fill you, to guide you, and to use your body for his glory.

Week 1

~~~~~~~~

Seeing and Acting

Skipped Aug 30 - Sept 3

MONDAY 9/6

THE INVISIBILITY OF THE POOR *Graig*

The LORD works vindication and justice for all who are oppressed.
— *Psalm 103:6*

For the next two months, our devotionals will focus on a life of compassion and social justice. Caring for the poor was a frequent topic for Jesus. In today's parable, the poor man Lazarus lies at the rich man's gate. The rich man, who remains nameless throughout the story, possesses all things in abundance, but is a man with no name.

The rich man never sees Lazarus. He is terribly blind. There Lazarus lies on the rich man's doorstep, slowly dying. And each day the rich man steps around Lazarus and continues his daily routine. Have the rich man's *wealth, comfort, and secure situation* blinded his eyes to the living corpse in front of him—someone there is still time to save? It seems that a carefree, comfortable existence has hardened the rich man's heart and blinded his eyes to those in much greater need around him.

Cyprian, an ancient Christian leader in North Africa, commented on the blinding effect riches can have on human perceptions: "You that are rich cannot do good works in the church, because your eyes, saturated with blackness and covered with the shadows of night, *do not see* the needy and poor."

Read: Luke 16:19–31

Reflect:

1. How might great wealth blind a person? Is it possible to be rich and still see and care for the poor? How?

2. Overfamiliarity with the poor can also cause blindness. If that describes you, take a moment to pray that God would give you fresh eyes for those in need.

TUESDAY

DOING WHAT JESUS SAYS

The Holy Spirit must come into the details of our lives, and we must look to these details so that we can begin to change. — Jean Vanier

Words can be empty. Isn't there a difference between people who say they believe what Jesus says is true and people who demonstrate that belief by living out the values of Jesus' kingdom?

In Matthew 7:21–27, which parallels today's passage in Luke, people call Jesus "Lord" and do powerful works in his name. Yet Jesus says, "I never knew you" (verse 23). Jesus is looking for more than just occasional acts of compassion. He wants our hearts and our lives. He wants friendship and relationship. "The love of Christ urges us on," the apostle Paul said (2 Corinthians 5:14). It's knowing the love of Jesus that gives us the strength to obey him. And in obeying, we find our lives being built upon rock.

Read: Luke 6:46–49

Reflect:

1. Why might someone call Jesus "Lord" but not actually do what he says?

2. How can we do what Jesus said to do without it becoming burdensome or legalistic?

WEDNESDAY

WHAT IS THE GREATEST COMMANDMENT? 9|8 Kelly

In everything do to others as you would have them do to you; for this is the law and the prophets. — Matthew 7:12

The Torah contains over 600 laws. What is the heart, the core, of all those laws? In today's reading, Jesus is asked this question by a Pharisee. Without hesitation, Jesus responds: love God with all that you are, and love your neighbor as yourself. The apostle Paul agrees. "The only thing that counts is faith working through love" (Galatians 5:6).

Allow the words of Jesus and Paul to percolate in your mind and heart, like coffee grounds in hot water.

The only thing that counts . . .

Love God. Love your neighbor.

These teachings are the foundation of social justice. Love God. Love your neighbor. This is the law, the prophets, and the heart of Jesus.

Read: Matthew 22:34–40

Reflect:

1. How are loving God and loving neighbor connected? Is it possible to do one without doing the other?

2. Jesus says to "love your neighbor as yourself." If you were to treat yourself poorly—for example, live in self-condemnation or a feeling of not being good enough—how would that affect your ability to love your neighbor?

3. Take a moment to speak aloud these core commands of Jesus: "Love the Lord your God with all your heart, and with all your soul, and with all your mind. . . . Love your neighbor as yourself." Bring them to mind throughout your day.

THURSDAY

AN UPSIDE-DOWN KINGDOM

It is not easy for the rich to allow themselves to be touched by the poor, to enter into communion with them, to let themselves be stripped of luxury and comfort. No, it is not easy for the rich and for the poor to sit down together at the same table. — Jean Vanier

In Luke 14, we find Jesus at a dinner. Most of the people who have been invited to this meal are Jewish religious teachers, well-known figures in their local communities; all are well-versed in the Law of Moses.

Behind Jesus' teaching in Luke 14 is a common belief shared by all at this supper. When the long-awaited Messiah appeared, he would feed Israel at the great messianic banquet, after the pattern of Moses feeding Israel with manna in the wilderness. At this dinner, Jesus takes these messianic expectations and turns them upside down in a manner that shocks the other guests.

The key question? Who would be invited to the great messianic banquet? Every teacher and scribe sitting with Jesus at this meal fully expected to be invited. Instead, Jesus points to the poor, the crippled, the lame, and the blind. Jesus was introducing an upside-down kingdom, one full of reversals, unexpected hopes, and unforeseen possibilities.

Read: Luke 14:12–14

Reflect:

1. Jesus is a king who deserved a grand entrance into the world and a life of luxury. Why instead did he choose a humble entrance and lifestyle? What did this accomplish that a rich and royal lifestyle wouldn't?

2. Jesus says to bless people who can't repay you because God will repay you later. Why is it better to be repaid later by God in the life to come? Are there rewards from God in the present life for serving the poor?

Month 9: The Compassionate Life

FRIDAY

DO JUSTICE, LOVE KINDNESS, WALK HUMBLY Susan 9/13

But you, God, see the trouble of the afflicted; you consider their grief and take it in hand. The victims commit themselves to you; you are the helper of the fatherless. — Psalm 10:14 (NIV)

In today's passage, Micah speaks with clarity, simplicity, and power. Both Micah and the Lord were not pleased with Israel. "The faithful have disappeared from the land, and there is no one left who is upright" (Micah 7:2). Violence is rampant; officials and judges are addicted to bribes; justice is perverted.

Things should not be this way. Through the preaching of Micah, the Lord reminds Israel that he has told them what is good and what the Lord requires of them: do justice, love kindness, walk humbly with your God.

Micah wants us to do more than simply think of justice. He wants us to *do* it. Micah wants us to do more than consider kindness. He wants us to *love* it. Micah realizes that the root of Israel's sin is pride, a bloated infatuation with its history and accomplishments. The antidote? Walking humbly with God.

Read: Micah 6:8

Reflect:

1. We may expect justice to appear here—Israel had become an unjust society. But why are kindness and humility equally important to God?

2. Ponder these three things: *do justice, love kindness, walk humbly with your God.* Take three minutes to ponder these in silence. Does one of the three stand out to you? If so, write a short prayer. For example, "God, how can I walk humbly with you?" Feel free to write anything you sense God may be saying in response.

Week 2

Social Justice in the Life and Parables of Jesus

MONDAY 9/17

WHAT HAS GOD CREATED US TO BE? No Pastor - See Friday

Then God said, "Let us make humankind in our image, according to our likeness. . . . So God created humankind in his image, in the image of God he created them; male and female he created them." — Genesis 1:26–27

All human beings are created in the image of God (Genesis 1:27); we are all God's image-bearers. We are also created in the image of the great image-bearer, Jesus Christ. Jesus, as Paul writes, "is the image of the invisible God, the firstborn of all creation" (Colossians 1:15).

Consider this carefully: Jesus was *fully human and fully divine*. So if you want to see what God looks like, look at Jesus. "Whoever has seen me has seen the Father" (John 14:9). And if you want to see what a real human being looks like—an unpolluted, sinless human being—look at Jesus.

Our understanding of who we are—God's redeemed image-bearers—is the foundation for what God has created us to do as we seek justice and righteousness.

Read: Colossians 1:15–17

Reflect:

1. Every person is made in the image of God. How does that relate to showing kindness and justice to one another?

2. Jesus showed us what God looks like. Do you have any ideas about God that look different than Jesus? If so, ask God for help to know Jesus more deeply so that you may see God more clearly.

TUESDAY

THE GOOD SAMARITAN

I was hungry and you gave me food, I was thirsty and you gave me something to drink, I was a stranger and you welcomed me. — Matthew 25:35

Many social justice themes come together in the well-known parable of the Good Samaritan. A Jewish "lawyer," or expert in the law, asks Jesus, "Who is my neighbor?" Jesus answers by telling this parable.

A man has been beaten by robbers and left for dead. The very people one expects to help him—a priest and a Levite—pass by the wounded man as though he doesn't exist. They see him, but don't see him. Filled with religious pride, they pass by on the other side of the road to avoid dealing with the situation.

Jews despised Samaritans and considered them outside of God's love and care. To hear Jesus tell of a Samaritan caring for a wounded man—doing justice, loving kindness, and walking humbly with God—would have been scandalous. Yet when Jesus asked, "Which one was a neighbor?" the lawyer couldn't deny that it was "the one who showed him mercy."

Read: Luke 10:29–37

Reflect:

1. What are some possible reasons why the priest and Levite passed by the wounded man?

2. Can you think of a parallel to the Samaritan in a modern context? How would people react to someone from a despised people group being the hero of the story? How would you react to it?

WEDNESDAY

AN UNEXPECTED FOOT-WASHING Robin 9/15

Do you not know that your body is a temple of the Holy Spirit within you, which you have from God, and that you are not your own? For you were bought with a price; therefore glorify God in your body.
— 1 Corinthians 6:19–20

Jesus knew he would soon be returning to his Father. What does he choose to do in his last hours with the disciples? He washes their feet! Jesus once again demonstrates the upside-down values of his kingdom.

When Jesus had finished his task, he reminds the disciples that "servants are not greater than their master" (John 13:16). If Jesus has washed their feet, so must they wash the feet of others. God's blessing will come when Jesus' apprentices *practice* what he has modeled. "If you know these things, you are blessed *if you do them*" (John 13:17).

John Vanier describes his attempt to help a mentally disturbed man. "He was quite a difficult man who absolutely refused to communicate with anyone." This man also suffered from a severe foot infection. So Vanier's community began washing his feet three times a day. "His whole attitude toward us changed. This showed us again the importance of the washing of the feet."

Read: John 13:1–17

Reflect:

1. Why was Peter so resistant to Jesus washing his feet?

2. If you had been with Jesus that night, what would you have felt as he approached you to wash your feet?

3. Whose feet might the Lord be asking you to wash? Who are you called to serve in a tangible and humble way?

THURSDAY

THE RICH FOOL

Put to death, therefore, whatever in you is earthly: fornication, impurity, passion, evil desire, and greed (which is idolatry). — Colossians 3:5

Although the main character in today's parable might demonstrate conventional wisdom, he is—in actuality—a fool. Here is a man who has no idea how to live well with God. The rich fool has been extravagantly blessed by the Lord but fails to discern the reason behind the blessing.

The rich fool never once considers the possibility that he has been blessed by God with such riches so that he can bless others. Rather, he builds even larger barns, storing away God's blessing solely for himself. Even more foolishly, once his barns are full, he considers himself secure for many years to come.

Little does the rich fool realize that his life will end that very night. He has placed his trust in what he possesses. After he dies, who will receive what he has stored away? "So it is," Jesus says, "with those who store up treasures for themselves but are not rich toward God."

Read: Luke 12:13–21

Reflect:

1. What is the rich fool's fundamental mistake? What is the reasoning behind that mistake?

2. Even if we aren't rich in money, most of us are rich in some area of life. How has the Lord blessed you? What might he be asking you to do with the blessing you have received?

FRIDAY

THE RICH YOUNG RULER

Do not store up for yourselves treasures on earth, where moth and rust consume and where thieves break in and steal; but store up for yourselves treasures in heaven, where neither moth nor rust consumes and where thieves do not break in and steal. For where your treasure is, there your heart will be also. — Matthew 6:19–21

In today's passage, Jesus sees something the rich young ruler did not see. His heart was wrapped too firmly around his possessions.

The rich young ruler was strongly pulled in two directions. He wanted Jesus. And he wanted his riches. He was fundamentally divided in his allegiances. And so, too often, are we. How would you respond if Jesus asked you to give away everything you owned? What are you clutching too tightly? Money? House? Reputation? Children? Vocation?

Read: Mark 10:17–23

Reflect:

1. Does Jesus ask everyone to give up their possessions? Why or why not?

2. Mark tells us that Jesus looked at the rich young ruler and "loved him" (verse 21). We can imagine Jesus' eyes filled with compassion, his tone of voice saturated with kindness. How does knowing Christ's personal love for us affect how we obey his requests of us?

3. Take three to five minutes in silence to ask God, "Is there anything in my life to which I am clinging too tightly and that is keeping me from the fullness of life you are offering now and forever?" Write down anything you sense, and perhaps a prayer like this: "Father, I release _____ to you. Please show me if there are any steps I need to take to release it further."

Week 3

~~~~~~

Christ's Peace, Pace, and Love in Ministry

MONDAY 9/20

65: 19-25

SHALOM Lillian
Peace

Peace will prevail one day; yes, and so prevail that the instruments of
destruction shall be beaten into other shapes and used for better purposes.
— Charles Spurgeon

Shalom is the Hebrew word for peace. God's longing for peace among individuals, cultures, and nations is reflected in today's reading.

God's vision for the world can help us as we pray and act. Shalom is not just the absence of conflict. It is the profound presence of the wholeness, health, and vitality that characterize a world that is completely in harmony with itself. Shalom is the realization of all the glorious potential God built into the world at creation; it is the state of serene concord and orderly creativity that allows the full, unhindered flourishing of all things—individually and collectively.

Isaiah's vision of shalom presupposes a right relationship with God as the foundation for healthy, full relationships throughout the world. *Isaiah is convinced there can be no real, lasting peace without God as its intimate, personal center.*

Read: Isaiah 2:2–4   65:19

Reflect:

1. Does the picture Isaiah paints of peace bring you hope or seem too good to be true?

2. Take a few minutes to pray for shalom—for wholeness, peace, and health. Pray for shalom with God, yourself, others, and the created world. Consider practices that will usher in shalom in these areas.

TUESDAY

THE PEACE JESUS OFFERS

As we pour out our bitterness, God pours in his peace. — F. B. Meyer

Jesus offers peace to his disciples, a peace different from that of the world. Jesus is clear that this peace is available to those who choose to follow and learn from him.

Michael Cassidy rightly distinguishes between folks who enjoy and manifest peace when everything is calm and those who reflect Christ's peace when things go badly. "The sort of person I am," Cassidy comments, "is largely determined by how I handle the negative situations in which I find myself."

Read: John 14:27

Reflect:

1. "Do not let your hearts be troubled," Jesus exhorts, "and do not let them be afraid." What do you think was the source of Jesus' inner fearlessness and courage?

2. What might be the relationship between fear and injustice? Fear and violence?

3. Consider one or two things that are troubling you, that cause you anxiety or fear. Then lift those things in prayer, also remembering what you are thankful for, so that the peace of God may guard your hearts and minds (Philippians 4:6–7).

WEDNESDAY

THE RHYTHM OF JESUS' MINISTRY

We will comprehend the mind of Jesus best if, in our own small way, we try to inculcate in our daily lives the values by which he lived and died.
— Michael Cassidy

Jesus had so much to do. His Father had given him the most important work in the history of the world. Yet isn't it interesting that Jesus never seems to be rushing? He carries out his ministry in a paced, discerning, wise way—never allowing the pressing needs of the moment to crowd out the intimacy he constantly shares with his Father in times of prayer and solitude.

Today's passage pictures for us the rhythm of Jesus' ministry. Can you hear the crowds crying out to Jesus? "Rabbi, heal my wife!" "Rabbi, my son just died!" "Rabbi, an evil spirit has taken over my daughter's mind and body!" "Rabbi, help us!" In the very next verse, Luke writes: "But Jesus often withdrew to lonely places and prayed" (verse 16 NIV).

Jesus could do what he did because *there were times when he did nothing other than being with his Father.* Here is the key to sane, wise, powerful ministry in the social justice stream, when it often seems there is endless work to be done. *Hard work. Silence, solitude, prayer. Hard work. Silence, solitude, prayer.*

Read: Luke 5:15–16

Reflect:

1. Why did Jesus put such a high value on being alone with his Father?

2. Do you struggle to say no to people in need whom you are capable of helping? How was Jesus able to do that?

3. Describe the rhythm of your week—considering all aspects: spiritual, vocational, mental, relational, physical. Does it match that of Jesus?

THURSDAY

~~~~~~~~~~~~~~~~~~~~

HESED

The steadfast love of the LORD never ceases, his mercies never come to an end. — Lamentations 3:22

The Hebrew word hesed is difficult to translate into other languages. It means unwavering compassion, steadfast love, lovingkindness. These terms describe God's unceasing hesed toward his wayward people, Israel. And toward all the wayward people made in his image.

Scripture calls us to model God's compassion for all people, but especially for the widow, the orphan, and the poor—folks often cruelly exposed to an uncaring world.

Murder. Robbery. Bribery. Exploitation. All these are horrible violations of God's covenant. All pollute the habitation of the widow, the orphan, the helpless, the poor. Hosea calls us to respond with hesed. How? By *imitating* God's unwavering compassion—God's *hesed*—with concrete acts of love.

Read: Hosea 6:6

Reflect:

1. Hosea says that the Lord desires steadfast love and knowledge of him rather than religious sacrifice and burnt offerings. But in the law of Moses, God had commanded sacrifice. Why then would God say this?

2. In what ways is it easier to sacrifice—to offer God religious service or to go through the motions—than to have a relationship with God and love others?

FRIDAY

LOVE YOUR ENEMIES

For if while we were enemies, we were reconciled to God through the death of his Son, much more surely, having been reconciled, will we be saved by his life. — Romans 5:10

If you were to make a personal enemies list, whose names would appear on it? Every name on your list represents harm and pain. Perhaps someone spoke an unkind word that remains branded in your memory. Perhaps someone harmed you physically or sexually. People have become our enemies for a reason: they have hurt us or those we love. And they are the last people on earth we desire to love, to pray for, or to bless—either in word or in deed.

Still, Jesus is insistent. "If you are my disciple, you must love your enemies. Were you not once my enemy? And I loved you most when you hated me most. The pattern of love I have left you is this: you must love your enemies."

Martin Luther King Jr. listed four reasons why we must love our enemies. First, "Returning hate for hate multiplies hate." Second, "Hate scars the soul and distorts the personality." Third, "Love is the only force capable of transforming an enemy into a friend." And fourth, "We must love our enemies, because only by loving them can we know God and experience the beauty of his holiness."

Read: Luke 6:27–28

Reflect:

1. Why would loving and serving our enemies help us to know God and experience the beauty of his holiness?

2. Who are your enemies? Though they may never reciprocate your love, how might you love them in a concrete manner that obeys the teaching of Jesus? Perhaps you might simply begin by asking God to bless your enemies lives.

Week 4

~~~~~~

Avoiding the Pitfalls of Self-Righteous Service

MONDAY 9/27 Group

TRUE SERVICE FLOWS OUT OF DIVINE PROMPTINGS

I find that [the Lord] never guides me into an intolerable scramble of panting feverishness. — Thomas Kelly

This month we have been looking at the call to live lives of compassion and to serve as agents of social justice. We are invited into a countercultural, world-changing partnership with God. Following Jesus' example, we offer bold and radical leadership by serving others.

Yet even something as beautiful and full of promise as our service to others can be easily distorted. In *Celebration of Discipline*, Richard Foster challenges us to guard against letting our acts of compassion become rooted in self-righteousness instead of divine initiative. This week we will explore five distinctions Foster makes between self-righteous service and true service.

The first distinction, says Foster, is that self-righteous service relies on human effort, whereas true service flows out of a relationship with God. "Listen to the promptings of God," Foster encourages us, "as you begin and lean on his strength to do the task."

Read: 2 Corinthians 12:8–10

Reflect:

1. Do you have a sense of being led and sustained by God when you serve others, or do you tend to rely on your own initiative?

2. What do you think the apostle Paul means when he says that his weaknesses allow the power of Christ to dwell in him?

3. How might the principle of "divine strength in human weakness" relate to when and how we serve others?

TUESDAY

TRUE SERVICE DOES NOT SEEK REWARD

Miss no single opportunity of making some small sacrifice, here by a smiling look, there by a kindly word; always doing the smallest right and doing it all for love. — St. Therese of Lisieux

Richard Foster points out a second set of distinctions: Self-righteous service is impressed with the "big deal," whereas true service makes no distinction between the large and the small. Furthermore, self-righteous service requires external rewards, whereas true service rests contented in hiddenness.

So how do we participate in true service? Remember that God often considers the small task the most important. And avoid doing things for others as a means of getting applause or reward, relying instead on the divine nod of approval.

Read: Matthew 6:1–4

Reflect:

1. How does it make you feel when something good you've done goes unacknowledged? Might that feeling reveal something about your underlying motivations for service?

2. Prayerfully consider if God might be inviting you into a hidden act of service this week. If so, try it!

WEDNESDAY

TRUE SERVICE IS COMMITTED FOR THE LONG TERM

The highest form of worship is the worship of unselfish Christian service. The greatest form of praise is the sound of consecrated feet seeking out the lost and helpless. — Billy Graham

A third way Richard Foster invites us to assess our service is in terms of its duration. Self-righteous service is temporary, he writes. It functions only while the specific acts of service are being performed. Having served, it can rest easy.

True service, on the other hand, is a lifestyle. It acts from ingrained patterns of living. It springs spontaneously to meet human need.

Read: 1 Peter 4:7–11

Reflect:

1. In today's passage, we are offered a picture of how a community of ongoing service might function. Make a list of the recurring acts of love and service described. Are any of the things on the list missing in your current communities?

2. How does a model of ongoing service rather than temporary acts of service affect your work and home life?

THURSDAY

TRUE SERVICE IS PATIENT AND SENSITIVE

[Love] does not insist on its own way. — 1 Corinthians 13:5

Are there ever occasions when acts of service do more harm than good? Richard Foster cautions us: Self-righteous service is insensitive. It insists on meeting the need even when to do so would be destructive. It demands the opportunity to help.

So how is true service different? True service can withhold the service as freely as perform it. It can listen with tenderness and patience before acting. It can serve by waiting in silence.

When we are offering true service, we are sensitive to what people really need, not merely what we think they need.

Read: Proverbs 18:2, 13

Reflect:

1. An expression says, "When you only have a hammer, every problem looks like a nail." Have you ever observed a one-solution-only approach to problems of poverty or social justice? How well has that worked?

2. Has anyone ever offered you help that did more harm than good?

3. Consider a time of prayer asking the Lord to show you how you can listen well to those you seek to serve.

FRIDAY

TRUE SERVICE BUILDS COMMUNITY

The greatness of a community is most accurately measured by the compassionate actions of its members. — Coretta Scott King

The final distinction we want to make between self-righteous service and true service has to do with the impact our actions have on our communities.

"Self-righteous service," Richard Foster warns, "fractures community. . . . It centers in the glorification of the individual. Therefore, it puts others into its debt and becomes one of the most subtle and destructive forms of manipulation known."

True service, on the other hand, "quietly goes about caring for the needs of others. It draws, binds, heals, builds."

Read: Philippians 2:1–11

Reflect:

1. Do you ever find yourself looking down on those you seek to serve? If so, how would your acts of service be different if you genuinely regarded those you were serving "as better than yourself" (Philippians 2:3)?

2. Have you participated in a social justice initiative that ended up fracturing community? How about one that built community? What makes the difference between an initiative that fractures community and one that builds community?

3. We have dedicated the past month to exploring the compassionate stream that flows out of the life of Jesus. Spend a few moments in silent prayer, asking the Spirit to show you one thing he wants you to focus on from the past four weeks of devotionals.

Week 1

~~~~~~

Justice for Every Person

MONDAY 10/4

SERVING THE LEAST IS SERVING JESUS

Our human compassion binds us the one to the other—not in pity or patronizingly, but as human beings who have learned how to turn our common suffering into hope for the future. — Nelson Mandela

This month we continue exploring the compassionate life—a life that serves the poor and needy and works for human justice and equity.

Today's passage is a powerful indictment of those who neglect the needy. Though it reads like a parable, it actually describes the future judgment of all the nations. Jesus gives us a picture of what that reckoning will be like. Like a shepherd separates sheep and goats, he will separate all people into two groups: those who cared for the needs of the hungry, thirsty, alienated, naked, sick, or imprisoned; and those who did not.

One detail in this story towers above all others. Jesus says that when people care for the needy, they care for him; and when people neglect the needy, they neglect him.

Read: Matthew 25:31–46

Reflect:

1. Why do you think Jesus so strongly identifies himself with the hungry, thirsty, alienated, naked, sick, and imprisoned?

2. Mother Teresa once said, "It is easier to give a cup of rice to relieve hunger than to relieve the loneliness and pain of someone unloved in our own home." Take a few moments to pray silently and ask God, "Is there someone I often see who feels alienated or lonely?" Pause to listen. If God brings someone to mind, write the name down along with one specific way you can love that person this week.

TUESDAY

ALL PEOPLE DESERVE TO BE TREATED JUSTLY

Human progress is neither automatic nor inevitable.... Every step toward the goal of justice requires sacrifice, suffering, and struggle; the tireless exertions and passionate concern of dedicated individuals.
— *Martin Luther King Jr.*

Throughout the history of the church, men and women have dedicated their lives to caring for the hungry, the poor, the naked, the alienated, the sick, and the imprisoned. The work of groups like Mother Teresa's Sisters of Charity and countless other charities testify to God's tender love.

Of course, the compassionate response demands more than a shipment of food or medicine. Bringing justice into a situation goes beyond temporary assistance. It involves helping people learn skills so that they can support themselves. The poor and the homeless not only need immediate food and shelter, but also ongoing help to overcome their plight. Many societal structures and institutions actually oppress needy people by denying them access to certain occupations, services, schools, housing, and more. Christ calls us to fight policies that discriminate on the basis of race, gender, class, and religion. All people are made in the image of God, so all people deserve to be treated justly.

Read: Isaiah 30:18

Reflect:

1. In today's passage, Isaiah reminds us that the Lord "will rise up to show mercy to you. For the LORD is a God of justice." Take time to reflect on the word *justice*. Where do you see instances of injustice in the world? In your local community?

2. Today's passage combines justice with waiting. Is it possible to combine actively working for justice with waiting on the Lord? What does that look like on a day-to-day basis?

WEDNESDAY

THE DULLING EFFECT OF SELF-INDULGENCE

No matter how much or how little we own, self-indulgence damages our character. — Jan Johnson

The picture the prophet Amos paints for us in today's reading is not a happy one. A few people have accumulated vast wealth and built for themselves "stone mansions" (Amos 5:11 NIV). The problem is that their prosperity has come at the expense of others. As Richard Foster notes, "All their wealth and affluence were the result of the sacrilegious oppression of the poor."

Self-indulgence quickly melts away our concern for justice for all people. Self-indulgence—a desire for just a little bit more—is never satisfied. "If I just had a bigger house," we sometimes say to ourselves. "I could really use another pair of shoes," we think, when we already have a closetful.

Yes, adequate housing is important. All God's image-bearers should have enough to eat. We all need to be clothed. In today's reading, though, Amos warns us that our concern for legitimate human needs, such as suitable housing, food, and clothes, can quickly transform into self-indulgence if we're not careful.

Read: Amos 5:11–12

Reflect:

1. How is self-indulgence related to a lack of compassion for others?

2. Is there any area in which you tend to be self-indulgent? If so, write it down.

3. Contentment is the opposite of greed and indulgence (see 1 Timothy 6:6–10). God wants for us a durable and lasting joy, rather than the fleeting pleasure of indulgence. Pray for this blessing, offering something like, "Lord, help _____ to experience your contentment and joy more deeply."

THURSDAY

~~~~~~~~~~~

WHAT DOES PURE RELIGION LOOK LIKE?

We care for orphans not because we are rescuers, but because we are the rescued. — David Platt

In today's reading, James describes pure and undefiled religion as "care for orphans and widows in their distress" and keeping oneself "unstained by the world."

James's teaching implies that it is possible to worship God in an impure and defiled manner. His words are clear and direct. Our worship of God and our compassion for other people should be intimately connected. Love for God and love for our neighbor are at the heart of genuine, pure, religious belief.

Today let's ponder together James's words carefully and offer prayer to the Lord for a relationship with God that ripples out in tangible love for those who are lonely, grieving, hungry, and parentless.

Read: James 1:27

Reflect:

1. What does it mean to "keep oneself unstained by the world"?

2. Who are the people you know who are in distress—God's image-bearers whom the Lord is asking you to notice and help in a concrete way?

3. Can you identify times in your own life when you were in distress and others reached out to you with love and compassion?

FRIDAY

〰〰〰

OVERCOMING DIVISION

Neighbor, says Jesus, is ... the person near us, the person in need. Jesus refuses to put walls around the word neighbor. No national heritage, no racial origin, no ethnic background, no barriers of class or culture can separate us from our neighbor. — Richard Foster

Most people in the ancient world viewed certain ethnic groups as irreconcilable enemies and certain social classes as unequal: Greek and Jew, slave and free, male and female. These divisions in Paul's world produced terrible injustices. Jews, for instance, struggled to believe that Gentiles could become part of God's new community—the church—apart from accepting circumcision, the mark of membership in Abraham's family. But in Christ, traditional walls of separation are broken down: "All of you are one in Christ Jesus."

In modern times, we also see what happens when people made in God's image refuse to recognize each other as neighbors. Hitler labeled the Jews as "vermin," and acted accordingly. Similarly, Hutus branded Tutsis as "cockroaches," and hundreds of thousands were slaughtered.

The unity we experience in Christ is a key antidote for the poison of injustice and oppression.

Read: Galatians 3:28

Reflect:

1. How did Christ break down the walls of separation? Why does his life, death, and resurrection make us all "one"?

2. Are there people that you struggle to consider your neighbor? Why?

3. Explore opportunities you may have to expand your circle of friends to new ethnic, social, or religious groups.

Week 2

The Vocabulary of the Compassionate Life

MONDAY

THE GOD OF MISHPAT

I the LORD love justice; I hate robbery and wrongdoing. — Isaiah 61:8

The Hebrew word mishpat—translated "justice" in today's reading—has a wide range of meanings that have important social, ethical, and religious implications. Richard Foster observes that mishpat "involves a morality over and above strict legal justice." We manifest mishpat when we care for others beyond what the letter of the law demands.

Keep in mind that "justice" and "righteousness" mean much the same thing. Both point to what is right and good in key human relationships. The just person, for instance, will be concerned that the orphan, widow, and stranger in the land are cared for. Psalm 103:6 declares, "The LORD works vindication and justice (*mishpat*) for all who are oppressed."

God delights in mishpat. God loves mishpat. And so should we as God's image-bearers.

Read: Jeremiah 9:23–24

Reflect:

1. God wants to be known as the one who acts with steadfast love, justice, and righteousness. Does this line up with your picture of God?

2. What would mishpat look like with your family? Your coworkers? Your neighbors?

3. What specific practices nourish mishpat?

TUESDAY

~~~~~~~

THE GOD OF HESED

The sword of judgment gives way to the trowel of reconstruction. The day of darkness . . . is replaced by a day of light. — David Allan Hubbard

The last word for the prophet Amos was mercy, not judgment. Even though Amos continually prophesied doom in light of Israel's sin, his book ends with a word of hope. This hope is expressed for us in today's reading.

A time is surely coming, Amos promises, when those plowing will overtake those reaping. Those treading grapes will overtake those sowing seed. The mountains will drip with wine and the hills will flow with the fruit of the vine. How can this blessed time of abundance possibly occur, especially when the nation of Israel has sinned so greatly?

The last word for Israel is hope because God is a God of *hesed*, a word you may remember from last month that expresses God's covenant loyalty to his people. God will always remain faithful to the covenant he has established with Israel. When Israel falls into sin, judgment comes. But with the nation's repentance, great blessing appears.

God's hesed guarantees that God will never give up on Israel. The purpose of God's judgment is cleansing, not destruction. Ponder carefully the covenant love expressed in today's reading.

Read: Amos 9:13–15

Reflect:

1. Much of the book of Amos expresses God's judgment upon his people for their sins, especially oppressing the poor. Why did God take this sin so seriously?

2. How has God's faithfulness, God's *hesed*, shown itself in your own life?

3. Are you facing difficult situations where God is asking you to remain faithful and loyal?

Month 10: The Compassionate Life

WEDNESDAY

THE GOD OF SHALOM

If mishpat and hesed are spotlights illuminating various dimensions of the Social Justice Tradition, then shalom is a great beacon. — Richard Foster

As we saw last month, shalom is the Hebrew word for "peace." Do you recall its broader meaning? Shalom is not just the absence of conflict. It is instead the profound presence of the wholeness, health, and vitality that characterizes a world in harmony with God and God's design for his creation.

Sin terribly disrupts shalom. Sadly, the world God loves so deeply has been wounded by a lack of shalom. The resulting brokenness is the great tragedy of our fallen world—and it is the driving force in the biblical storyline, as God acts to reverse the havoc sin unleashes. The God of shalom, as the psalmist in today's reading celebrates, promises to make all things right once again.

God is constantly, actively, zealously in pursuit of loving communion and shalom with his beloved image-bearers. In turn, God's redeemed image-bearers are called to be hands and feet of shalom in the world today. "Righteousness and peace will kiss each other" (Psalm 85:10).

Read: Psalm 85:10–13

Reflect:

1. Why does sin—acting outside of the way God intended things to be—disrupt shalom?

2. What concrete steps can you take to be an agent of God's shalom in your family, neighborhood, or church?

3. Are there a situations in your own life where you need God's shalom? If so, pray to experience God's shalom in these areas.

THURSDAY

~~~~~~~~~

THE GOD WHO SEES AND REMEMBERS

They asked only one thing, that we remember the poor, which was actually what I was eager to do. — Galatians 2:10

The God of compassion sees and remembers. No human being is ever forgotten or unseen by God. In today's reading, the writer of Hebrews asks us to imitate the divine pattern of sight and remembrance.

God calls us to widen our vision, to lengthen our memory. We must honestly ask ourselves, "Who have we forgotten?" and "Who do we no longer remember?"

Gary Haugen, founder of International Justice Mission, writes, "Scriptures are confident that if we imagine we are the child prostitute, the torture victim, the child laborer, we would not want to be forgotten. Surely, it is God's job to remember *all* the victims of injustice in our world, but might there not be one child, one prisoner, one widow, one refugee that I can remember?"

Read: Hebrews 13:1–3

Reflect:

1. Ponder the thought that you may be "entertaining angels" when you care for the outsider. How might that affect how you care for people?

2. As we did last month, pray for fresh eyes to see and a compassionate heart to remember the needy.

FRIDAY

THE GOD OF LOVE

From everlasting to everlasting the LORD's love is with those who fear him, and his righteousness with their children's children—with those who keep his covenant and remember to obey his precepts. — Psalm 103:17–18 (NIV)

The Spirit-empowered pursuit of justice is a difficult task. We can become discouraged and even angry as we daily encounter evil and the suffering it causes. The struggle seems endless.

So let's use today's reading to pause and remember why we're doing what we're doing. We seek justice for the poor and oppressed because God is love and he calls us to imitate his love for all people. Love is why we do what we do.

Spend time again with Paul's description of love. Love is patient and kind. It does not envy or boast; it is not proud, self-seeking, or easily angered. Love does not add up the evil things people do and hold their sins against them. It rejoices with the truth. It always protects, trusts, hopes, and perseveres. Love never fails. Faith, hope, and love are essential for those who seek justice. "But the greatest of these is love."

Read: 1 Corinthians 13:1–13 (NIV)

Reflect:

1. Paul says, "If I give all I possess to the poor . . . but do not have love, I gain nothing" (1 Corinthians 13:3 NIV). Social justice, he seems to say, can be done without love. It can also be done as an act of love. What's the difference? Is it an outward difference, or only an inward one?

2. Of all the characteristics of love mentioned in today's passage, is there a particular characteristic that stands out to you? Take a few moments to write a short prayer about it.

Week 3

~~~~~

Potential Perils of the Compassionate Life

MONDAY

THE PERIL OF SELF-RIGHTEOUSNESS

The deceitfulness of the heart of man appears in no one thing so much as this of spiritual pride and self-righteousness. — *Jonathan Edwards*

Richard Foster writes that those committed to social justice "are most prone to rigidity and judgmentalism." Why would this be?

First, because social justice is concerned about concrete action and lifestyle, we can easily judge other people on the basis of superficial outward standards. "People's level of commitment to a simple lifestyle, for example, is often based on the kind of housing they live in or the transportation they use or the clothing they wear."

Second, because social justice focuses on critical issues of human life, Foster writes, "Standards of who is in and who is out, who is right and who is wrong, become more and more narrowly defined. It is a danger we tend to fall into because the stakes are so high."

In today's reading, Jesus teaches us first to ponder our own obedience to the standards we use to judge others. Do we judge others too quickly and too harshly? Yes, those committed to social justice must often speak a strong word on injustice to those who commit it. Let us always be willing to speak just as loudly to ourselves.

Read: Matthew 7:1–5

Reflect:

1. How can you stay committed to justice without falling into self-righteousness?

2. Are there specific areas where you tend to judge others too quickly? Do you tend to judge others in the areas where you yourself struggle?

3. How can you "take the log out of your own eye" without falling into self-condemnation?

TUESDAY

THE PERIL OF DISCOURAGEMENT

What is required of a man or a woman who is called to enter fully into the turmoil and agony of the times and speak a word of hope?
— Henri Nouwen

Elijah could have identified with Nouwen's question. Imagine Elijah's situation. He had faithfully followed the Lord and spoken on the Lord's behalf. He had trusted God and the Lord had sent fire from heaven, consuming Elijah's burnt offering and spurning the sacrifice of the prophets of Baal (1 Kings 18:36-40).

Yet in today's reading we find Elijah running for his life. Jezebel, the wicked consort of the evil King Ahab, is furious over the death of her pagan priests and vows to kill Elijah. Elijah is deeply discouraged. "I alone am left, and they are seeking my life, to take it away" (1 Kings 19:10, 14).

Like Elijah, those who long for justice will experience discouragement. We too will sometimes feel that we aren't accomplishing anything. What Elijah learns is that he was never alone. God was working with him all the time.

Read: 1 Kings 19:1-18

Reflect:

1. God chose to speak to Elijah through "a gentle whisper" (1 Kings 19:12 NIV). Why do you think God chose to speak this way?

2. How do you tend to respond to discouragement?

3. What have been sources of discouragement for you over the past year? Write them down without judgement, and ask the Holy Spirit for comfort and redemption in these areas.

WEDNESDAY

THE PERIL OF HATING OUR ENEMIES

I am certain that Jesus understood the difficulty inherent in the act of loving one's enemy. He never joined the ranks of those who talk glibly about the easiness of the moral life.... So when Jesus said, "Love your enemy," he was not unmindful of its stringent qualities. Yet he meant every word of it.
— *Martin Luther King Jr.*

In the ancient Christian world, the phrase "Repetition is the mother of learning" was a well-known principle for learning and study. So today we want to return to a text we pondered last month: Jesus' teaching on loving our enemies.

This text is especially important to those of us who are deeply engaged in social justice work. Almost daily we encounter people who consider us their enemies.

Jesus unequivocally states that we must love our enemies. This command can seem so unreasonable, so unrealistic. Martin Luther King Jr. again offers wise advice for responding to our enemies: First, develop and maintain the capacity to forgive. Second, remember that we can love people we don't like. Third, love with *agape* love, a love that imitates God's unconditional love for us.

Read: Matthew 5:43–48

Reflect:

1. How would you define "forgiveness"?

2. Does loving our enemies mean we must like them? Why or why not?

3. How is God's *agape* love different from the way we normally express love to other people?

THURSDAY

~~~~~~~~~~

THE PERIL OF FEAR

Peace I leave with you; my peace I give to you. I do not give to you as the world gives. Do not let your hearts be troubled, and do not let them be afraid. — John 14:27

Those who try to live a compassionate life and work for social justice will often be in situations of conflict and sometimes danger. Anger, intimidation, and violence are daily realities. Some of those devoted to justice have paid with their lives.

If anyone had reason to fear, it was Jesus. Yet Jesus, knowing the horrific torture and death on a cross that awaits him, encourages the disciples: don't be afraid. Despite this forbidding future, Jesus offers them peace and the antidote for fear. The enemies of God may destroy the body, but they cannot destroy the soul. We are safe in the hands of God.

Read: Matthew 10:28–31

Reflect:

1. In today's passage, fearing God ("Fear him who can destroy both soul and body in hell") is mentioned alongside God's fatherly care ("You are of more value than many sparrows"). When you think of fearing God, do you also think of God's loving care?

2. How does fearing God free us from fearing people?

3. Consider your fears. Perhaps you fear physical harm or death. Perhaps you fear criticism or rejection. Take a moment now to write down one or two fears. Later, spend ten minutes alone with God to ask what the root cause of your fear is. Consider sharing this with a trusted friend or pastor who can pray with you.

FRIDAY

THE PERIL OF MISPLACED PRIORITIES

You can't get second things by putting them first; you can get second things only by putting first things first. From which ... would follow ... the question, What things are first? — *C. S. Lewis*

In today's reading, Jesus warns that we can prioritize our concerns about food and dress—surely important things for those who care for the poor—over seeking first God's rule in our own lives.

God must reign in our lives if God's purposes are to reign in the world. Do you know people whose hearts were once on fire for God but who were overcome by the demands of social justice work and lost their faith in God?

Mother Teresa said she could never have carried out her ministry in Calcutta if she had not first begun each day with mass. Some relief organizations encourage their staff to pause throughout the day to pray, and then return to their work.

Worship and prayer? These are first things. Service to the poor and the oppressed? These are second things that are empowered by our commitment to first things.

Read: Matthew 6:25–33

Reflect:

1. What does it mean in practical terms to "strive first for the kingdom of God?"

2. Can you identify instances in which you have pursued a second thing as a first thing?

Week 4

~~~~~~

Boldness and Perseverance in Doing Good

MONDAY

THE BOLDNESS OF A LIONESS

How can we expect righteousness to prevail when there is hardly anyone willing to give himself up individually to a righteous cause? — Sophie Scholl

Unjust people often put on a bold face. They bully and intimidate. But inwardly they are often cowards. According to Proverbs 28:1, "The wicked flee when no one pursues." But the proverb goes on to say that the righteous are just the opposite. Rather than fleeing, they "are as bold as a lion."

Sophie Scholl was only twenty-one years old when she was guillotined by the Nazis, executed two days after being arrested for distributing leaflets that criticized Hitler. As she walked to her execution, she boldly said, "I have to go, but what does my death matter if through us, thousands of people are awakened and stirred into action?"

Scholl was a strong Christian, a Spirit-filled lioness, and the wicked hunters brought her down. Yet who was finally victorious? Sophie Scholl is considered by young Germans today to be one of the most important Germans of all time.

Remember that God delights in using his courageous, bold image-bearers in the most surprising ways.

Read: Proverbs 28:1

Reflect:

1. Are you ever tempted to wonder, "What difference can my life make—I'm only one person?"

2. What bold lioness or lion whom you know or have read about inspires you?

3. Are there areas where God is asking you to be bolder in your pursuit of justice?

TUESDAY

PERSEVERANCE IN DOING GOOD

Evil is recalcitrant and determined, and never voluntarily relinquishes its hold short of a persistent, almost fanatical resistance.
— *Martin Luther King Jr.*

Opposition to evil can tire us out. It seems we are pushing against an immovable force. Sometimes we're tempted to think that nothing will ever change. We wake up, look out the window, and everything appears the same. The same injustices face us that we fought against yesterday. One perpetrator is sent to jail, and another quickly replaces him. The evil we face is unrelenting. Haven't we all asked, "Am I really making a difference?"

In today's reading, Paul shows us the process God uses to bring about transformation. Suffering produces perseverance; perseverance, character; and character, hope" (Romans 5:3–4). We persevere because Christ is at work within us through the power of the Holy Spirit. He is transforming us, producing the character we need to do what he's asking us to do. When we remember that the Lord of the universe is present with us, working in us and transforming us, our hope is revived and our endurance strengthened.

Read: Romans 5:3–5

Reflect:

1. Can you name one or two instances when the persistence of evil has tempted you to give up?

2. Suffering in some people produces bitterness while in others it produces perseverance. Why? What thoughts regarding suffering lead to bitterness and what thoughts lead to perseverance?

3. What spiritual disciplines might you practice to help you better respond to suffering?

WEDNESDAY

THE ENCOURAGEMENT OF HOPE

Let us not become weary in doing good, for at the proper time we will reap a harvest if we do not give up. — Galatians 6:9 (NIV)

Paul understood that those who do good can grow weary. What does he—along with the psalmist in today's reading—propose as the remedy? Hope.

Hope is the Spirit-inspired willingness to look at time from the perspective of who God is and what God has done, is doing, and will do in the future. God promises that the harvest will come if we don't give up.

The psalmist encourages us to "Seek the LORD and his strength." We simply do not have the strength to do the work God is asking us to do. The Lord realizes this. It is his strength, not ours, that will bring our tasks to their completion.

The psalmist also asks us to lengthen our memory. "Remember," he exhorts, "the wonderful works he has done, his miracles, and the judgments he has uttered." A long memory, the psalmist promises, will carry us through the occasional moments of weariness and discouragement.

Read: Psalm 105:4–5

Reflect:

1. Review where your thoughts tend to go. Do you tend to "live" in the past, present, or future? Why?

2. Spend a few moments in silence and ask God to bring to mind specific ways he has worked in your life in the past. To nourish hope, record these instances where you can reference them later.

THURSDAY

~~~~~~~~~~

LET US RUN WITH PERSEVERANCE

In light of faith I am strong, constant, and persevering. — Catherine of Siena

In today's reading, the author of Hebrews exhorts us to "run with perseverance." The metaphor of the Christian as an athlete running a race before a great "cloud of witnesses" is both encouraging and challenging.

Have you had the opportunity to go for a long run? When we are just beginning to get in shape, running is difficult. Our lungs burn. Our hearts pound with exertion. Our legs tire quickly.

If we persevere in running, things start to get better. But that takes some discipline, doesn't it? Perhaps we get up early when we would rather stay in bed. We put on running shoes instead of soft slippers.

So, too, our spiritual lives require exercise and exertion. Yet, as the writer of Hebrews reminds us, we are not alone. Christians before us have also persevered in the race the Lord gave them to run. And now they surround us, cheering us on, encouraging us not to give up, to cross the finish line. Can you see Jesus running with us, setting the pace, smiling and saying, "You can do this! Don't give up! I'm with you!"?

Read: Hebrews 12:1–2

Reflect:

1. What was the joy set before Jesus that allowed him to persevere?

2. Name some people, past and present, who have encouraged you not to give up.

3. God wants us to be honest with him about our struggles—think of David's honesty in the Psalms. Consider a difficult challenge in your life right now. Take a few minutes to write an honest prayer about it. You might try the pattern of Psalm 13. Begin with your feelings: "How long, O LORD?" (verse 1). Then end with a statement of perseverance: "But I trust in your unfailing love" (verse 5 NIV).

FRIDAY

GOD IS WITH US

If we are to better the future we must disturb the present. — *Catherine Booth*

In today's reading, Moses is soon to die. We see him passing the mantle of leadership to Joshua. As this momentous change occurs, Moses encourages Joshua and reminds him that the Lord "will be with you."

The words of Moses to Joshua are a fitting conclusion to our study of social justice and the compassionate life. As we have seen, God's call to a life of compassion and justice can be daunting. We may be tempted to be fearful or timid. Those we desire to love may resist us. What God asks us to do as we seek justice for all people may seem too hard for us to attempt. Yet the promise of God is clear. God will be with us. He promises that he will never leave us or forsake us (Hebrews 13:5).

Things that seem impossible become possible with God at our side.

Read: Deuteronomy 31:7-8

Reflect:

1. God promises to be with us as we seek justice for all people. Consider how the promise of God's constant presence with us can strengthen us in the work God asks us to do.

2. Can you recall times when God's faithfulness and presence were particularly clear to you?

3. Dozens of Scripture passages remind us that God is with us and thus we should not be afraid. Consider choosing one of those passages now—perhaps today's reading from Deuteronomy, or Matthew 10:28-31, or John 14:27—and memorizing it. A simple memorization method is to say the verse aloud ten times each day for ten days.

Week 1

～～～

What Is the Word-Centered Life?

MONDAY

THE WORD

The soul can do without everything except the word of God, without which none at all of its wants are provided for. — Martin Luther

When Christians talk about "the Word," they are usually referring to the Bible. That's true, yet there is more. In fact, God uses three central ways to reveal himself to people: the written Word (Scripture), the living Word (Jesus), and the spoken word—truth proclaimed from the written Word, along with personal testimony of the living Word, Jesus.

For the next two months our focus will be on the Word-centered life. We'll explore each of these three ways that God communicates.

Read: Luke 4:16–20a; 42–44

Reflect:

1. What does the term "Word of God" mean to you?

2. How did you first become aware of the good news of the kingdom of God? Did you hear it proclaimed by a person, or did you read about it in the Bible?

3. What was the good news that Jesus was proclaiming to the poor? What made it so good?

TUESDAY

ALL THE SCRIPTURES

The New Testament lies hidden in the Old and the Old Testament is unveiled in the New. — Augustine

In today's reading, we find two disciples walking together on the road to the village of Emmaus. One of the two is identified as Cleopas (Luke 24:18); the other is unnamed. They do not know that Jesus has been raised from the dead. These disciples are discussing the events of recent days (Jesus' arrest, trial, and crucifixion). The risen Jesus joins them on their journey, but they don't recognize who he is.

Did you notice that Jesus challenges these two followers for not understanding the Old Testament's central message? Take a close look at Jesus' words. He chides these disciples, teaching that if they had read the writings of Moses, the prophets, and "all the scriptures" with faith, they would have understood what God was doing in and through Jesus.

Read: Luke 24:13–27

Reflect:

1. Can you identify portions of the Old Testament that clearly point to the story of Jesus?

2. Are there verses or chapters of the Old Testament that have nourished your relationship with Jesus? If so, write a few of them down to incorporate into your prayers today.

WEDNESDAY

~~~~~~~~~

GOD'S PRESENCE IN THE LIVING WORD

Our Lord is called the Word because those things that were hidden were revealed through him, just as it is through a word that the hidden things of the heart are made known. — Ephrem the Syrian

John begins his Gospel with a breathtaking statement: "In the beginning was the Word, and the Word was with God, and the Word was God." Then in verse 14 of chapter 1, John writes that "the Word became flesh and lived among us." Jesus, as God's "Word" to us, explains and models—in word and deed—what God is like.

When you think of God, what image comes to mind? Some people think of God as a distant, demanding parent. Others imagine God to be a divine military officer, always screaming at his soldiers to perform better. And still others imagine God to be an unworried grandfather, whose "highest hope," as C. S. Lewis writes, "is that at the end of the day everyone had a good time." Thankfully, none of these views of God is true. How do we know?

God is like Jesus.

Read: John 1:1–14

Reflect:

1. Out of all the ways John could have described Jesus, why do you think John called him "the Word"?

2. Do you have any ideas about God—potentially negative ideas—that are different than what you see in Jesus?

THURSDAY

~~~~~~~~

JESUS IS THE FULLNESS OF GOD'S WORD

Jesus said . . . "Whoever has seen me has seen the Father." — John 14:9

As we saw in yesterday's reading, Jesus "the Word" has entered our world to teach us what God is like.

In today's reading, the apostle Paul further expands our understanding of who Jesus is. "He is the image of the invisible God, the firstborn of all creation" (Colossians 1:15). And "in him all the fullness of God was pleased to dwell" (verse 19). So Jesus is not only God's Word to us; he is the very image of God. We can be confident that when we look at Jesus—studying and meditating on his words and actions—we are seeing God in the flesh, God incarnate (John 1:14). Jesus mirrors God. When we look at Jesus, we see a rich, full understanding of what God is like.

During times of physical pain, emotional stress, and spiritual dryness, we may begin to question the goodness of God. Remember that in Jesus, God the Son has entered our real-life situations in a very tangible way. Jesus experienced human pain. He witnessed and responded to human suffering. He willingly suffered and died on the cross. He knows what it is to experience human life, in all its joys and sorrows.

To sum up Paul's words, Jesus is the great image-bearer. Again, as we've seen in other readings this week, if you want to know what God is like, take a close look at Jesus.

Read: Colossians 1:15–20

Reflect:

1. We all experience physical and emotional pain; some of us have suffered deeply. During times of suffering, what have you been tempted to think God is like?

2. As your knowledge of Jesus grows, are your ideas about God changing?

FRIDAY

~~~~~~~~~~

WHICH IS GOOD NEWS, INDEED!

Do not be so frightened in the presence of such a gentle baby, smiling at you and holding out his arms to you. He is your God, but he is all smiles and gentleness. Do not be afraid. — Charles de Foucauld

The events surrounding Jesus' birth are filled with joy, beauty, and amazement. The angel Gabriel invites Mary to be the mother of Jesus, the incarnate Son. With great faith she accepts God's invitation, knowing it comes with great cost.

An angel greets shepherds in the fields and proclaims good news to this ragtag group. They too have a role in God's plan.

Eight days after his birth, the baby is circumcised and officially given the name Jesus. A month later, the parents bring their baby to the temple. Simeon and Anna—two well-known figures in the temple complex—offer their blessings to the Holy Family. Simeon exclaims that at last his eyes have seen the promised Messiah. More good news!

In these wonderful events, God is acting to rescue the world—to save those made in his image from their sins and invite them into his kingdom. *God has not remained separate from us.* God's immense love for us is demonstrated in the events surrounding Jesus' birth.

Read: Luke 2:8–38

Reflect:

1. Take time to ponder the events surrounding Jesus' birth. Which events especially impress or encourage you?

2. Sometimes the good news Jesus offers can become familiar, stale, or distant. With this passage in mind, take a few moments in thankful prayer. You might write down a few things or pray aloud something like "Thank you, Jesus, for your humility," or "Thank you, God, that you came to rescue us and forgive us."

Week 2

~~~~~~

Scripture: The Written Word

MONDAY

THE WORD OF GOD WRITTEN

The Bible is one of the greatest blessings bestowed by God on the children of men. It has God for its author; salvation for its end, and truth without any mixture for its matter. It is all pure. — John Locke

Most of us are familiar with the Bible, God's written Word. The first section, the Law (or Torah), was written on parchment scrolls that were passed from generation to generation. Later the Israelites added the scriptural components known as the "Prophets" and the "Writings." God has used the Scriptures to communicate directly with his people for millennia.

Followers of Jesus call the Hebrew Scriptures the "Old Testament" and have added other writings, called the "New Testament," to form the Bible. In the New Testament, we learn about Jesus in the Gospels, the beginnings of the church in Acts, faithful living in the Epistles, and our ultimate destiny in Revelation. Followers of Jesus know the two testaments together as the written Word of God.

Read: 2 Timothy 3:16–17

Reflect:

1. What does it mean that Scripture is "God-breathed" (2 Timothy 3:16 NIV)?

2. There is great variety in Scripture. God spoke through each author's style and particular cultural context. What does this tell you about how God likes to work?

3. What parts of the Bible do you find most life-giving? Are there some parts you find confusing and avoid? If so, perhaps offer this honest prayer: "God, there are parts of Scripture that don't make sense to me. But I trust you are good, and I ask for your help in understanding the whole of Scripture."

TUESDAY

GOD'S WORD IN COVENANT

Hoping against hope, [Abraham] believed that he would become "the father of many nations," according to what was said, "So numerous shall your descendants be." — Romans 4:18

In Genesis 12, God promised to make Abraham's name great, to give him descendants, and to give him land. In today's reading, God confirms these covenant promises.

Now we find Abraham afraid and discouraged. Why? Many years have passed and God's promises to him still have not been fulfilled. He has no children from Sarah. How can he possibly have descendants when his wife is beyond the normal age for bearing children?

God's promises to Abraham would be fulfilled; God's covenant with Abraham would hold true. Here is the pattern of covenant: God makes a promise to a person, the person responds in faith, and eventually the promises are fulfilled, *though sometimes in very surprising ways.*

Sometimes hundreds of years must pass before God's covenant promises are fulfilled. For those to whom the promises are made, this delay in fulfillment can be very hard and deeply discouraging. Yet when we *take the long view* and see the biblical story unfold—often over hundreds and hundreds of years—God's faithfulness to his promises appears clear. God is not a liar. What God has promised will come to pass.

Read: Genesis 15:1–6

Reflect:

1. As we have seen in other readings, God's promises are often fulfilled in strange and unexpected ways. Have you seen this pattern in your own life?

2. In what ways might God be asking you to "take the long view"?

WEDNESDAY

~~~~~~~~~~~~~

GOD'S WORD IN PROPHECY

If we confess our sins, he who is faithful and just will forgive us our sins and cleanse us from all unrighteousness. — 1 John 1:9

Today we continue to see the covenantal pattern of promise and fulfillment. We move forward to the time of Jeremiah, one of the great Old Testament prophets. The context for our reading? Israel has repeatedly disobeyed God's law. Jeremiah sees God's judgment moving toward Israel. It will soon arrive.

Yet, with judgment on the horizon, Jeremiah buys a field in the land of Israel. By all appearances, the land seemed lost forever. Through the purchase of this field, Jeremiah indicates that the promises made to Abraham remain firm.

In Scripture, prophecies of judgment often appear in Israel's life with God. But the last word God speaks is mercy, not judgment.

And so it is with us. God does not take our sin lightly. But thankfully, the word we receive from the apostle John is that when we confess our sins openly and honestly, God—with an eagerness soaked in mercy—forgives us (1 John 1:9).

Read: Jeremiah 32:1–15

Reflect:

1. Why does God take sin so seriously?

2. Identify times in your life when you knew you deserved judgment, but instead you received mercy. What effect did this have on you?

3. Unconfessed sin can weigh us down. Silently on your own, ask God if there is anything he wants to bring into the light for the sake of forgiveness and freedom. If so, write down, "I confess that I have _____. I receive your forgiveness and your mercy in Jesus."

THURSDAY

~~~~~~~~~~~~~~

GOD'S WORD IN POETRY

The LORD is my shepherd, I shall not want. He makes me lie down in green pastures; he leads me beside still waters; he restores my soul. He leads me in right paths for his name's sake. — Psalm 23:1–3

Isn't it true that there are some things that can only be expressed well in a poem or song? Think of a favorite. What is it about a piece of poetry that has touched your mind and heart in a manner that simple prose could not express?

In today's reading, we have a selection from Psalm 119, the longest poem in the Old Testament. We've selected one verse out of this long psalm to ponder together. The writer describes God's word as a "lamp" and a "light."

Imagine walking down a forest path at night. You have lost your way. You reach into your backpack and pull out a flashlight. With a flip of the switch light beams onto your path. What had been a fearful, confusing, threatening situation is instantly transformed. "Oh," you say to yourself, "there's the trail. Now I can find my way home."

As our reading teaches, God's word sheds light on our path, transforms what was fearful into the familiar, and guides us home. Indeed, God's word is a lamp to our feet and a light to our path.

Read: Psalm 119:105

Reflect:

1. Have you ever written a poem or song? Or do you prefer prose?

2. Recall a specific instance when you felt confused, fearful, or lost and a phrase or sentence from Scripture shed light on your situation.

3. Do you have some favorite psalms? What is it about these poems that you have found especially helpful?

Month 11: The Word-Centered Life

FRIDAY

GOD'S WORD IN WISDOM

The fear of the LORD is the beginning of knowledge; fools despise wisdom and instruction. — Proverbs 1:7

What is your definition of "wisdom"? What are the attributes of a wise person? Who are the wise people you have known? What characterized their lives? Their choices? Their responses to difficult and puzzling situations?

Proverbs is the wisdom book of the Old Testament. Many proverbs come from Solomon, the wisest king in the history of Israel. Today's proverb describes wisdom.

What is "the fear of the LORD"? Fear of God is profound reverence for God. When we fear God, we remember who God is, in all his majesty and glory. We recognize that God is not a creature like us. We acknowledge that God is the transcendent Lord of the entire universe. In reverence we welcome God into the smallest details of our lives and ask God to reign there.

Reverence also applies to our relationship with Jesus. One day we will see the ascended Christ reigning on his throne in heaven. He is the King of kings and Lord of lords. *How will you feel as you step into the presence of the king of the universe?*

Read: Proverbs 9:10

Reflect:

1. What does the fear of the LORD look like in a modern context?

2. What are concrete steps you can take to have a greater reverence for God?

3. Take a few moments to pray for greater reverence. Perhaps something like, "God, help me to see you rightly, to have the kind of reverence that draws us closer together. You are the Creator and I am a creature, yet you call me friend. You could destroy us, yet you save us. The power of your mercy amazes me."

Week 3

~~~~~~~~

Jesus: The Living Word

MONDAY

JESUS IS THE MESSIAH, THE SON OF THE LIVING GOD

Then [Jesus] said to Thomas, "Put your finger here and see my hands. Reach out your hand and put it in my side. Do not doubt but believe." Thomas answered him, "My Lord and my God!" — John 20:27–28

In today's reading, Jesus asks his disciples a very important question: "Who do people say that the Son of Man is?" (Matthew 16:13). Peter, clearly the leader of the group, quickly and rightly responds, "You are the Messiah, the Son of the living God" (verse 16). Jesus is pleased with Peter's response. "Blessed are you, Simon son of Jonah! For flesh and blood has not revealed this to you, but my Father in heaven" (verse 17).

Ponder what has been revealed to Peter. The Messiah, the anointed one of Israel, is "the Son of God." Jesus is fully human and fully divine.

How has Peter come to this amazing conclusion? He has heard Jesus' teaching firsthand. He has witnessed his great miracles. The Father has revealed to Peter the meaning of Jesus' words and works.

Jesus continues to ask generation after generation, person after person: "Who do you say that I am?"

Read: Matthew 16:13–17

Reflect:

1. If Jesus asked you directly, "Who do you say that I am?" how would you respond?

2. Can you recall words or works of Jesus that indicate his exalted stature as the Son of God?

TUESDAY

THE WORD BECAME A HUMAN BEING

See what love the Father has given us, that we should be called children of God; and that is what we are. — 1 John 3:1

Have you ever wondered whether God loves you? All of us struggle with this question from time to time. Especially when we experience physical or emotional pain, or times when our circumstances are terribly difficult, God's love can seem distant or even nonexistent. Even in our normal daily life we sometimes wonder, "Does God love me?"

In today's reading, the apostle John declares, in the strongest terms possible, that God loves us. "God's love was revealed among us in this way: God sent his only Son into the world so that we might live through him" (1 John 4:9).

The proof of God's love is this: God the Father has sent his Son into our world so that we might live through him. How did the Son come? As a human being—a human being like us in every way, apart from sin. Jesus had a real human body, a real human mind, and a real human will.

So when moments of illness, sorrow, doubt, or pain occur, we can be assured that Jesus is near us and loves us. He has entered our world. He has become what we are. He has died for our sins. He has risen from the dead. And he will come again.

Read: 1 John 4:7-11

Reflect:

1. Can you identify specific life experiences when it was difficult to believe God loves you?

2. God's love is manifested in the Father's willingness to send the Son on our behalf. How can we *imitate* this divine self-giving more effectively?

WEDNESDAY

THE WORD WAS CONCEIVED BY THE POWER OF THE HOLY SPIRIT

The initiator of a new birth had to be born in a new way. — Tertullian

In yesterday's reading, we pondered the love shown to us by the Father in sending his Son into the world. Now we are invited to consider the unique and miraculous conception of Jesus in Mary's womb by the power of the Holy Spirit.

Today's reading tells us the story of Jesus' conception. God's spoken word comes to Mary through the angel Gabriel: she will conceive and bear a son whose name is to be Jesus, which means "the Lord saves." Mary has a choice. She could say yes to Gabriel's invitation or she could say no. Mary responds in faith to what Gabriel has said, and miraculously the promised child is conceived.

In Mary, the Holy Spirit fulfills the plan of the Father for saving his people from the disease of sin. In a wonderful combination, Mary's faith combines with the Holy Spirit's power and gives birth to the Son of God.

Read: Luke 1:26–38

Reflect:

1. In Mary, we see great faith in God, despite the promise of what seems impossible from a human perspective. Can you identify experiences in your own life where God accomplished what seemed impossible to you?

2. Mary responded in faith to a direct promise of Gabriel. Can you identify promises in the Scriptures that have been fulfilled in your own life?

THURSDAY

〰〰〰〰〰

JESUS, THE INCARNATE WORD, PROCLAIMS THE KINGDOM OF GOD

When Jesus heard this, he said ... "I came not to call the righteous, but sinners." — Mark 2:17

In today's reading, Jesus proclaims that the kingdom of God is "has come near." Throughout his ministry, and particularly in his parables, Jesus teaches that in him the kingdom of God is breaking into this world in a new and unexpected way.

Jesus says *everyone* is called to enter God's kingdom. Yes, Jesus first announces the kingdom to the people of Israel. Yet as God's plan unfolds in Jesus' life, death, resurrection, and ascension, we see that his messianic kingdom is intended for people from all the nations of the world.

God's kingdom especially belongs to *the poor and lowly*. Jesus is sent by the Father to "bring good news to the poor" (Luke 4:18). He declares the poor blessed, "for yours is the kingdom of God" (Luke 6:20). Indeed, Jesus shares the life of the poor, from his cradle to the cross. He experienced what it is to be poor: to hunger, to thirst, and to often be deprived of life's basic necessities.

Jesus invites *sinners* to his kingdom. He invites sinners to conversion in his kingdom and teaches about the depth and breadth of God's mercy. And in his sacrificial death on the cross, Jesus demonstrates his love for all.

Read: Mark 1:14–15

Reflect:

1. Jesus' invitation to God's kingdom is made to all people. Who might be the people we tend to exclude from his kingdom or to declare beyond the hope of the kingdom?

2. Why do you think that Jesus has a special place in his kingdom for the poor and lowly?

FRIDAY

JESUS AS THE TRANSFIGURED WORD

He is the reflection of God's glory and the exact imprint of God's very being.
— Hebrews 1:3

In our first reading this week, we examined Peter's declaration that Jesus is the Messiah, the Son of God. From that time in Jesus' life, he "began to show his disciples that he must go to Jerusalem and undergo great suffering . . . and be killed, and on the third day be raised" (Matthew 16:21). This was not welcome news for Peter and the other disciples.

It is within this context of imminent suffering and death that the mysterious event of Jesus' transfiguration occurs. On a high mountain, Jesus is transfigured before Peter, James, and John. Jesus' face and clothes are transformed, or transfigured; and Moses and Elijah appear, "speaking of his departure, which he was about to accomplish at Jerusalem" (Luke 9:31). Suddenly a cloud descends upon the gathered group, and a voice from the cloud declares, "This is my Son, the Beloved; with him I am well pleased; listen to him!" (Matthew 17:5).

In the transfiguration, Jesus reveals his divine glory, confirming Peter's earlier confession of him as the Son of God. But Jesus also manifests his glory as he dies on the cross and is raised from the dead on the third day. For Jesus, suffering on behalf of others for the sake of his kingdom is intimately connected to the transcendent glory he reveals to Peter, James, and John.

Read: Matthew 17:1–8

Reflect:

1. Why do you think Jesus chose such a small group—Peter, James, and John—for the transfiguration, rather than making it a more public event?

2. How does the suffering of Jesus uniquely demonstrate his glory?

3. In your life, is glory—honor and victory and beauty—ever linked to suffering? Why do these two things often go together?

Week 4

~~~~~~

The Gospel: The Spoken Word

MONDAY

THE POWER OF GOD FOR SALVATION

The kingdom of God depends not on talk but on power.
— 1 Corinthians 4:20

In today's reading, Paul stresses the power of the gospel. Many of those receiving Paul's letter to the Romans had grown up in Rome, the most powerful city in the ancient world. What did the Romans believe about power and how it should be exercised?

Caesar was king. Caesar was considered divine. Caesar demanded absolute political and religious allegiance and, in the case of a Roman soldier, military loyalty and sacrifice. Honor was the highest Roman value. Shame was abhorred.

How striking to find Paul writing, "I am not ashamed of the gospel." For the Roman, to be crucified was to experience horrible public humiliation. For the Christian, Christ's crucifixion was the supreme manifestation of God's power, wisdom, and love.

Power to do what? To save God's children from the curse of sin, to break the power of evil and wickedness, to provide supernatural power to live a transformed life, to empower us to love our enemies rather than kill them.

Read: Romans 1:16–17

Reflect:

1. Paul was unashamed of something that his culture considered shameful. What gave him this boldness?

2. What have you experienced from those who exercise power? Has your experience been positive or negative?

TUESDAY

FOOLISHNESS TO THOSE WHO ARE PERISHING

Christianity is unique. The world's religions have certain traits in common, but until the gospel of Jesus Christ burst upon the Mediterranean world, no one in the history of human imagination had conceived of such a thing as the worship of a crucified man. — Fleming Rutledge

It's possible for us to forget how strange, how unexpected, how "foolish" the message of the gospel appeared in the ancient world. For many, when they first heard that Christians worshiped a crucified man, the response, essentially, was "That's crazy!" Who could possibly believe that a crucified man could save anyone?

And yet Paul is insistent. What appears foolish to the unbelieving world is the manifestation of the power of God. As Christ dies—naked on a Roman cross—he cracks the spine of the devil, conquers sin and wickedness, and offers forgiveness to every person who honestly says to him, "Yes, Lord, I have sinned. Save me. Deliver me. Help me."

Read: 1 Corinthians 1:17–18

Reflect:

1. The wisdom of God is often found in words or actions that the world finds foolish. Can you identify instances of this?

2. God delights in manifesting his power through our weaknesses. How might your own weaknesses—and God's power manifest in them—illustrate this?

WEDNESDAY

THE WORD BRINGS PEACE

Peace with God comes only from acceptance of his gift of life in his Son (Romans 5:1–2). We are then assured of the outcome of our life and are no longer trying to justify ourselves before God and others. — Dallas Willard

In today's reading, Jesus promises his disciples peace, but teaches that the peace that he brings is not "as the world gives." What type of peace might the world offer? The peace of mind that comes from financial security? The peace derived from a good reputation? The peace of freedom from political tyranny?

Financial security is important. A good reputation is a gift from God. Freedom from political tyranny is, without doubt, a value to be pursued. But Jesus offers a more significant, fundamental peace.

In a word, believers in Jesus know how things will turn out. They take the long view. They are often able to find peace in the midst of difficult circumstances.

Read: John 14:27

Reflect:

1. Ponder the areas in your life where you know you have yet to experience the peace that Jesus offers. What are some specific steps you can take toward peace in these areas?

2. Today's passage is short but powerful. Do something today to keep the passage in your memory. Perhaps write the word *peace* on the palm of your hand or tie a string around your wrist. Whenever you feel hurried or anxious, take two minutes to pray, "Jesus, I receive the peace you promised."

THURSDAY

THE WORD PRODUCES HOPE

The solid facts about the future hope of Christians are a powerful motivation for constant faith and costly love in the present. — N. T. Wright

James Bryan Smith highlights four aspects of the Christian hope the apostle Paul speaks of in his letter to the Colossians:

We have died with Christ (Colossians 3:3).

We have been raised with Christ (Colossians 2:12).

Christ has ascended into heaven and is seated at the right hand of God (Colossians 3:1).

Christ will return (Colossians 3:4).

These truths offer us great hope, hope that can help us to be formed more deeply into the image of Christ. The old "you" has died in Christ and a new "you" has been raised to new life in Jesus. As we walk with Jesus at our side into each new day, the values of his kingdom can increasingly shape our values and perspectives. Our hope for the future deepens.

Read: Colossians 1:3–6

Reflect:

1. Try to identify issues or situations where you may have lost hope. Is Jesus offering you hope in these areas in a way you may not have recognized?

2. Smith mentions four aspects of Christian hope. Which touched you most deeply?

FRIDAY

THE WORD IS WORTH IT ALL

If any want to become my followers, let them deny themselves and take up their cross and follow me. — Mark 8:34

In today's reading, Paul speaks, with genuine grief, of those who "live as enemies of the cross of Christ." What characterizes these folks? They believe the lie that human fulfillment is found in "earthly things" such as a stomach filled with rich food and the satisfaction of every desire that crosses the fallen human mind, despite how shameful such desires and actions may be.

Both Paul and Jesus warn that the result of such ideas is destruction—human misery on a grand scale, in this life and in the life to come.

A better word, a word of hope, is needed to move us beyond these destructive patterns. And Paul delivers it: remember who you are and where you come from—you are citizens of heaven. Even more, you have a Savior who will transform you totally to look like him.

That's a word worth staking your life on.

Read: Philippians 3:17–21

Reflect:

1. Paul writes that he is in tears over the enemies of the cross. How does tearful grief over our enemies differ from judgmental anger?

2. Paul says to watch and learn from those who are living Christlike lives. Who is someone you look to in this way? What is it about them that you admire?

3. Sometimes we forget who we are and where we come from. Take a few minutes to pray based on today's passage. For example, "Thank you that I am a citizen of heaven. And thank you that Jesus is coming back to set all things right and give me a transformed body."

Week 1

~~~~~~

Memorize and Teach Scripture

MONDAY

HIDE GOD'S WORD IN OUR HEARTS

The most obvious thing we can do is to draw certain key portions of Scripture into our minds and make them a part of the permanent fixtures of our thought. This is the primary discipline for the thought life. . . . A good way to do that is to memorize them and then constantly turn them over in our minds as we go through the events and circumstances of our life.
— Dallas Willard

How do we "treasure," or "hide," God's Word in our hearts, with the happy result that sin is progressively drained out of our lives? Try Scripture memorization.

In memorizing Scripture, we are concretely imitating the pattern the psalmist offers us in today's reading. Christians have often benefited from the discipline of Scripture memorization. What might be some practical ways to practice this key spiritual discipline?

You might try memorizing a passage that has been particularly helpful to you. Try writing a verse on a small card that you can put in your pocket or attach to your computer screen. One verse a day works for some people. Others set a goal of one verse per week.

As your memory strengthens, try memorizing chapters from the Gospels or one of Paul's epistles. Some people like to memorize the Psalms. Memorization takes time, but what's the rush? We are treasuring God's Word in our hearts.

Read: Psalm 119:11

Reflect:

1. Have you tried to memorize verses or sections of the Bible? What method of memorization has worked best for you?

2. Consider memorizing a passage from the Bible with a friend. Colossians 3:1–17 is a wonderful option. You might challenge each another to memorize it or another passage by the end of the year. Discuss this possibility with a prayer partner.

TUESDAY

TEACH GOD'S WORD TO OUR CHILDREN

I believe God has a special plan for parenting. It is as if He hands us this tiny human, and says, "Now let's learn some really great stuff." — Thea Lee

Did your parents introduce you to the Bible in childhood? Or are you now learning the Bible for the first time as an adult? In today's reading, Moses emphasizes the importance of teaching children God's Word in general and God's commandments in particular. "Recite them to your children and talk about them when you are at home and when you are away, when you lie down and when you rise" (Deuteronomy 6:7).

Ponder prayerfully the opportunity we have to help form a biblical memory in our children—little ones God has entrusted to us for their ever-deepening formation into the image of Jesus.

Read: Deuteronomy 6:1–9

Reflect:

1. If you have children, what are some specific steps you can help them with in their understanding of the Bible?

2. If you don't have children, how can you help teach the children who are part of your church, family, or community circle?

WEDNESDAY

LET THE WORD OF CHRIST DWELL IN YOU RICHLY

It is the practice of the Christian community to cultivate habits of reading that sharpen our perceptions and involve us in getting this word of God formatively within us. — Eugene Peterson

In today's reading, Paul exhorts us to crack open space within our minds for the "word," or "message," of Christ to dwell in us "richly." If Paul finds such encouragement necessary—in this case to the Colossian church—then it must surely be possible for us to allow the word of Christ to dwell in us poorly.

What would such a poor dwelling look like? Maybe we find ourselves caught up in a work and home schedule that has made it extremely difficult to find time for Bible study and prayer. Perhaps the technology we use daily is distracting us from more important things. Young people in some countries check their cell phones eleven times per hour.

Read: Colossians 3:16

Reflect:

1. What do you think it means to "let the word of Christ dwell in you richly"?

2. Is it possible to have an unhurried heart and still work quickly and productively? Describe what that might look like.

3. Take a few moments in silence. Ask God if you have any unhealthy habits that might be distracting you from healthy habits like reading Scripture. Write them down. Instead of trying hard to change, simply commit to saying a simple prayer about it for the next couple mornings. For example, "Lord, I give my phone to you. Help me to use it well."

THURSDAY

〜〜〜〜〜〜

LET THE WORD OF GOD TEACH US

All this I have spoken while still with you. But the Advocate, the Holy Spirit, whom the Father will send in my name, will teach you all things and will remind you of everything I have said to you. — *John 14:25–26 (NIV)*

God has not remained silent, but has chosen to speak to human beings, his image-bearers. Paul emphasizes to Timothy the usefulness of the Scriptures for wise, loving living.

In a word, the Bible is the school of the Holy Spirit, the curriculum the Spirit uses to help us grow in our relationship with the Lord and with other image-bearers. Eugene Peterson writes that "readers become what they read." He's right. "Christians feed on Scripture. Holy Scripture nurtures the holy community as food nurtures the human body."

To stay spiritually healthy, then, we need to feed on God's Word. Without food, we eventually die. So it is with the Bible. If we neglect the nourishment it offers, our spiritual life withers. Paul invites us to absorb the Scripture's nourishment. As Eugene Peterson says, we can take "it into our lives in such a way that it gets metabolized into acts of love, cups of cold water, missions into all the world, healing and evangelism and justice in Jesus' name, hands raised in adoration of the Father, feet washed in company with the Son."

Read: 2 Timothy 3:14-17

Reflect:

1. For any job, it's important to be properly equipped. How does Scripture "equip you for every good work"?

2. Family meals are often carefully planned. How can we also plan to feast on the Word of God?

3. What time of day do you normally eat? Consider feasting on the Bible as well—read a passage before or after a meal.

FRIDAY

~~~~~~~~

TO HEAR AND OBEY IS BLESSED

The most important question we ask of this text is not, "What does this mean?" but "What can I obey?" A simple act of obedience will open up our lives to this text far more quickly than any number of Bible studies and dictionaries and concordances. — Eugene Peterson

In today's reading, Jesus warns that it's possible to "hear" his words without hearing them at all. He wants us to put his words into practice, to build our lives upon their foundation, to listen with constant attention to how we might obey what he is teaching. We are listening with our ears, our mind, and our hands and feet!

How do we learn to put Jesus' words into practice? We do so by slowing down, quieting down, and purposely asking as we read, "What is Jesus asking me to live out in this text?"

When we meditate on a text, we go slow. Imagine yourself chewing on Jesus' words like a dog gnawing on a bone. There is nourishment here to be enjoyed. "O taste and see that the LORD is good" (Psalm 34:8).

What is the result of this slow feeding? Growth in knowledge and growth in obedience.

Read: Matthew 7:24–27

Reflect:

1. What separates the "wise man" from the "foolish man" in Jesus' teaching? How can you become wiser in your reading of the Bible? What specific steps can you take?

2. What are some specific difficulties you have experienced in putting Jesus' words into practice?

Week 2

~~~~~~

Read and Pray Scripture

MONDAY

LISTEN EAGERLY AND STUDY THE SCRIPTURES

Those who are attentive to a matter will prosper, and happy are those who trust in the LORD. — Proverb 16:20

These days much is said about the accuracy of news reports. Is that story in the paper real? Is that online article fabricated? Some people trust too quickly without searching out the truth of a matter. Others trust nothing, using suspicion as a shield against being deceived.

The people in today's passage display a remarkable balance: receptive hearts and thoughtful minds. "They welcomed the message very eagerly *and* examined the scriptures every day to see whether these things were so" (Acts 17:11). Nothing indicates that suspicion or fear sparked their study—as if they were looking for biblical ammunition to shoot down Paul and Silas. Rather, they wanted assurance that this good news being preached to them aligned with the reliable source of truth found in the Scriptures. They listened eagerly and studied Scripture daily—a wonderfully balanced model to follow.

Read: Acts 17:10–12

Reflect:

1. What do you think these people heard from Paul and Silas that made them welcome the message "very eagerly"?

2. When you read a book or hear a sermon, do you find yourself being suspicious and skeptical, overly trusting, or somewhere in between?

3. Describe what it looks like to have a balance of a receptive heart with thoughtful searching out of the Scriptures.

TUESDAY

MEDITATE UPON GOD'S LAW

It is reverence that makes us persevering in our exposure to God's word. We recognize the limitations of an existence without God and we want to provide as many openings as possible for God to enter our life and to influence our living of it. — Michael Casey

How do wise believers develop the profound happiness the psalmist describes in today's reading? First, they are very careful about who they choose to listen to for counsel. They are wise in whom they imitate. They do not "follow the advice of the wicked, or take the path that sinners tread." Second, they avoid "the seat of scoffers." And what is a scoffer? Someone who laughs at things that aren't funny; someone who scoffs at the truth and ridicules the holy. A scoffer has lost any sense of reverence for God and the things of God.

Notice *the positive things* these happy people delight in. "Their delight is in the law of the LORD, and on his law they meditate day and night." Imagine yourself taking a long drink from a clean, cool stream on a hot day. As you quench your thirst, you sense your energy being restored; life is flowing into your body and your mind. The Scriptures represent just such a living stream. As we drink, we grow. Over time, we become "like trees planted by streams of water," living fruitful, joy-filled lives.

Read: Psalm 1:1–6

Reflect:

1. Give a practical example of "sitting in the seat of scoffers."

2. Describe what it means to delight in Scripture, in God's law and ways.

3. Those who are focused on God's Word are described as "trees planted by streams of water." How does this metaphor speak to you?

WEDNESDAY

READ GOD'S WORD TO ALL

I say to the LORD, "You are my God; give ear, O LORD, to the voice of my supplications." — Psalm 140:6

Our reading from Nehemiah is sad. How far the people of Israel had wandered from God. The nation had gone through a terrible exile, and now the leaders of the restored community—Nehemiah and Ezra—are calling the survivors of the exile to repentance and renewal.

Did you notice the first step in this process? Ezra, the scribe and priest, simply stands in the square and reads the Law of Moses to the people. Some of these listeners had never heard the Law before. Ezra provides them with an intense listening experience from early morning until midday and, with the help of other teachers, explains to the people what the text means.

Repentance, renewal, and refreshment—either individually or corporately—is ignited with a return to God's Word. Are there areas of your life where you sense the Lord inviting you to a significant change of heart or behavior?

New beginnings are always possible. And they often begin by turning our minds and our hearts to Scripture.

Read: Nehemiah 8:1-3; 9-12

Reflect:

1. When the people heard the Law of Moses, what caused them to weep?

2. Soon after the people "make great rejoicing, because they had understood the words that were declared to them." How does understanding lead to rejoicing?

3. Has there been a time in your life when a passage of Scripture has been an epiphany—like a light bulb coming on?

THURSDAY

〰〰〰〰〰〰

PRAY FOR SALVATION

... pray for us as well that God will open to us a door for the word ... so that I may reveal it clearly, as I should. — Colossians 4:3–4

Assyria was a terribly wicked and idolatrous nation—the power center of Jonah's world. It had wreaked havoc against Israel and its neighbors. This was the last place Jonah wanted to go. He hated the Assyrians and all they represented. So he fled from the Lord's command.

The Lord was not going to let Jonah escape. As you may know, Jonah was thrown overboard by sailors, swallowed by a huge fish, and vomited up on the shore. He had been delivered, and his mission to Assyria's great city of Nineveh lay before him.

For whom is the Lord asking you to pray for salvation and deliverance from sin and evil? Is the Lord opening a door for you to proclaim the wonder, beauty, and forgiveness of Christ?

God's mercy is wide and deep. He loves our enemies and calls us to do so too. Are there people we have crossed off our prayer list and consider too depraved for God to save, people we consider beyond the hope of salvation? Today's reading reminds us that nobody is beyond the love and mercy of God offered in Christ.

Read: Jonah 3:1-10

Reflect:

1. What does it say about God that he is willing to forgive and receive even the worst sinners?

2. How do we bless our enemies without condoning their actions?

3. Who have you been tempted to consider beyond the hope of salvation? Take a few minutes now to pray silently or aloud.

FRIDAY

PRAY GOD'S PRAISE

Praise the LORD! Praise God in his sanctuary; praise him in his mighty firmament! Praise him for his mighty deeds; praise him according to his surpassing greatness! — Psalm 150:1–2

In today's reading, we meet Hannah, a woman who was loved by her husband Elkanah but had been barren for years. Finally Hannah bears a son, Samuel, and she erupts in praise and thanksgiving.

Can you identify times in your life that reflect the pattern of Hannah? Indeed, perhaps you recall the birth of a child, the wedding of a son or daughter, a college graduation, or the provision of a job. God's provision often elicits our praise and thanks.

Might the Lord be asking you to remember times such as these? God's provision is always present, though sometimes unrecognized or forgotten by us. *Praise grows in a lengthened memory.* As today proceeds, take time to recall how God has provided for you over the years—in ways large and small.

Consider writing down on your calendar when future provision and blessing occurs. And as you do so, clearly—and perhaps loudly—express your praise to the Lord.

Read: 1 Samuel 2:1–3

Reflect:

1. In the midst of her praise, Hannah advises, "Let not arrogance come from your mouth." Why does she say this? How do praise and humility go together?

2. Sometimes we don't recognize God's provision and our praise disappears. Have there been times like these in your life?

3. Take a few moments to recall a time or two when God undoubtedly provided for you, perhaps in answer to a specific prayer. Write these down and offer a simple prayer of thanksgiving for each.

Week 3

Proclaim the Gospel with Words

MONDAY

PROCLAIM THE GOSPEL BOLDLY

Princes, kings, and other rulers of the world have used all their strength and cunning against the Church, yet it continues to endure and hold its own.
— John Foxe

In today's reading, we find Paul in prison, behind bars because of his bold and joyful proclamation of the gospel. While Paul's opponents rejoiced over the suffering he was experiencing in prison, events turned in a remarkable direction: Paul's Christian brothers and sisters were speaking the gospel more confidently.

Persecution attempts to use fear to crush a cause. In the case of the gospel, it often empowers the messengers and furthers the message. Why is that?

Read: Philippians 1:12–14

Reflect:

1. The passage says that people who learned of Paul's imprisonment spoke "with greater boldness and without fear." Why would persecution cause this to happen?

2. Consequences can follow when we speak boldly for a worthy cause like the gospel. Have you experienced this, positively or negatively?

TUESDAY

PROCLAIM THE GOSPEL WISELY

Who is wise and understanding among you? Show by your good life that your works are done with gentleness born of wisdom. — James 3:13

As Jesus prepares to send the apostles out to preach the gospel of the kingdom, he warns them to expect stiff opposition. "See," Jesus warns, "I am sending you out like sheep into the midst of wolves." And what do wolves do with sheep? They attack them, scatter them, and eat them.

Despite the dangers inherent in preaching the good news, Jesus sends his disciples out advising them to "be wise as serpents and innocent as doves."

Why would Jesus choose the snake and the dove as helpful illustrations in this puzzling teaching? In Jesus' day, snakes were described as wise, shrewd, cautious, and cunning. Serpents know how to live in a dangerous environment; they normally avoid danger rather than confronting it directly. Doves were viewed as innocent, harmless, and gentle. Doves were a sign of purity and sometimes of the presence of God.

So Jesus was teaching his disciples that as they preached the kingdom, they should act wisely in their environment, expect resistance and persecution, avoid offending people unnecessarily, and speak the truth with gentleness.

Read: Matthew 10:16–25

Reflect:

1. Knowing that Jesus can only act out of love—wanting and working for the good of others—why would he send out his disciples into danger? What good did Jesus know would result from their endangerment?

2. Did any wise, gentle people share the gospel with you in the manner Jesus describes? On the other hand, have you encountered any angry, self-righteous, judgmental people preaching the good news of the kingdom? What was the result?

WEDNESDAY

PROCLAIM THE GOSPEL WITH INTEGRITY

Let the gold of your life back up the currency of your words. — Unknown

Almost every week we hear of a Christian leader who has fallen into sin and whose ministry has been destroyed. For one leader, it's sexual sin. For another, it's mismanaged money. For yet another, power has been abused and people's lives have been destroyed.

It can be terribly discouraging to hear of the discrepancy between our leaders' words and actions. But before we accuse anyone else of a lack of integrity, we must ask ourselves a tough question: How do I behave when I think no one is watching? If someone followed me around 24/7—and I didn't know they were watching—what would they see? Are the words I speak and the life I live consistent?

Read: 1 Corinthians 10:31—11:1

Reflect:

1. People-pleasing—trying at all costs to be liked by everyone—can cause a person to live one way in public and another way in private. What is the difference between people-pleasing and what Paul talks about in this passage: "I try to please everyone . . . not seeking my own advantage"?

2. Paul said, "Be imitators of me, as I am of Christ." Why would he say this instead of simply "Be imitators of Christ"?

3. Wise living comes from a Christlike heart, not from strict rule-following. Still, we can put wise, practical habits into place. For example, some Christian leaders never travel alone because they want to be accountable to another Christian. What other kinds of practical habits can make it easier to live wisely?

THURSDAY

~~~~~~~~~~

PROCLAIM THE GOSPEL UNCEASINGLY

Paul was occupied with proclaiming the word. — Acts 18:5

As you read the accounts of Philip preaching in Samaria (Acts 8:4–8) or Paul preaching in Corinth (Acts 18:5–11), what immediately catches your attention? Wherever they go, these men unhesitatingly proclaim the gospel of the kingdom. Their minds and hearts are on fire for God. Why? They have experienced the power of the gospel in their own lives. They have encountered Jesus.

Not all of us are evangelists. Yet are there people in our lives who may be silently asking us, "Would you please explain to me why you believe that Jesus is the Lord, the promised Messiah?" The world is filled with people like these—people in our families, neighborhoods, towns, and cities.

Do you see them? Has Jesus brought you into a relationship where he longs for you to have a wise, gentle conversation? It may be someone you have known for a long time or someone you just met. Jesus urges us to be constant witnesses to the gospel of the kingdom, sometimes with our words and sometimes with our actions. The need is unceasing, and so, then, is our proclamation.

Read: Acts 8:4–8

Reflect:

1. The crowds "listened eagerly" to Philip (Acts 8:6). Why do you think they were so attentive to Philip's message?

2. Do you find it easy, or difficult, to talk with others about the gospel?

3. Take a moment to pray. Ask God to lead you to someone in the next week with whom you can share about Jesus. Then be alert for the opportunities that God provides.

FRIDAY

PROCLAIM THE GOSPEL COMPASSIONATELY

When [Jesus] saw the crowds, he had compassion for them, because they were harassed and helpless, like sheep without a shepherd. Then he said to his disciples, "The harvest is plentiful, but the laborers are few; therefore ask the Lord of the harvest to send out laborers into his harvest."
— Matthew 9:36–38

Isn't the encounter between the Ethiopian eunuch and Philip interesting? First, an angel of the Lord directs Philip to a specific spot: "the road that goes down from Jerusalem to Gaza." There Philip meets the official, who at that very moment is reading a passage from Isaiah that he doesn't understand. This seeker needs help in understanding the Scriptures, and Philip supplies just that.

Have you experienced God-directed encounters like the one between Philip and the Ethiopian? Pause for a moment and think back over the past month or so. Perhaps there was a time you sensed God's direction. "There's someone I'd like you to talk to. He needs me. Help him out on my behalf."

Read: Acts 8:26–39

Reflect:

1. Why do you think God uses Philip to explain the gospel instead of simply speaking directly to the Ethiopian? How might God's use of people to proclaim the gospel bring him more glory and pleasure?

2. Have you ever sensed God's guidance to talk to someone about the gospel?

Week 4

~~~~~~

Proclaim the Gospel with Actions

MONDAY

BE LIKE TABITHA

Whatever you do, in word or deed, do everything in the name of the Lord Jesus, giving thanks to God the Father through him. — Colossians 3:17

For some of us, talking comes easy. For others, action and service are easier. Tabitha sounds like the latter. "She was devoted to good works and acts of charity" (Acts 9:36). Shortly before Peter prayed for Tabitha and she was raised from the dead, other widows showed him "tunics and other clothing that [Tabitha] had made while she was with them" (Acts 9:39). This clothing was not for Tabitha's own wardrobe. No, it was for widows and other people in need.

Some of us might feel afraid or inadequate when we think of verbally sharing the gospel of the kingdom with others. Thankfully, Tabitha's example can be an encouragement to us. Her acts, not her words, were what people remembered about her and what impressed people.

Yes, the Lord needs our mouths to speak on his behalf. But he also needs our hands. As Tabitha sat at her loom, weaving garments for the poor, Jesus was weaving through her. And the kingdom of God was extended.

Read: Acts 9:36–42

Reflect:

1. Is it truly possible to "preach the gospel without words," or are some words necessary?

2. What might those for whom speaking comes naturally teach those for whom service comes naturally? And the other way around?

TUESDAY

BE LIKE BARNABAS

Barnabas himself walked in the way of light. He did not exalt himself, but saw himself as a servant. He was not full of himself, nor was his head swollen with big plans. He just did what needed to be done—an excellent model of service for us all. — Bert Ghezzi

Attention to need—material and spiritual—characterized Barnabas. Overshadowed by Paul, he served humbly. Sometimes our love for big plans can paralyze us. If we aren't doing something "big," we feel that our efforts to serve God are less important or less fruitful than those who are writing best-selling books or standing on a stage speaking to thousands.

Not so. At our funeral, those who love us will not be remembering whether we wrote many books or spoke many words. Our spouses will remember whether we loved them and remained faithful to them. Our children will remember if we spent time with them and invested our lives in them.

Richard Foster writes, "The big deal is the little deal." Barnabas got this right. He was known as an encourager and a giver. Do you know people like that? They don't want to draw attention to themselves. They prefer to stay in the background unless God pushes them into the limelight. They carefully observe what's going on, and when a need arises, they are quick to respond.

Read: Acts 4:36–37

Reflect:

1. Have you ever felt discouraged that you aren't doing something "big" in your life? Why?

2. What day-to-day needs—unknown to most, but known by God and those closest to you—might God be asking you to be faithful with?

WEDNESDAY

BE LIKE CORNELIUS

I am afraid that as the serpent deceived Eve by its cunning, your thoughts will be led astray from a sincere and pure devotion to Christ.
— *2 Corinthians 11:3*

Consider the words Luke uses to describe Cornelius in today's reading. Cornelius was a "devout man." He "feared God." He "gave alms generously to the people." He "prayed constantly to God." Devotion. Reverence. Generosity. Prayer. Which of these words touches you most deeply?

Some of us may sense that our *devotion* to God—our loyalty, faithfulness, commitment, and allegiance—needs to be strengthened.

Others might be aware that our *reverence* for God must grow. We ask ourselves, "How can awe for God increase in my mind and heart?"

Still others may realize we have failed to be *generous* toward God and neighbor. In repentance, we ask the Lord to renew our compassion for those in need around us.

Finally, some may discern that God is calling us to a deeper *prayer* life. As Richard Foster writes, God "is inviting you—and me—to come home, to come home to that for which we were created. His arms are stretched out wide to receive us. His heart is enlarged to take us in." The pathway home is prayer.

Read: Acts 10:1–4

Reflect:

1. The angel said to Cornelius, "Your prayers and your alms have ascended as a memorial before God." What does this say about God's attention to our prayers and generosity?

2. Which of Cornelius's character traits do you wish to deepen in your own life? Take a few minutes to pray about these areas.

THURSDAY

〜〜〜〜〜〜

BE LIKE LYDIA

Be doers of the word, and not merely hearers who deceive themselves.
— *James 1:22*

As you read today's text, take note of how Lydia is described as listening. "Lydia, a worshiper of God, was listening to us. . . . The Lord opened her heart to listen eagerly to what was said by Paul" (Acts 16:14). Lydia's intense, eager listening birthed faith in her heart and the generous offer of her home to Paul as he ministered in Philippi.

Two Greek words for listening are used here. The first word carries the idea of hearing audible sounds with the ear. The second word goes deeper. It means "to turn the mind to, to be attentive to, to apply oneself to." This is true listening, the kind that includes action and obedience.

Read: Acts 16:11–15

Reflect:

1. What is the difference between simply hearing someone—perhaps even nodding in approval—and truly listening in such a way that leads to action?

2. Notice that at first Lydia "was listening," but then "The Lord opened her heart to listen eagerly." What does this tell you about God's role in helping people listen to his Word? Do you think there is anything we can do to help ourselves and others to "listen eagerly"?

FRIDAY

BE LIKE THE CHURCH IN PHILADELPHIA

To the present hour we are hungry and thirsty, we are poorly clothed and beaten and homeless, and we grow weary from the work of our own hands. When reviled, we bless; when persecuted, we endure; when slandered, we speak kindly. — 1 Corinthians 4:11–13

As our focus on the Word-centered life closes, let's look at an example of a group of Jesus-followers who stayed faithful to his word.

Christ offers special commendation to the church at Philadelphia in the book of Revelation. What characterizes this praiseworthy church? They patiently endured in the midst of great trials.

When we face situations today that seem too difficult to endure, we may be sorely tempted to deny what we know to be true about God and Jesus. Perhaps marriage or family situations are rocky. Perhaps a battle with sickness goes on and on.

The Lord says to us in the midst of our struggles, "Endure for me. I will never desert you. I understand. I am with you. Your suffering is not foreign to me. Remember my little church in Philadelphia. I was with them. I am with you. Persevere with me in this present evil age. I promise that the outcome of your faith will be honor, glory, and life eternal. I will return. Suffer with me, then, for this little while."

Read: Revelation 3:7–13

Reflect:

1. Are you currently facing situations that demand great faith and endurance?

2. Have you ever been tempted to deny your deepest beliefs? If so, when?

3. If Jesus were to say a word of encouragement to you, what do you think it would be?

Week 1

*How Do We Become More Like Jesus
in All Aspects of Life?*

MONDAY

THE INCARNATE SON

Theology is never an end, but is always a means for understanding and developing transformed living. — Thomas Langford

For the next two months we will explore what it means to become more like Jesus in all aspects of life. It's tempting to separate our "spiritual lives" (everything pertaining to God) from our "material lives" (everything pertaining to our daily living—the world of "matter"). But as we'll see, the material world is important to God. Nowhere is that clearer than in the incarnation (God becoming human in the person of Jesus).

Before Jesus was born at Bethlehem, he existed as the Son of God in a wonderful communion of love with the Father and the Holy Spirit. Then, at a particular point in time, the Son entered our world as the son of Mary, fully human. In a wonderful movement of divine love, "The Word became flesh and lived among us" (John 1:14). Or as *The Message* puts it, "The Word became flesh and blood, and moved into the neighborhood."

Read: John 1:14–18

Reflect:

1. Why is it important for us to have an image of the invisible God?

2. At the start of this devotional, we worked on gaining a right understanding of God. It's a good thing to revisit. For you, does God the Father—in his actions, emotions, personality—look like Jesus? Or do God the Father and Jesus seem different?

TUESDAY

GOD AFFIRMS THE GOODNESS OF MATTER

God is the cause of things through his mind and will, like an artist of a work of art. — Leonardo Boff

In Genesis 1, God announces the goodness of creation. As each day of creation passes, we hear the resounding phrase: "And God saw that it was good." Quite evidently, God delights in creation. God loves to create. God likes matter. God loves "stuff."

Have you ever had a chance to look at the images only an electron microscope can see? The lens of the microscope makes visible exquisitely beautiful crystalline structures that for thousands of years were hidden from humans. And yet there they were—breathtaking beauties that only God could see and in which God delighted.

Pause for a moment to ponder all that God has created: mountains, stars, oceans, starfish, eagles, monarch butterflies, elephants, diamonds, cypress trees. Thousands of pages would not suffice to list all the wonders God has created. Why has God done so? Simply put, God loves to use matter to produce great beauty and diversity. And God will never stop loving to do so.

Read: Genesis 1:28–31

Reflect:

1. God delights in creation and matter. What does that mean for how we relate to and treat the created world, animals, and people made in his image?

2. People are made in the image of God, and God is a creator. What do you find joy in creating? When you create, do you feel more alive and connected to God? How so?

WEDNESDAY

THE SPIRIT HARMONIZES THE SPIRITUAL AND MATERIAL

Everything created by God is good. — 1 Timothy 4:4

Let's return to Genesis. Notice the role the Holy Spirit plays as God speaks all creation into existence. Bringing order out of chaos, "The Spirit of God was hovering over the waters" (Genesis 1:2 NIV). (NRSV translates this phrase, "A wind from God swept over the face of the waters.") In Genesis 2:7, God breathes into the first human the breath of life.

The Spirit is giving value to matter. Our bodies aren't something to be escaped but something to be sanctified—made holy and purified. God is very concerned about how we live as embodied creatures. We are not angels who do not have bodies. Image-bearers have bodies, brains, blood, hands, and feet, and God uses all this "matter" to further his purposes in our lives and to facilitate our spiritual growth.

Matter matters! Matter is a help rather than a hindrance to a healthy spiritual life, a life empowered by the Holy Spirit.

Read: Genesis 1:1–5

Reflect:

1. Do you think of the spiritual and the material working in harmony or working against each other?

2. First John 2:15 says, "Do not love the world or the things in the world." What kind of love is this referring to? What is a healthy love of matter?

THURSDAY

THE IMPLICATIONS OF THE INCARNATION

When you use your life for God's glory, everything you do can become an act of worship. — Rick Warren

In Jesus, God took on the form of a human. And for about thirty years—nine-tenths of his life—the life of Jesus was, as far as we can tell, quite normal. His brief miracle-working ministry was preceded by a long period of mundane life. He lived in obscurity. He likely worked in his earthly father's trade of carpentry. He did all the things humans do, and he did them for the glory of God.

Want further proof beyond Genesis 1 that God works through matter and creation? We need look no further than Jesus. He is the greatest evidence that God values our bodies and our everyday actions.

Read: 1 Corinthians 10:31

Reflect:

1. Why do you think Jesus spent so much time in obscurity and living a relatively normal life before entering public ministry?

2. In practical terms, how do you "eat or drink" or work or play for the glory of God? What does that look like?

FRIDAY

THERE IS NO DIVISION BETWEEN THE SECULAR AND THE SACRED

We, the ordinary people of the streets, believe with all our might that this street, this world, where God has placed us, is our place of holiness.
— *Madeleine Delbrel*

Have you ever found yourself dividing your world up into spiritual practices and places and unspiritual ones? For example, we might think it "spiritual" to go to church or read a Christian book but "unspiritual" to go to a football game or read a book on hairstyling. Why do we divide our world up in such a way? Did Jesus?

We find Jesus, surely the most spiritual person who has ever lived, providing wine at a wedding, enjoying meals with friends (and sometimes enemies), fully engaged with nature, providing a meal of bread and fish—all while continuing to attend synagogue and making regular trips to Jerusalem to worship at the temple.

He didn't divide life into "worldly activities" and "spiritual activities." Why? "All things have been created through him and for him" (Colossians 1:16). If so, there is nothing good that would not interest him— *nothing.*

Read: Colossians 1:15–17

Reflect:

1. Does it feel strange, or natural, that Jesus is interested in all of life? Why do you think that might be?

2. Is there any area of life—work, play, hobby—that you've considered separate from God? If so, take a few moments to pray silently to invite God into that area. Perhaps a prayer like "God, I repent for thinking that you aren't interested in [some activity], and I want to do that activity with and through you."

Week 2

~~~~~~~~

No Divide between Sacred and Secular

MONDAY

JESUS HEALED ON THE SABBATH

Shabbat [Sabbath] is like nothing else. Time as we know it does not exist for these twenty-four hours, and the worries of the week soon fall away. A feeling of joy appears. — Nana Fink

The Sabbath day was provided by God for rest and worship. Does this mean that only "spiritual" things can be done on the Sabbath?

Jesus often healed people on the Sabbath. Why? For one thing, he was teaching the Pharisees that their Sabbath-day restrictions missed the point of why God had established the Sabbath in the first place.

Yes, Jesus taught, *the Sabbath is a time to worship.* But the Sabbath was also a time to *rest*, a God-provided time to experience a pause from the normal patterns of work engaged in during the other six days of the week.

Rest also included, in Jesus' perspective, the restoration of health. As Jesus healed on the Sabbath day he was acting out an important lesson for God's kingdom-dwellers. "I have provided this day for you. Rest in it. Relax in it. Worship in it. Be restored in it. I did not create the Sabbath to be another burden for you. It is a joy to be anticipated, a day to be made well, a day to be restored and renewed."

Read: Luke 6:1–11

Reflect:

1. Do you find it difficult to practice the rhythm of a Sabbath day? Why?

2. What are some ways that you bring patterns of rest and renewal into your Sabbath?

3. Challenge yourself to experience Sabbath in a different way, being open to the ways the Lord wants to be with you "in the flesh" during this time.

TUESDAY

JESUS' DISCIPLES GLEANED ON THE SABBATH

The streams of religion run deep or shallow, according as the banks of the Sabbath are kept up or neglected. — Matthew Henry

In today's reading, once again the Jewish religious leaders are upset with Jesus. Why? Again, Jesus is allowing his disciples to do something on the Sabbath that the Pharisees had classified as "unspiritual."

Notice how Jesus responds: with Scripture. David and his troops entered the tabernacle and ate the consecrated bread, which only the priests were allowed to eat. Meeting the human need was more important than keeping the law of the temple.

Jesus then makes a more important point. He—the Son of Man—is Lord of the Sabbath. It is his day, and it is he who decides what occurs on it. For the disciples to move fully and restfully into the Sabbath, they needed to eat. So he allowed them to glean and rub the grain kernels with their hands.

Jesus never denied that the Sabbath day was special; he simply reclaimed, as its Lord, its original intent. The Sabbath isn't a day of rules that people were created to follow. It's a day created *for* people, a day of rest and worship

Read: Mark 2:23–28

Reflect:

1. Have you ever needed to act in a countercultural way to live as a disciple of Jesus? What did that feel like when others confronted you?

2. Jesus is the Lord of the Sabbath. Ask him to show you how to practice rest and worship in a way that pleases him.

3. As you work to alleviate hunger, does the spiritual aspect of your vocation ever get drowned out by the practical considerations?

WEDNESDAY

JESUS MADE BREAD A SACRED EVENT

"Like the sacramental use of water and bread and wine, friendship takes what's common in human experience and turns it into something holy."
— *Eugene Peterson*

At the end of Jesus' life, on the very night he was betrayed and arrested, Jesus had a special meal with his disciples. During the meal, Jesus took bread and wine, the staples of life for every Jew, and set them apart for a sacred use. Taking a loaf of bread, Jesus broke it and said, "This is my body, which is given for you." Taking a cup of wine, Jesus said, "This cup that is poured out for you is the new covenant in my blood."

Here again, we see a very important principle at work. God delights in using matter—in this case, bread and wine—to communicate his presence to us. In the hands of God incarnate—the one who had created bread and wine for the needs and the joy of his image-bearers—what is used for common use becomes sacred. Through the means of matter, God's blessing is given. Here we see the *incarnational principle* clearly at work. God the Son, now the incarnate Jesus, provides very tangible, spiritual nourishment for his embodied image-bearers.

Read: Luke 22:14–20

Reflect:

1. What are some "common" spaces or things in your life that God has made sacred through meeting you in them in a special way?

2. How does participating in the remembrance of Communion shape your identity in Christ?

THURSDAY

~~~~~~~~~~

JESUS CURSED A FIG TREE

How pitiful the man ... who has all the outward appearance of leading a fruitful life, but is not sincerely attempting to yield fruit! — Josemaria Escrivá

The cursing of the fig tree can seem confusing, strange, nonsensical. Why would Jesus curse a tree for not bearing fruit, especially if the time for fruit-bearing was not at hand?

Once again, Jesus is borrowing from nature to make a graphic point about the spiritual life of the nation of Israel. For whatever reason, a tree that should have been a fruit-bearer remained sterile, barren, unproductive. Something was amiss.

So too, in this case, with the nation of Israel. In the Bible, Israel is often described as God's vine, God's fig tree. Israel had been given everything it needed to bear fruit. And it had failed to do so. Judgment was soon to arrive.

Isn't it striking that in today's reading Jesus chooses a part of the natural world he had created to illustrate what is happening in the life of Israel itself?

Read: Mark 11:12–14, 20–21

Reflect:

1. Why do you think Jesus chose to make this particular parable (see Luke 13:6–9) come to life for his disciples? Why was this an important lesson for them to see "in the flesh"?

2. What were the leaves on the fig tree hiding? In Genesis 3:7, Adam and Eve used fig leaves to try to hide their nakedness from God. How are these related?

3. Are you in a flourishing season or a barren season? Prayerfully ask God to reveal what you need in order to be fruitful for the kingdom.

FRIDAY

JESUS COOKED BREAKFAST

For Jesus, his physical body wasn't just something that he "wore" while on earth, but part of his very being. And for us, our bodies are not something solely for this life which we forever discard at the time of death.
— *Chris Singer*

Today we find ourselves on the shore of the Sea of Galilee. So much has happened between Jesus and his disciples. They had failed terribly. They all had fled when Jesus was arrested. Most horribly, Peter had denied his friend and Lord three times. How could they ever be welcomed back into fellowship with Jesus? Jesus takes the initiative.

What does Jesus do? Not only does he direct the disciples to a huge catch of fish, but he waits for them on shore. And what has he prepared? A meal. He is restoring table fellowship with his friends who had failed him so seriously. It is as though Jesus is saying, "Yes, we need to talk. You've made some serious mistakes. But first let's eat together. I've prepared some good fish and bread for you. We're going to begin our friendship anew. I have lots in store for you all."

A charcoal fire. Fish. Bread. Fellowship. New beginnings.

Read: John 21:1–14

Reflect:

1. Why do you think it was important for Jesus to draw the disciples' efforts into this breakfast? What did that communicate to his disciples?

2. Does your perception of Jesus carry with it the weight of matter? Will you be shocked to see Jesus presiding over a wedding feast— eating and drinking in heaven?

3. What are some memorable meals you have shared with others? What do you remember most about them? Why?

Week 3

~~~~~~

Becoming More Like Jesus in Our Public Actions

MONDAY

WHAT DOES IT MEAN TO ACT JUSTLY?

Never forget that justice is what love looks like in public. — Cornel West

"What does the LORD require of you? To act justly . . ." (Micah 6:8 NIV). To "act justly" is to act in accordance with what a relationship requires. For example, a college professor can act justly or unjustly toward his students. If he prepares well for class, teaches well, grades fairly, and invests himself in his students, he is acting justly toward them. He is doing what a "just" or "righteous" professor should do in his relationship with his students. If, however, he is a lazy, uncaring, unjust professor, he won't be prepared for class, will teach poorly, will spend little time with his students, and will grade unfairly. He is an unjust professor.

Of course, the same is true for students. Hardworking, studious students are acting in a "just" manner toward their professor and each other. Lazy, inattentive students are acting "unjustly."

The same dynamic applies to all public relationships. You have just medical doctors and unjust ones. Just lawyers and unjust ones. Righteous employers and unrighteous ones. Righteous employees and unrighteous ones.

When we act justly and receive justice from others, societies flourish. And just the opposite is true. Injustice always increases human misery. Always.

Read: Micah 6:8

Reflect:

1. If you had to come up with a one-sentence definition of "justice," what would it be?

2. Think over the past week. Is there an instance of injustice you witnessed or experienced—or maybe even helped to cause? Consider possible steps you could take to move those situations toward justice. Then commit them to the Lord in prayer.

TUESDAY

WHAT DOES IT MEAN TO LOVE MERCY?

Go and learn what this means, "I desire mercy, not sacrifice." For I have come to call not the righteous but sinners. — Matthew 9:13

"What does the LORD require of you? To . . . love mercy . . ." (Micah 6:8 NIV). What characterizes a person who "loves mercy"? Think of Jesus' relationship with the apostle Peter. Peter utterly failed Jesus at his time of greatest need. Surely Peter should have been judged and punished. After all, judgment and punishment are what our moral failures deserve. Right?

The person who loves mercy values relationship more than punishment. Today we look again at John 21. Pay attention to the mercy that Jesus showed Peter. First, Jesus prepares a meal for his disciples. He is inviting them back into fellowship. *He wants to be in relationship with them despite their failure and sin.*

Second, he restores Peter. Peter had denied Jesus three times. So Jesus asks Peter three times if he loves him. Peter expresses his love for Jesus in terms of friendship (Greek, *phileo*), but Jesus asks him to deepen his love (Greek, *agapao*).

This conversation is filled with mercy, for Jesus loves mercy. Rather than punish, Jesus forgives, restores, and then releases Peter into his vocation as an apostle.

Read: John 21:9–17

Reflect:

1. Do you think it was merciful for Jesus to ask Peter if he loved him three times? Why or why not?

2. Someone once defined mercy as "compassion for those in need— regardless of the reason for the need." Do you find it easier to be merciful toward an innocent victim than toward someone whose own poor choices have created his or her problems? Is mercy still required, even if it's the second case? Why or why not?

WEDNESDAY

WHAT DOES IT MEAN TO WALK HUMBLY?

To be humble is to live as close to the truth as possible. — Ignatius of Loyola

"What does the LORD require of you? To . . . walk humbly . . ." (Micah 6:8). When you think of a humble person, what characteristics come to mind? Someone who is quiet, withdrawn, and prone to let others run over her?

Consider this description of Moses, the great prophet who led Israel out of Egyptian bondage: "Now the man Moses was very humble, more so than anyone else on the face of the earth" (Numbers 12:3). Is it surprising to hear Moses described that way?

Now consider Jesus, especially the last hours of his life: his betrayal, arrest, trial, and crucifixion. At any point in these horrific events, Jesus could have called upon legions of angels to deliver him from his agony. Yet as he was mocked, scourged, and nailed to a cross, he remained silent. Why? He knew who he was: God incarnate. And he knew what he was here to do: rescue humanity through his death and resurrection.

He showed us that true humility isn't self-loathing or timidity. It is walking in the truth and agreeing with God. It is becoming obedient to God—no matter the cost.

Read: Philippians 2:5–11

Reflect:

1. Were you raised to admire humility or to try to avoid it?

2. Think of a situation—perhaps at work, in your family, or in your church—where you feel an urge to prove yourself. If you could "empty yourself" like Jesus, how might you behave differently in that situation?

3. Is there a way to know your strengths clearly and still be humble?

THURSDAY

WHAT DOES IT MEAN TO WALK WITH GOD?

As you walk with Jesus, resting your head on His heart, you will learn to know His Word, His will, and His ways. You will want to obey Him, not out of forced compliance, but out of heartfelt connection. Your joy will abound as you remain in His love. — Sue Detweiler

We have worked through phrases found in Micah 6:8. Today we ask what it looks like to not just "walk humbly," but to "walk humbly with your God."

The Bible says it is possible to live one's life not only thinking about, worshiping, and obeying God, but walking alongside him. In the Old Testament, Enoch "walked with God" (Genesis 5:24) and God promised his people, "I will walk among you" (Leviticus 26:12). In the New Testament, Jesus takes it even further, promising that "the Spirit of truth . . . abides with you, and he will be in you" (John 14:17).

God does not watch us from a distance, but comes alongside and invites us to take each step with him. Saint Patrick caught a glimpse of this in his prayer: "Christ with me, Christ before me, Christ behind me, Christ in me, Christ beneath me, Christ above me, Christ on my right, Christ on my left, Christ when I lie down, Christ when I sit down, Christ when I arise . . ."

Read: 2 John 4–6

Reflect:

1. What does it mean to "walk with God," or as John puts it, to "walk in the truth"?

2. John mentions "walking according to [God's] commandments." How do we do this in a way that is life-giving rather than legalistic?

3. Consider writing out the words from St. Patrick's prayer above and going for a walk while repeating those phrases ("Christ with me," "Christ before me," etc.) with each step.

FRIDAY

WHAT DOES IT MEAN TO LIVE FULLY?

We glorify God by living lives that honor Him. — Billy Graham

The Lord invites us to act justly, to love mercy, to walk humbly, and to walk with him. These are invitations that are not limited to our "personal" or "religious" life. They require us to live out every facet of our lives in step with God—our jobs, our families, our hobbies, our roles in the community. Are we acting justly when we drive in traffic? Are we merciful when our neighbors are rude? Are we walking humbly with God when we are inching forward in a frustratingly long line at the market?

Although we must each make a choice to walk with Jesus, that personal decision always has public implications. The more we walk in step with God, the more we can expect justice, mercy, and humility to become a part of every single facet of our lives.

Read: Romans 12:1–21

Reflect:

1. Romans 12 gives a remarkably complete picture of what a life lived fully in step with God looks like. Write down a list of the characteristics described. Does anything on the list jump out to you as something the Spirit is inviting you to cultivate more fully in your life? If so, circle it.

2. Spend some time praying for the characteristics you circled—ask the Spirit to work within you so that your lives come to resemble the list from Romans 12 more and more.

Week 4

~~~~~~

Becoming More Like Jesus in Our Relationships

MONDAY

~~~~~~

WHAT DOES RIGHT RELATIONSHIP WITH GOD LOOK LIKE?

The basic purpose of prayer is not to bend God's will to mine but to mold my will into his. — Timothy Keller

Most of us resist the Holy Spirit in some way. We put up a barrier that excludes God, even though we are his children. We might think of this as an invisible shield, an extra layer of protective skin that we cover ourselves with to keep God out.

This shield may be in place as a defense mechanism against past pain, shame, or disappointment. It may simply be our strongly bent will to have things our way. Whatever the cause, the result is that we don't fully experience the life God intends for us now—a life connected to God in the midst of everyday joys and sorrows.

Jesus, on the other hand, had zero resistance to the Holy Spirit—even when it was extremely costly and painful. May it be so with us.

Read: Luke 22:39–42

Reflect:

1. Who do you know who regularly obeys God in ways that may seem risky or difficult? What is the result of obedience in that person's life and in the lives of others?

2. Why do you think we often resist the Holy Spirit in some way or hold parts of ourselves back from God?

3. If you sense any "invisible shield" you have up with God, take a few moments to pray, "God, I remove this barrier; I ask you to penetrate my life and make me whole."

TUESDAY

WHAT DOES RIGHT RELATIONSHIP WITH OURSELVES LOOK LIKE?

It is evident that man never attains to a true self-knowledge until he has previously contemplated the face of God, and come down after such contemplation to look into himself. — John Calvin

For Christians, right relationship with ourselves begins with knowing God. Early in this devotional, we talked about the fact that what we believe about God is the most important thing about us. Why? Because the truth about God allows us to face the truth about ourselves.

When we know God's holiness, character, beauty, gentleness, and grace, we can face ourselves honestly without despair or self-condemnation. We can forgive ourselves because God in Christ Jesus has forgiven us. We can lose our lives—lay down that burden of always having to provide for ourselves and map out a plan to get what we want—because we trust that Jesus, the Good Shepherd, will provide our needs. We relinquish self-preservation, self-punishment, self-righteousness, self-hatred. Quite simply, we relinquish self. And in the wondrous economy of God, the more we do that—the more we lose our life for Jesus and his kingdom—the more we find our life and become our true selves.

Read: Matthew 10:39

Reflect:

1. Do you agree that knowing God comes before knowing self, or do you think it's the other way around?

2. Jesus says that we need to "lose our life." Thinking ahead to your day and week, are there any areas in which you may be tempted to hold onto your life—for example, your reputation, work, or money? Write it down and ask God for grace to surrender this area.

WEDNESDAY

WHAT DOES RIGHT RELATIONSHIP WITH FAMILY LOOK LIKE?

When we have sat at Jesus' feet through all four Gospels, and he has won our trust, and our allegiance, and our utter devotion, the overwhelming sense we have is that everything has changed. No relationship will ever be the same again. — John Piper

Those who come to Scripture for neatly packaged answers will be disappointed. Instead, the text gives us a rich tapestry of law, story, poetry, and parable—sometimes in tension with each other. The wise person holds seemingly contradictory passages together before God and asks for wisdom to understand.

Today's passages represent two such examples. How can "hate father and mother" and "honor father and mother" go together?

The first of the Ten Commandments in Exodus 20 is "You shall have no other gods before me." Why? Is God arrogant or insecure? Not at all. This command, like all of God's commands, flows out of God's desire for our good. You see, God knows that anything besides him that is elevated to the first position in our life—even family—will ultimately fail us. Our love for Jesus must have no equal. Loving Jesus supremely means all other loves look like hate in comparison. What's amazing is that putting Jesus first actually opens the way for us to truly love and serve our family. We serve our family—change diapers, wash dishes, work our job—for the sake of God instead of for our own sake or to be loved by our family in return.

Read: Luke 14:26; Ephesians 6:1–3

Reflect:

1. Have you heard Jesus' words about the need to "hate" your family before? What have you understood that to mean?

2. How does putting God first help us to better love others, including our family?

THURSDAY

〰〰〰〰

WHAT DOES RIGHT RELATIONSHIP WITH STRANGERS LOOK LIKE?

Our citizenship is in heaven, and it is from there that we are expecting a Savior, the Lord Jesus Christ. — Philippians 3:20

In today's text, God commands his people not to oppress the stranger, the foreigner, the alien. After all, the Israelites themselves were once foreigners in Egypt.

In an age of extreme nationalism and fear of the other, it is worth reminding ourselves that our citizenship is in heaven. Our allegiance, first and foremost, is to the kingdom of God and to Jesus its King. We are ambassadors of that kingdom here on earth. That doesn't mean we can't love our country and even defend it from malicious attacks. But it does mean that we are called to welcome the stranger and befriend the foreigner, especially those in distress. For as citizens of heaven, Christians are themselves foreigners here on earth.

Read: Leviticus 19:33–34

Reflect:

1. Why was it so important to God that the Israelites welcomed strangers? Why is it important that we do so?

2. How do we maintain healthy boundaries with aliens, both personally and nationally, while still welcoming them in appropriate ways?

FRIDAY

WHAT DOES RIGHT RELATIONSHIP WITH CREATION LOOK LIKE?

The earth is the LORD's and all that is in it, the world, and those who live in it. — Psalm 24:1

God gave humans dominion over the earth (Genesis 1:26). We can choose to rule poorly, as dictators who pillage the earth for our own gain, or we can choose to rule wisely, as stewards who respect and care for the earth as God calls us to do. The benefits of the former are instant but eventually run out—if not our lifetime, surely in our grandchildren's. The benefits of the latter—of being good stewards—grow slowly and flourish over time. Today's passage gives practical instructions on one aspect of how to do this.

It's worth noting that, as with anything good, environmentalism can degrade into legalism. The cure for this is the same as the cure for other kinds of legalism: friendship with God. Staying connected with God and his heart allows us to care for the earth out of joy rather than out of obligation or fear.

Read: Leviticus 25:1–7

Reflect:

1. Why did God command his people to let the land rest every seven years?

2. What is a legalistic example of caring for creation? What is a healthy example?

Week 1

~~~~~~

Partnering with the Trinity

MONDAY

AFFIRMING THE GOODNESS OF CREATION

God saw everything that he had made, and indeed, it was very good.
— Genesis 1:31

In today's reading, the word good occurs repeatedly. Dry land and seas, plants and seeds, sun, moon, and stars—all are good. Birds and creeping things, cattle and even sea monsters—God says, "It's good." Human beings, made in the image of God, are good. Indeed, all creation is described as "very good."

How can we partner with God to affirm the goodness of creation, a goodness so clearly declared by the writer of Genesis? Perhaps you might study astronomy. The wonder, beauty, and complexity of the universe are breathtaking. Or you might learn more about God's oceans. Or God's animals.

Some might respond, "I don't have enough time for such things. I want to devote my time to 'spiritual' matters." The main point of today's reflection is this: to affirm the goodness of God's creation *is a spiritual matter and a key spiritual discipline.*

Read: Genesis 1:1–31

Reflect:

1. If God called all of creation good, how might that affect how we treat it?

2. Have you ever experienced the beauty of God's creation in such a way that caused you to worship God? Share a story or two.

3. Does studying space, oceans, or animals sound like a waste of time to you? Why or why not?

TUESDAY

UNDERSTANDING OUR STATUS AS IMAGE-BEARERS

For whatever was the form and expression that was then given to the clay, it was in God's thoughts that Christ would one day become man. — Tertullian

When you look in the mirror, whose face do you see? Most of us would answer "My own." And of course we would be right.

The creation accounts in Genesis 1–2 picture things somewhat differently. Genesis 1:26–27 describes human beings—male and female—as created in the image of God. When we look at God, as God's image-bearers, we can see our own reflection.

Human beings are unique. No animal in the Genesis creation accounts is called God's image-bearer. When we move to the New Testament, things get even more specific. Paul introduces us to the perfect image-bearer, Jesus himself. "He is the image of the invisible God," Paul writes in Colossians 1:15.

To be God's image-bearer is both a gift and a calling. It is the gift of being able to reason and choose. And it is the call to grow ever more deeply into the perfect image of the incarnate Son. *Jesus shows us what we have been created to be.* If you want to see what a real human being looks like, look at Jesus.

Read: Genesis 1:26–27; 2:1–7

Reflect:

1. Reflect on the phrase "made in the image of God." What specific aspects of God's image did Adam and Eve reflect that the rest of creation didn't?

2. How does being made in God's image affect the way we treat and care for people?

3. Take a few moments to pray around this theme. You might pray something like "God, thank you for making _____ in your image. What a wonder that you would give that gift. Help him/her/me to become more like the perfect image-bearer, Jesus."

WEDNESDAY

LIVING WELL AS EMBODIED SELVES

I appeal to you therefore, brothers and sisters, by the mercies of God, to present your bodies as a living sacrifice, holy and acceptable to God, which is your spiritual worship. — Romans 12:1

The term embodied self might at first glance seem strange or unfamiliar. It simply means that we are a whole person—body and soul.

God loves bodies. Jesus' body was raised from the dead, and our bodies will also be raised (1 Corinthians 15:50–57). We are not simply souls or spirits. We possess souls, but our souls indwell bodies—bodies that we can use to live well in God's kingdom.

When we invite Jesus into our lives, the Holy Spirit takes up residence in our bodies (1 Corinthians 6:19). Think of the fruit of the Spirit mentioned by Paul in today's reading. Every characteristic in Paul's list manifests itself through our bodies. Loving people demonstrate their love through how they conduct themselves in their bodies; the same can be said for joy, peace, patience, kindness, generosity, faithfulness, gentleness, and self-control.

So Christian spiritual life is *embodied spiritual life*. That is, *our bodies are the means by which we manifest the reality of God's kingdom.*

Read: Galatians 5:22–23

Reflect:

1. Why is it important to think of ourselves as a whole person—body and soul—rather than as a soul that will escape the body at death?

2. Practically speaking, how can you "present your body as a living sacrifice" (Romans 12:1) today?

THURSDAY

~~~~~~~~~~~

COOPERATING WITH THE TRIUNE GOD

You have never seen people more active than those who have been set on fire by the grace of God. — Dallas Willard

Spiritual growth is not a passive affair. As we saw yesterday, we have been created with human bodies and we can decide how we are going to live in them as we receive God's grace and the power of the Holy Spirit.

In today's reading, consider carefully the active phrases Paul uses to describe the process of spiritual transformation: "Put to death." "Get rid of all such things." "Clothe yourselves." "Bear with one another." "Forgive each other." "Do everything in the name of the Lord Jesus, giving thanks to God." Every phrase shows the role we play in responding to the grace we have received in Jesus. Paul beckons us to respond to and cooperate with God's gracious work within us.

Read: Colossians 3:1–17

Reflect:

1. In past devotionals, we've talked about how grace is opposed to earning but isn't opposed to effort. This is a good time to review— What's the difference between cooperating with God (effort) and striving for God's approval (earning)?

2. Three times in this passage Paul refers to "clothing yourselves." Why does he use that metaphor? What, practically, does this mean for us?

3. Paul also mentions being thankful multiple times. Take a few minutes now to write down two specific things that you are thankful for from the last month.

FRIDAY

REVISITING THE SACRED/SECULAR DIVIDE

The biblical message is not just about some isolated part of life labeled "religion" or "church life."… We don't have to accept an inner fragmentation between our faith and the rest of life. — Nancy Pearcey

There is no area of human life that is separate from God's concern and care. None.

Yet, do you ever find yourself dividing your life into the secular and the sacred? When we fall into the secular-sacred divide, we tend to separate or distinguish things, people, and places that we consider to be *sacred* from those we consider to be *secular*. We consider certain vocations or jobs to be "spiritual"—pastoral ministry, for instance—and others to be separate from God's life or interest.

The Bible simply doesn't support this divide. In today's reading, Peter urges his readers to "serve one another with whatever gift each of you has received" (1 Peter 4:10). It is just as important to practice law well as to preach well; to govern well as to evangelize well; to conduct our business affairs well as to serve the poor well. In whatever we do, the key is to "maintain constant love for one another" (1 Peter 4:8).

Read: 1 Peter 4:7–11

Reflect:

1. Do you consider certain gifts or jobs more sacred or spiritually important than others? Why?

2. Think through your day ahead. What is one mundane, seemingly "unspiritual" activity you will have to do? For example, filling out paperwork or washing the dishes. Purpose now to do that activity with God—that is, to be in an interactive conversation with God in the middle of the activity, consciously aware that Christ is there with you through the Holy Spirit.

Week 2

~~~~~~

Going Deeper with the Apostles

MONDAY

CHOOSING MATTHIAS

I handed on to you as of first importance what I in turn had received: that Christ died for our sins in accordance with the scriptures, and that he was buried, and that he was raised on the third day in accordance with the scriptures. — 1 Corinthians 15:3–4

With Judas gone from the twelve apostles, a replacement was needed. This person had to meet two requirements: he had to have accompanied the apostles from the start of Jesus' ministry and be a witness of the resurrection.

Matthias, then, had known Jesus and spent time with him for the three years of Jesus' public ministry. And Matthias had seen Jesus after his resurrection. Matthias's job description? To bear faithful witness to the fact that Jesus had risen from the dead.

The selection of Matthias makes two things very clear: *the early Christian community was very concerned to preserve and pass on accurately the events of Jesus' life, ministry, and teaching.* All the apostles could do this, because they had been with Jesus for three years. And second, *the resurrection of Jesus from the dead was—and is—at the core of Christian faith.*

Read: Acts 1:15–26

Reflect:

1. This is the last mention in Scripture of casting lots, a method used in the Old Testament to determine God's will. Why might that be?

2. The resurrection of Jesus is the heart of the Christian faith. What are one or two implications of the resurrection for your everyday life?

3. Have you ever read through a Gospel in one sitting? Consider blocking out some time on your calendar to read the Gospel of Mark. Reading Scripture this way gives us a better picture of Jesus' life, death, and resurrection.

TUESDAY

SHARING ALL THINGS

Never turn away the needy; share all your possessions with your brother and call nothing your own. If you and he share what is immortal in common, how much more should you share what is mortal! — The Didache

The description of the church's life in today's reading is both encouraging and challenging. Goods were held in common. Some of the Christians sold their property to meet the needs of poorer believers. People were of one heart and soul," and this unity manifested itself in significant sharing of material goods.

How might we imitate this ancient pattern of sharing in our modern context? Two ancient Christian ideas come to mind.

First, *stewardship.* We are overseers of the material goods God has given us, not owners.

Second, *moderation.* Wealth is neither good nor evil. What matters is *how we respond to our prosperity.* If we respond self-indulgently, our material blessing can easily be our downfall. It is better to enjoy what God has given to us in *moderation,* with the rest distributed to the needs of the poor who are always present to us—if we have eyes to see.

Read: Acts 2:43–47

Reflect:

1. What compelled these early followers of Jesus to voluntarily have all things in common? What would this look like practically in our modern culture?

2. How does being a steward of something differ from being its owner?

3. God owns everything and has no lack—that liberates us to share. Today, meditate on the first verse of Psalm 23. Write it on a card to put in your pocket or carry some other object that when you see it, it will remind you to return to the Scripture: "The Lord is my Shepherd, I shall not want."

WEDNESDAY

THE WHOLE MESSAGE ABOUT THIS WAY OF LIFE

We must also "seek first his kingdom and his righteousness." What is the object of our quest? The Church? Heaven? No; we are to seek God's righteousness—His sway, His rule, His reign in our lives. — George Eldon Ladd

Today we find the apostles just months after they abandoned Jesus in his hour of greatest need. Yet here they are, emboldened by the resurrection and filled with the Holy Spirit, working miracles and being arrested for the sake of the gospel.

There in prison, an angel opens the doors, frees them, and charges them to go to the temple and speak. Pay attention in verse 20 to what the angel says they are to speak. It can be translated, "all the words of this Life" or "the whole message about this way of life."

Recall that our theme over these two months is about becoming like Jesus in all of life. The good news of Jesus isn't only about his death and resurrection. That is the foundation, to be sure—apart from which we have no hope. But the whole message is more: Jesus has died and risen to make the kingdom of God available to us now and forever. He has made possible a new way of living, a new life in and through and with him.

Read: Acts 5:12–21a

Reflect:

1. Today's passage lines up with the Great Commission: "Then instruct them in the practice of all I have commanded you" (Matthew 28:20 The Message). What "all" did Jesus command? What is "the whole message about this life" (Acts 5:20)?

2. Why was there such opposition against the apostles preaching this life? What were the religious leaders afraid of?

THURSDAY

PETER AND PREJUDICE

I refuse to accept the view that mankind is so tragically bound to the starless midnight of racism and war that the bright daybreak of peace and brotherhood can never become a reality. — Martin Luther King Jr.

For centuries, God's work in the world had been largely limited to God's call on Israel to be his special people. Now, in Jesus, God's purposes and actions are broadening out to the Gentiles, a movement that was initially hard for the first Jewish Christians to understand and embrace.

Our text relates that Peter received a vision from God of a sheet descending from heaven containing many "unclean" animals. Not only does he see the sheet, but a voice commands him to eat the animals the sheet contains. It is likely that Peter recognizes the divine voice as that of Jesus, for he replies, "By no means, Lord." Jesus responds, "What God has made clean, you must not call profane."

The injunction issued to Peter remains applicable today. Though most Christians recognize that persons of all ethnicities are invited to be members of Christ's body, we are still prone to separate from people who are different from us. How ironic and sad that Sunday remains the most deeply segregated day of the week for Christians in many countries around the world, especially in the West. It need not be so.

Read: Acts 11:1–18

Reflect:

1. Try to identify your prejudices. Are there people made in God's image you might be tempted to exclude or ignore?

2. Why are we often so quickly suspicious of those who are different from us?

3. What specific steps can you take to overcome prejudice within the church?

FRIDAY

PAUL IN THE TEMPEST

For I am convinced that neither death, nor life, nor angels, nor rulers, nor things present, nor things to come, nor powers, nor height, nor depth, nor anything else in all creation, will be able to separate us from the love of God in Christ Jesus our Lord. — Romans 8:38–39

In today's reading, Paul is in a genuinely dangerous situation. He is traveling to Rome as a prisoner and the ship on which he is sailing is enveloped in a huge storm. By all appearances, it appears that all on board are soon to lose their lives.

How does Paul respond? He sees beyond his immediate circumstances and discerns God's deeper purposes. Indeed, an angel appears to Paul, "an angel of the God to whom I belong and whom I worship" (Acts 27:23). And what does the angel say? "Do not be afraid, Paul; you must stand before the emperor; and indeed, God has granted safety to all those who are sailing with you."

Though the winds are howling and the ship is breaking apart, Paul is entirely safe because God's purposes for Paul's life have not yet been completed. There is still work for Paul to do.

The same is true for every believer in Christ. Yes, storms will come. But Jesus himself is the captain of our ship. He voyages with us and will lead us safely to harbor, our final home.

Read: Acts 27:13–26

Reflect:

1. When do you tend to become afraid?

2. Try to identify one or two instances when it was clear that God delivered you from danger.

Week 3

~~~~~~

How Do We Live with Jesus in Our Workplaces?

MONDAY

THE GOOD GIFT OF WORK

Pastors are not the only ones who have been given a sacred trust. Through the orders of creation, all our work is a sacred trust. — Kai Nilsen

Most people most of the time have work to do. We might be tempted to see work as a necessary evil. But according to Genesis, God intended engagement in fruitful work to be part of what it means to thrive. Richard Foster suggests we need the following understanding of our work:

> *We have a sense of calling, a God-given ability to do a job linked with a God-given enjoyment in doing it. We have a sense of responsibility to do something in our own time that has value. We have a sense of freedom from the burden of the workaholic, for we are not asked to do more than we can. We have a sense of creativity that enables us to place the autograph of our souls on the work of our hands. We have a sense of dignity, for we value people over efficiency. We have a sense of community, for we know that our life together is more important than the end product. We have a sense of solidarity with the poor to empower them to do what they cannot do by themselves. And we have a sense of meaning and purpose, for we know that we are working in cooperation with God to bring the world one step closer to completion.*

We'll spend this week exploring our work as a sacred trust.

Read: Genesis 2:15–24

Reflect:

1. What work did God invite the first humans to do in the garden?

2. Do you see any correlation between Adam and Eve's first tasks and your own work?

3. We explored the idea earlier this month that nonreligious work is as "sacred" as religious work. Is your understanding of "sacred work" changing? Why or why not?

TUESDAY

〰〰〰

CALLING AND RESPONSIBILITY

The place God calls you to is the place where your deep gladness and the world's deep hunger meet. — Frederick Buechner

Our work includes all we do to produce good in the world, including our paid employment. We often refer to work as our vocation, a word which comes from the Latin word *vocare* meaning "to call."

What are you called to do?

What are you good at? What brings you joy? Where do your abilities and passions intersect with the needs around you?

Richard Foster reminds us that we should approach our work with both a sense of calling ("a God-given ability to do a job linked with a God-given enjoyment in doing it") and a sense of responsibility ("to do something in our own time that has value").

Approaching work this way doesn't mean that every task will be enjoyable—sometimes hard things must be done. But it does mean that, when the choice is there, we should look for work that most aligns with our gifts and passions. It also means that we bring our whole selves to whatever task is before us, enjoying our responsibility to serve others and create value in our own unique ways.

Read: Romans 12:4–8

Reflect:

1. Do you currently feel you are able to use your gifts and passions in your vocation? If not, are there adjustments you can make to your tasks? How about to the way you approach your tasks?

2. Think about others you know through your workplace or other group contexts. Can you see the way different gifts are in use? Are there adjustments that can be made to allow your teammates to more fully express their calling?

WEDNESDAY

FREEDOM AND CREATIVITY

He who cannot rest, cannot work; he who cannot let go, cannot hold on; he who cannot find footing, cannot go forward. — Harry Emerson Fosdick

Author Parker Palmer warns that many God-followers are operating as "functional atheists." We believe "that ultimate responsibility for everything rests with us. This is the unconscious, unexamined conviction that if anything decent is going to happen here, we are the ones who must make it happen."

The truth is that God is holding the universe together and our work is an opportunity to partner with him in what he's already doing. Our work should be marked, says Richard Foster, by "freedom from the burden of the workaholic, for we are not asked to do more than we can."

We can trust God in our work *and* in our rest. Too much work and we become joyless and driven—functional atheists. Too much rest and we miss our opportunity to partner with God in cultivating good things. In following Jesus, we find healthy rhythms of work and rest that leave us both challenged and rejuvenated. The more we follow the pattern established by the Creator, the more we can undergo our work with creativity and freedom.

Read: Genesis 2:1–3

Reflect:

1. Why do you think the account in Genesis mentions the fact that God created for six days and then took a day of rest?

2. Have you been able to cultivate a Sabbath pattern in your own life (either one day of rest per week or regular intervals of rest throughout the week)? Why or why not?

3. What do you think of Parker Palmer's idea of "functional atheism"? Have you ever observed it in your own life?

THURSDAY

DIGNITY AND COMMUNITY

It is possible to do Jesus things but not in the Jesus way. — Eugene Peterson

God-centered work, Richard Foster tells us, is marked by a sense of dignity, "because we value people over efficiency." And God-centered work nurtures community, "for we know that our life together is more important than the end product." For those of us working in contexts where there are too many tasks and not enough time, these two characteristics are countercultural.

During his time on earth, Jesus highly valued the dignity of each person and the cultivation of community. The Gospels describe many journeys Jesus undertakes with his friends. He almost always travels "the long way"—taking extra time to talk, teach, heal, or have dinner in people's homes. He is constantly interruptible, sometimes to the great exasperation of his disciples.

If we want to live out our vocations the "Jesus way," we have to value people over processes (even though good processes may be helpful.) The people who interrupt us from our work may actually be our most important work of all.

Read: Luke 8:40–48

Reflect:

1. Why do you think Jesus stopped and recognized the woman who touched his clothes while he was on his way to another important healing?

2. Are you ever tempted to make checking off your to-do list more important than loving the people in your path?

3. Is there a tension between cultivating efficiency and safeguarding the value of each person's dignity and the gift of community? If so, what might be some ways to mitigate this tension in real-world situations—at work, school, in volunteer groups, etc.

FRIDAY

SOLIDARITY WITH THE POOR; MEANING AND PURPOSE

The important thing is not to do a lot or to do everything. The important thing is to be ready for anything, at all times; to be convinced that when serving the poor, we really serve God. — Mother Teresa

Richard Foster's description of God-centered work ends with two important and related hallmarks. The first is "solidarity with the poor," which he defines as empowering the poor "to do what they cannot do by themselves." God's heart is so aligned with the poor that whatever we do for them, we do for him (Matthew 25:40).

When our work empowers the lives of the marginalized, we can rest assured that we are partnering with God in his project to "make all things new" (Revelation 21:5). This gives our lives deep meaning and purpose. As we sync up our hearts with Jesus, we will naturally desire to do Jesus things in the Jesus way.

Read: Luke 4:16–21

Reflect:

1. In this devotional series we've looked at this passage before, but it is worth revisiting at regular intervals. From this passage, how do you think Jesus (at least in part) defined his vocation?

2. When you reach the end of your life, what will you need to have done (or not done) to be able to say your work had meaning and purpose?

3. Take some time to lift up your work or group life to God, asking for a sense of calling and responsibility, a joyful freedom and creativity, the ability to safeguard dignity and community, and a solidarity with the poor that generates deep meaning and purpose.

Week 4

~~~~~~

How Do We Live with Jesus at Home?

MONDAY

〜〜〜〜〜〜〜

THE SACRED IN THE ORDINARY

God made us to spend our days in rest, work, and play, taking care of our bodies, our families, our neighborhoods, our homes. What if all these boring parts matter to God? — Tish Harrison Warren

Nowhere is more familiar than the home in which we live. And the familiar places can be the easiest in which to exclude God. Perhaps, we feel, God has more important matters to tend to: wars and refugees and forest fires. Why should God waste his attention on one person making a sandwich in the kitchen?

The truth is that God is fully present wherever he is. And he's everywhere. He sees the king and he sees the sparrow with equal attentiveness. His attention is never divided. To exclude God from our ordinary lives is to say, in effect, that God isn't great enough to care about small things. But he is—and he does.

Our challenge—and great joy will be found in rising to it—is to recognize God beside us when we wake, around us as we brush our teeth, within us as we dress. Every moment is an opportunity to be in communion with God in prayer and thanksgiving, with or without words.

Read: 1 Thessalonians 5:16–18

Reflect:

1. Do you find it easy or difficult to recognize God's presence with you at home? Why?

2. How could one possibly "pray without ceasing" and get anything done?

3. This week choose one activity you do at home every day and intentionally recognize God's presence in it. For example, imagine Jesus beside you as you brush your teeth at night; and as you do, give thanks for the day.

TUESDAY

HOME WORK

We must accept the circumstances we constantly find ourselves in as the place of God's kingdom and blessing. God has yet to bless anyone except where they actually are. — Dallas Willard

The picture of the woman in Proverbs 31 nearly leaps off the page. She is smart and diligent, kind and compassionate. She does all this while she "fears the Lord." We can almost see God smiling at the way she lives her everyday life.

All this is in a place and time in which women were not always honored, and the culture viewed men as having the important jobs. She could have easily thought her work was unimportant and done it half-heartedly. Yet she took her job of caring for matters at home as a calling from God and glorified God in everything she did.

Read: Proverbs 31:10–31

Reflect:

1. What in particular from this passage stands out to you about the way this woman lives her life?

2. What does it mean to fear the Lord or to live in the fear of God?

WEDNESDAY

THE CALLING OF PARENTHOOD

How do we as parents serve our children? We serve them through compassionate discipline . . . by training our children for increased independence . . . by being available and vulnerable . . . by respecting them. We serve them by introducing them to the spiritual life. — Lacy Finn Borgo

Much humanitarian effort is expended to set right what went wrong during childhood. It's a powerful reminder that, for those of us who are parents, perhaps our highest calling is raising children.

Here again, our hope isn't in our strong resolve to do a good job and our willpower to carry that out. On our own we'll fall into one ditch or another, being harsh or aloof or overindulgent or worse. Our hope is parenting with God and learning from Jesus the way of loving discipline.

When a child comes to us with a problem, we learn to turn our hearts, even for a second, to God for wisdom. We learn from Jesus the way of relationship, connection, and service, rather than the way of legalism, law, and punishment.

And for those who are not parents, you likely know a child without good parents or without parents at all. Know that your love—even the simple act of listening—has far-reaching effects.

Read: Ephesians 6:1–4

Reflect:

1. What are some ways that fathers or mothers provoke their children?

2. What are some practical ways to "bring children up in the discipline and instruction of the Lord"?

THURSDAY

LORD OF POTS AND PANS

We ought not to be weary of doing little things for the love of God, who regards not the greatness of the work, but the love with which it is performed. — Brother Lawrence

Few books remain in print a decade. Fewer still a generation. And exceedingly few stand the test of centuries. One of those books is The Practice of the Presence of God. What makes this more incredible is that its author had no special skills or education, no fame, no wealth, no notable position. In fact, Brother Lawrence was a seventeenth-century monk who served as a cook in the monastery kitchen. This "lord of pots and pans," as he called himself, was a very ordinary man who discovered an extraordinary way to interact with God.

The book is made up of letters never meant to be published. Thank God, for our sake, that they were, for it is one of the greatest treasures to help us live everyday life with God.

Brother Lawrence broke down all barriers between sacred and secular. He learned through patient practice ("For the first ten years I suffered a great deal," he notes) how to be with God at all times. "It isn't necessary that we stay in church in order to remain in God's presence. We can make our hearts personal chapels where we can enter anytime to talk to God privately."

Read: Colossians 3:15–17

Reflect:

1. How do you "let the word of Christ dwell in you richly"?

2. Although today's passage was used in a recent devotional, it is worth revisiting. Take a few minutes now, if you haven't already, to memorize verse 17. Say it aloud three times. Then intentionally do one of your mundane tasks today while being aware of Christ's presence.

FRIDAY

~~~~~~

CO-LABORING WITH GOD

Whatever your life's work is, do it well. — Martin Luther King Jr.

Let's sum up the last two months.

There is no divide between sacred and secular.

It is possible to pray without ceasing.

God wants all of our life.

Joy is the result.

Through the work of Jesus, God the Holy Spirit has taken up residence in us. Our bodies are portable sanctuaries. God is with us wherever we go—we need only recognize it. We are ambassadors of heaven, called to bring the kingdom of God to whatever "kingdoms"—family, home, work, school—in which we have influence. The Christ-life in us isn't confined to church. It is for all of life.

"Come to me," Jesus invites us. "Take my yoke upon you" (Matthew 11:28–29). A yoke goes on two oxen. That means we're working together with Christ. He's carrying the heavy load and we're carrying the light one. But we carry it together. We get to live *with* God. We get to play and sing and invent *with* God. We get to join Martin Luther King Jr. in saying "I have a dream" and come up with creative solutions to the world's most pressing needs—all *with* God. It's what we were made for: vibrant collaboration with our Savior, Teacher, Lord, and Friend.

Read: John 10:10, Matthew 11:28–29

Reflect:

1. Looking back over the last two months of this devotional, is there anything you sense God bringing up and wanting you to remember?

2. In what areas of your life do you want to recognize God's presence more? Write them down. Then pray for greater awareness of God's presence in these areas.

Week 1

~~~~~

Questions Jesus Asks

MONDAY

WHY DID JESUS ASK SO MANY QUESTIONS?

God wants to enter into a conversational relationship with each one of us.
One way in which God shows this deep desire is by asking questions.
— *Trevor Hudson*

Have you ever noticed how many questions Jesus asks in the Gospels?
According to some counts, Jesus is recorded asking other people at least
307 different questions, while he is asked 183 questions, of which he
directly answers less than 10.

We know that Jesus was a Jewish rabbi, and rabbis were and are
famous for using questions as teaching aids. But even beyond a common
educational style, Jesus' questions seem motivated by a genuine interest in the inner lives of other people. Over the next two weeks, we'll walk
with Jesus by paying attention to the questions he asks—letting those
questions invite us into a deeper, more conversational relationship with
him..

Read: Luke 2:41–52

Reflect:

1. Today's Scripture selection contains Jesus' first recorded words in
   the Bible. What role do questions play in this passage?

2. Have you noticed previously that Jesus asks a lot of questions in the
   Gospels? Why do you think he may have done that?

3. Do you enjoy spending time with people who ask you questions?
   Do you tend to lead with questions or statements in your own
   conversations with people?

TUESDAY

〰〰〰〰

WHAT ARE YOU LOOKING FOR?

Your desire for more of God than you have right now, your longing for love, your need for deeper levels of spiritual transformation . . . is the truest thing about you. — Ruth Haley Barton

In today's passage, Jesus asks the two men who are following behind him, "What are you looking for?" Strikingly, he poses this question repeatedly in various forms in the Gospels. For example, when blind men call out to him, he asks, "What do you want me to do for you?" (Matthew 20:32; Mark 10:51). To the mother of James and John, he inquires, "What do you want?" (Matthew 20:21).

Jesus does not assume what people want or offer them aid without giving them the dignity of first articulating their needs and desires. He invites each of us to become aware of our own desires—to be able to discover for ourselves what it is we are really longing for.

Read: John 1:35–40

Reflect:

1. What is the significance of Jesus asking people what they want before he does anything for them? Does that pattern have any relevance for your own vocation?

2. Take a few moments to reflect silently. Imagine that you are one of the disciples trailing behind Jesus on a hot, dusty day. He turns, looks you in the eyes, and asks, "What are you looking for?" How would you answer him? Write down anything that comes to mind.

WEDNESDAY

WHO DO YOU SAY THAT I AM?

Peter replied, "Master, to whom would we go? You have the words of real life, eternal life." — John 6:68 MSG

In today's exchange, Jesus asks his disciples two questions. The first is Who are people saying that I am? The second question is more personal: Who do you say that I am?

These questions invite us to look into our hearts and ask ourselves at least four additional ones.

Do I believe Jesus is who he says he is?

Can I say I hold an accurate picture of the Jesus revealed in the Gospels?

Can I say I know Jesus relationally and intimately?

The last is the most personal: *Who is Jesus to me?* In other words, *How does who Jesus is affect who I am and the way I live my life?*

Read: Matthew 16:13–17

Reflect:

1. Why did Jesus ask these two questions of his disciples? Didn't he already know the answer?

2. In the culture around you, what do people believe about who Jesus was and is?

3. Take a few moments to reflect silently. Imagine that you are walking with Jesus down a dirt road in Caesarea Philippi. He turns, looks you in the eyes, and asks, "Who do you say that I am?" How would you answer him? Jot down anything that comes to mind.

THURSDAY

WHAT ARE YOU DISCUSSING?

I believe that although the two disciples did not recognize Jesus on the road to Emmaus, Jesus recognized them, that he saw them as if they were the only two people in the world. And I believe that... he also sees each of us like that. — Frederick Buechner

Two people are walking the seven-mile road from Jerusalem to Emmaus, speaking in low, heartbroken tones. It is now the third day since the horrific crucifixion of Jesus of Nazareth. They can't believe they had allowed themselves to place their hopes in him. And they can't believe it all came to such a humiliating and tragic end.

Someone else joins them. As readers, we have the insight of knowing this man is the resurrected Jesus. But the travelers' eyes are kept from seeing him. Jesus joins their conversation. And where we might expect him to clear his throat and announce his identity, he does something different. He asks not one, but two questions (verses 17 and 19).

Read: Luke 24:13–35

Reflect:

1. Why do you think Jesus asks the two people he is walking with to put their doubts and disappointments into words, rather than just immediately revealing who he is?

2. Take a few moments to reflect silently. Imagine that you are walking with Jesus, and he asks you to put into words any doubts or disappointments that you carry in your heart. What might you say to him? Jot down anything that comes to mind.

FRIDAY

DO YOU BELIEVE THIS?

The father of the child cried out, "I believe; help my unbelief!" — Mark 9:24

In the Gospels, we see that Jesus frequently asks individuals to examine the faith and the doubt in their own hearts. "Why did you doubt?" he asks Peter, after Peter successfully walks on water and then begins to falter (Matthew 14:31). "Why are you frightened, and why do doubts arise in your hearts?" he asks the disciples when he appears to them after his resurrection (Luke 24:38).

It might be tempting to hear Jesus' questions as accusations, or as tests to pass. But the more we keep company with Jesus in the Gospels, the more we see the love behind his questions. Just as we might gently ask a child who has woken up from a nightmare, "Why are you afraid?" Jesus' questions about the state of our own belief (and unbelief) are invitations to have a conversation with him about what is really in our hearts.

Read: John 11:17–27

Reflect:

1. What does it mean to doubt something and to believe something? Be as specific as possible. Can you force yourself to believe something?

2. Why do you think Jesus asks Martha if she believes what he is telling her?

3. Looking back at the four questions we considered this week, what resonates the most with you? Close your time in prayer, asking Jesus to continue speaking to your heart.

Week 2

More Questions Jesus Asks

MONDAY

DO YOU WANT TO BE MADE WELL?

God wants to free you and me. However, we need to be willing to go on a journey of change and risk and obedience. — Trevor Hudson

The Gospels are full of stories of miraculous healing. But Jesus never forces that healing on anyone. Almost always he asks the person involved to make an initial commitment or take a risk of obedience— whether that's filling up empty wine jugs with water (John 2:7), answering a challenging question, or, as the invalid in today's passage, rising up and walking.

Most of us have areas of our lives where we feel paralyzed and desire healing. Jesus comes to us and asks us if we really want to be made well—or whether we've actually become so accustomed to our dysfunction that it's hard to give it up. If we really want to be well, some risk of obedience may be required. Is there a secret we need to reveal? A situation we must walk away from or someone we need to walk toward? Is there forgiveness we need to extend or receive?

Read: John 5:1–9

Reflect:

1. When Jesus asks the man at the pool if he really wants to be made well, what does the man's response reveal?

2. Take a few moments to reflect silently. Is there an area of chronic pain or dysfunction in your life? Let Jesus ask you, "Do you want to be made well?" How do you respond? Jot down anything that comes to mind, possibly including a step of obedience you are being invited to take.

TUESDAY

〜〜〜〜〜〜〜

WHY ARE YOU AFRAID?

Here is the world. Beautiful and terrible things will happen. Don't be afraid.
— Frederick Buechner

One of the most oft-repeated phrases in Scripture is "Fear not." In the Christmas story, it is striking to notice the words the angels emphasize every time they appear: "Do not be afraid." "Look at what's happening here," they seem to be saying. "Look at the lengths God will go to in order to reach you with his love. You're not alone, and you never will be. You don't have to be afraid."

Dallas Willard writes, "Jesus brings us the assurance that the universe is a perfectly safe place for us to be." But looking around, the universe doesn't seem safe at all. Sometimes we might suspect, like the disciples in today's passage, that a storm is about to overtake us and that God seems to be sleeping. But if the apostle Paul is right that nothing, not even death, can separate us from the love of the one who holds the universe together (Romans 8:38–39)—then the universe really is a perfectly safe place to be.

Read: Matthew 8:23–27

Reflect:

1. Fear and anxiety seem to be dominant emotions in many modern cultures. What might be some of the underlying causes for this?

2. Take a few moments to reflect silently. Is there an area of deep fear or anxiety in your life? Let Jesus ask you, "Why are you afraid?" How do you respond? Jot down anything that comes to mind.

3. Read Psalm 23 aloud as a closing prayer.

WEDNESDAY

HOW MANY LOAVES DO YOU HAVE?

When we make available to God whatever we are holding in our hands, we will always be astounded by what God can do with it. — Trevor Hudson

In today's passage, the disciples are faced with feeding a crowd of thousands when they don't have sufficient food. Jesus, however, gets them to focus on what they do have—seven loaves of bread and a few small fish. Their meager resources, when handed over to Jesus, are miraculously transformed into a feast.

There is a similar exchange between God and Moses in Exodus 3:1—4:17. When God asks Moses to help deliver his people from oppression, Moses gives a classic list of reasons he is not qualified. Trevor Hudson summarizes these excuses as *I'm nobody. I don't know enough about God. What happens if I fail? I don't have what it takes. Someone else could do it better.*

God responds by asking Moses, "What is that in your hand?" (Exodus 4:2). Moses replies that he is holding a shepherd's staff, and God proceeds to show him the miraculous things he can do with it.

We all hold certain "loaves" and "staffs" in our hands—our abilities, our life experiences, and even our awareness of our inadequacies. These we can give to Jesus. In his hands, these small resources are multiplied into what the world needs.

Read: Matthew 15:32–38

Reflect:

1. What are some helpful ways to respond to being under-resourced to deal with the needs around us?

2. Imagine that Jesus is asking you, "How many loaves do you have?" or "What is that in your hand?" What might you offer him? Jot down anything that comes to mind.

THURSDAY

~~~~~~~~~~~~

DO YOU UNDERSTAND WHAT I HAVE DONE FOR YOU?

The way of Jesus is radically different. It is the way not of upward mobility but of downward mobility. It is going to the bottom, and choosing the last place! Why is the way of Jesus worth choosing? Because it is the way to the Kingdom, the way Jesus took, and the way that brings everlasting life.
— *Henri Nouwen*

After the extraordinary, holy moments when Jesus washes his friends' feet during their last supper together, he says something striking. "For I have set you an example, that you also should do as I have done to you" (John 13:15). This passage is the only place in the Gospels where Jesus is recorded explicitly saying that he has set a new example, or pattern, for living.

What is this new example? It is the way of "downward mobility" —of walking away from status, power structures, or entitlements to serve others in love. What Jesus has done for us is to give us a beautiful picture of an entirely different kind of life

Read: John 13:1–17

Reflect:

1. The apostle John writes in verse 3 that Jesus knew "that the Father had given all things into his hands, and that he had come from God and was going to God." Why are these details important to the story? How does knowing your identity in Jesus help you to serve?

2. Take a few moments to reflect silently. What are your honest thoughts about being a servant for Jesus' sake? Is there an area where you sense Jesus inviting you to serve? Discuss it with him.

3. Close in prayer, asking Jesus for the willingness and ability to follow his example.

FRIDAY

WILL YOU LAY DOWN YOUR LIFE FOR ME?

It is much easier to die than to lay down your life day in and day out with the sense of the high calling of God. — Oswald Chambers

When we hear the question from Jesus in today's passage—"Will you lay down your life for me?" (John 13:38)—what might come to mind is the shining examples of martyrs throughout history. Women and men who have willingly and even joyfully died for Jesus inspire us.

Yet it is worth noting that the Greek word used for "life" in this passage is not *bios*, the word for physical life, but rather *psuche*, the word that describes the inner life of thoughts and feelings. So Jesus is asking: *Will you lay down your internal orientations and agendas? Are you willing to pattern your life around my example? Will you let your heart come into sync with mine, until you care about the same things I do?*

There might seem to be a great distance between the first question we considered—"What are you looking for?"—and today's question, "Will you lay down your life for me?" And yet in conversation with Jesus we discover the truth of these words from Henri Nouwen: "Beyond all our desires to be appreciated, rewarded, and acknowledged, there lies the simple and pure desire to give."

Read: John 13:33–38

Reflect:

1. Take a few moments to reflect silently. Hear Jesus asking you, "Will you lay down your life for me?" Have an honest conversation with him about your response.

2. Looking back over the past few days, which of the five questions we considered this week resonates with you the most? Close your time in prayer, asking Jesus to continue drawing you more deeply into another kind of life.

Week 3

~~~~~~

Invitations from Jesus

MONDAY

I AM THE BREAD OF LIFE

To know much and taste nothing—of what use is that? — Bonaventure

Hunger is an interesting phenomenon, isn't it? Several times a day we're nudged by our body with a distinct message: Feed me. And what happens if we don't respond to this urging? Initially, we're simply hungry. If our failure to eat continues, though, we become fatigued, irritated, out of sorts. After days and weeks without nutrition, our biological systems start to break down—we're literally starving.

In today's reading, Jesus invites us to feed on him as "the bread of life." He knows there is a hunger within us that only he can satisfy: a hunger for forgiveness; a hunger for meaning; a hunger for relationship; a hunger for healing, a hunger for renewal; a hunger for new beginnings. He invites us to a rich meal, a feast that will never end.

Jesus offers us food that no one else in all creation can provide: the bread of his body, the wine of his blood. "Do you wish to be fed?" he asks us. "I offer myself as your food and drink."

Read: John 6:35–58

Reflect:

1. When Jesus talked about the need to "eat my flesh," many people were shocked and stopped following him (John 6:66). What did Jesus mean, and why did he say it this way?

2. If Jesus invited you to have breakfast with him this morning or dinner with him this evening, what would you ask from him?

3. Ask Jesus, "Are you offering me any meal that I have refused to accept?"

TUESDAY

From the standpoint of this present age, there is darkness; faith however is luminous, because it opens a window to a hidden world of light.
— Michael Casey

All of us have dark areas of our lives that are off limits to others and often to ourselves. What have we hidden away in these closed closets and iron boxes of our life's story?

Are there areas of your life that you've never shared with another human being? Perhaps it is a habitual sin or addiction. Or a piercing grief that clings to you like a gray, wet blanket. Maybe a past experience continues to radiate shame into your mind and body.

Thankfully, Jesus invites us to open our hidden places to the light that radiates from him. He is the darkness-dispeller, the light-bringer. As God incarnate, Jesus' very being is light. He has come to dispel darkness in many ways and on multiple levels.

It can be daunting to expose our dark places to Jesus. But can you remember a single instance in the Gospels when someone humbly confessed to Jesus and he walked away in disgust? Jesus' most joy-filled moments occurred when people came to him, opened the locked closets of their lives, and invited his light in.

Read: John 8:12; 9:5

Reflect:

1. Why do we hide our darkness from Jesus? Why do we hide it from other people, even people who we know would offer us grace?

2. Do you have a trusted friend, pastor, or mentor to whom you can reveal the parts of yourself that you keep in the shadows? If not, take a moment to ask God to provide someone.

WEDNESDAY

I AM THE GATE FOR THE SHEEP

This new epidemic of distraction is our civilization's specific weakness. And its threat is not so much to our minds. . . . The threat is to our souls.
— *Andrew Sullivan*

Why do shepherds keep sheep in fenced fields or gated pens? Because they wander off! Sheep get easily distracted, and the next thing you know they're lost.

It's extremely important that sheep live and thrive in an environment that protects them from walking distractedly into danger. As we see in today's passage, Jesus provides this for his beloved sheep. Indeed, he is the gate for their pen.

Although Jesus is talking about sheep, he's referring to us—his special creatures made in the image of God. We tend to be distracted. As the day passes, do you find that your attention is often diverted from important to less significant things? Or how about unexpected, heated temptations that suddenly arise?

Jesus invites us to *attentiveness*. He desires for us to be alert to our environment and aware of its dangers. An inattentive sheep is soon a dead sheep. But a sheep attentive to its master's voice "will come in and go out and find pasture" (John 10:9).

Read: John 10:7–10

Reflect:

1. What sins are a result of distraction? What kinds of good and beautiful and productive things happen when we're focused and attentive?

2. How much time, unrelated to work, do you spend on a screen each week? What is the fruit of that time?

3. Take a moment to create a simple plan for media use today through Sunday. Perhaps no screens after 8 p.m., or no phone on Sunday. Think of this not as a guilt-driven legalism, but as a way to be more attentive to Jesus and the abundant life he offers.

THURSDAY

I AM THE GOOD SHEPHERD

Suppose one of you has a hundred sheep and loses one of them. Doesn't he leave the ninety-nine in the open country and go after the lost sheep until he finds it? — Luke 15:4 (NIV)

Jesus is not only the sheep gate, but he's also the good shepherd. Why does Jesus use good to describe the kind of shepherd he is?

The answer is straightforward. Some shepherds, Jesus teaches, are like a hired hand. If a wolf attacks the flock, this self-interested shepherd runs away. Why? He cares nothing for the sheep. But Jesus is the good shepherd. He loves his sheep. And his sheep recognize his voice.

Consider sheep for a moment. What do they offer? They eat grass. They wander. They fertilize the ground with their droppings. They get distracted. Their wool grows without any effort on their part. They are simple animals. Yet the good shepherd loves them, protects them, and will search high and low for a single sheep who wanders from the flock.

We are of much more value to Jesus than sheep. Yet our value, like that of our wooly friends, is not based on how much we do on God's behalf. And like sheep, we wander. When we do, Jesus calls us home with a voice we will recognize if only we slow down, quiet down, and listen.

Read: John 10:1-6, 11–15

Reflect:

1. What are all the things that a good shepherd provides for the sheep.
2. How might you raise the level of your attentiveness to Jesus' voice?
3. Meditate today on the first line of Psalm 23: "The LORD is my shepherd, I shall not want." Bring it to mind and say it aloud, especially in moments when you feel lost or in need.

FRIDAY

I AM THE RESURRECTION AND THE LIFE

How would I live today if my life were not to extend beyond a year, a month, or even less? Today is the day when infinite possibilities remain open before us if only we can . . . reimagine a different future. —Michael Casey

This very second, the moment you are reading these words, Jesus is alive, well, and reigning over the universe. So pause for a moment and ponder the resurrection life he offers you. Imagine Jesus saying, "I'm asking you to look at your world differently. I want you to view your life and future within the solid, unwavering, unending truth of my resurrection. For truly I am alive."

Dallas Willard encourages us to allow the wonder of the resurrection *to expand our field of vision* and how we think of the future. "Our life—yes, that familiar one we are each so acquainted with—will never stop. We should be anticipating what we will be doing three hundred or a thousand or ten thousand years from now in this marvelous universe."

Read: John 11:25–26

Reflect:

1. What does it mean to your everyday life that Jesus is alive and reigning over the universe?

2. Revelation 22:5 says that followers of Jesus "will reign forever and ever." How might our life now affect how we'll live and create and reign with Jesus after we die?

3. If you only had eighteen months to live, would you do anything differently than you are now?

Week 4

~~~~~~~

More Invitations from Jesus

MONDAY

I AM THE WAY, THE TRUTH, THE LIFE

Jesus Christ became Incarnate for one purpose, to make a way back to God that people might stand before Him as they were created to do, the friends and lovers of God Himself. — Oswald Chambers

It's important to know the time frame of today's passage: Jesus' death will be occurring the very next day. He now focuses on the most important things. At the top of the list is that he is "the way, and the truth, and the life" (John 14:6). If the disciples are to know God, they must know Jesus intimately. The same, of course, is true for us.

Admittedly, there are many religious or philosophical options open to people today, all of them claiming to be the path to God and the way of truth. This is nothing new. People in Jesus' own day were deeply religious and interested in many philosophies. In Israel, other men occasionally claimed to be the Messiah, and religious choices in the Roman and Greek world were multiple.

Still, Jesus clearly focuses attention on himself and invites us to an intimate, personal relationship with him. "I am the way, and the truth, and the life." Perhaps today we can simply pause to ponder this statement. Jesus invites us to himself—a relationship that leads to God, truth, and life.

Read: John 14:1–7

Reflect:

1. "No one comes to the Father except through me" (John 14:6). Does this feel constraining or liberating to you? Explain.

2. In a sentence or two, define "truth." Next, do the same with "life." When Jesus says he is the truth and the life, what does he mean?

TUESDAY

JESUS INVITES US TO ABIDE IN HIM

I am like a green olive tree in the house of God. I trust in the steadfast love of God forever and ever. — Psalm 52:8

For a moment, picture yourself as a branch of a green, healthy vine. You swing gently in the wind, heavy with large, plump grapes—each full of juicy life.

Jesus describes himself as the true vine and his Father as the master gardener. The Father constantly tends the vine: trimming some branches, cutting off others that have borne no fruit. We are invited by Jesus into fruitfulness through our union with him, the true vine. As we abide in Jesus and his words—his teaching—abide in us, the Father is glorified as our life bears the fruit of love.

Did you notice how Jesus connects love and obedience in this teaching? "If you keep my commandments, you will abide in my love, just as I have kept my Father's commandments and abide in his love" (John 15:10). The sweet result of abiding and obedience? *Deep, lasting gladness and joy.* "I have said these things to you so that my joy may be in you, and that your joy may be complete" (John 15:11).

Read: John 15:1–17

Reflect:

1. This metaphor of the vine is alive and organic, an example from nature. Why did Jesus use this instead of a mechanical, man-made metaphor?

2. In nature, a branch does nothing by its own effort to bear fruit. It is simply pruned and remains in the vine. How does this apply to our spiritual life?

3. One practical way for Jesus' words to abide in us is to read the Gospels. This week try reading the Gospel of John in one or two sittings. Or you might try listening to an audio version on your phone or computer.

WEDNESDAY

~~~~~~~~~~~~~

JESUS INVITES US TO REST

Times come when we yearn for more of God than our schedules allow. We are tired, we are crushed, we are crowded by friends and acquaintances, commitments and obligations. The life of grace is abounding, but we are too busy for it. — *Emilie Griffin*

If you were to rate your level of fatigue on a scale from one to ten, what would your number be? Many studies indicate that most people are physically and emotionally tired. Some are exhausted. Many of us are not getting enough sleep.

Some fatigue is unavoidable. There will be times in our lives when we are pushed to the limit. A loved one may be sick and in need of constant care. Relationships within the home may be strained and tense for extended periods of time. The demands of work may be ever present. Occasionally, Jesus himself was tired. John writes that "Jesus, tired out by his journey, was sitting by the well. It was about noon" (John 4:6). Soon a long discussion with a Samaritan woman would occur.

Still, despite the times of weariness that may occasionally be unavoidable, Jesus invites us to rest in him. Jesus links his offer of rest to his yoke and his desire to teach us, a topic we'll discuss more tomorrow.

Read: Matthew 11:28–30

Reflect:

1. What kind of rest is Jesus talking about? What are the people he is speaking to weary from?

2. Are you tired because of circumstances beyond your control or because you have simply taken too much on? Is Jesus asking you to say no more often?

3. Take a few moments to pray. If you are feeling weary or weighed down, simply pray, "Jesus, I give you this burden and I receive your rest."

THURSDAY

JESUS INVITES US TO THE EASY YOKE

What then are we afraid of? Can we have too much of God? Is it a misfortune to be freed from the heavy yoke of the world, and to bear the light burden of Jesus Christ? — François Fénelon

Dallas Willard comments that a yoke is a device to train us in our relationship with Christ. "When we put ourselves in the yoke with Jesus, we are learning that posture of a life beyond death that brings forth much fruit."

Our willingness to receive Christ's yoke is an act of self-surrender. When we bow our neck to receive his yoke, we are saying to him, "Lord, I am safer trusting in you rather than in me. Left to myself I so quickly wander off to dangerous, twisted trails. I surrender to the training you offer me. I trust you. I know your yoke is gentle, not harsh. I surrender to your loving training."

Let's revisit yesterday's reading and see what God might have in store for us today.

Read: Matthew 11:28–30

Reflect:

1. Why does Jesus talk about a yoke and say "My burden is light" instead of "I'll take your entire burden"? What does this say about how Jesus wants to do things *with* us instead of just *for* us?

2. To receive a yoke is to surrender to a master trainer. Name the points of resistance within you to Jesus' invitation to surrender. Why do you think you are resisting?

FRIDAY

LIVING WATER FOR THE REST OF OUR LIVES

"Those who drink of the water that I will give them will never be thirsty. The water that I will give will become in them a spring of water gushing up to eternal life." — Jesus (John 4:14)

The Reservoir concludes today. Our prayer is that your reservoir has been filled to overflowing, and that you'll replenish it by abiding in Jesus and practicing the things he practiced.

Jesus promises us he will never stop giving us the water we need to flourish. And our reservoirs must remain full of fresh water if our speech, actions, and lives are to quench the thirst of those around us. Here are some practices that will help us keep our reservoirs full:

- Immerse yourself in the life and teachings of Jesus. Read the Gospels continually.
- Review your habits on a regular basis. Come up with concrete plans for eradicating unhelpful ones and nourishing good ones.
- At the end of every year, spend a day in reflection. How has God been involved in your life?
- Each day is important. Take five minutes before bed to ponder what has happened and why. What has God been up to?
- Develop a life of gratitude. Every evening write down two things you are thankful for.
- Memorize Scripture. Start small. Meditate on the text as you memorize it; allow it to sink from your mind into your heart.

Read: John 7:37–39

Reflect:
Take a few minutes to ask God to bring to mind a key concept or two that he wants you to remember from the last fifteen months. Then ask God what spiritual practices you should engage in over the next three months. Write those down and share them with a friend.

 Renovaré

Visit **renovare.org**
for articles, podcasts, online courses,
to learn more about the two-year Renovaré Institute,
or to order bulk copies of *The Reservoir*.

CPSIA information can be obtained
at www.ICGtesting.com
Printed in the USA
FSHW020955191220
76782FS